Music in the School

About the author

Dr Janet Mills began her career teaching music (and mathematics) in a comprehensive school in Keighley, West Yorkshire. Since then she has not strayed from the classroom—or from music—and has worked in various capacities in over 800 primary, secondary, and special schools. From 1983–1990, in posts at Westminster College in Oxford and the University of Exeter, she was a teacher educator working mainly with aspiring and serving primary teachers. From 1990–2000 she was an HM Inspector of Schools working in all aspects of education, and she was Ofsted's specialist adviser for music from 1995. Since the end of 2000 she has been based at the Royal College of Music in London, where she is a Research Fellow.

Janet Mills is author of *Music in the Primary School* and many articles in books, magazines, and research journals. She has given talks on school music throughout the UK, and overseas. She studied music and mathematics at the University of York, trained as a teacher at the University of Leeds, and completed a DPhil at the University of Oxford. In 2004 she won a National Teaching Fellowship.

Music in the School

Janet Mills

MUSIC DEPARTMENT

OXFORD
UNIVERSITY PRESS

OXFORD
UNIVERSITY PRESS

Great Clarendon Street, Oxford OX2 6DP

Oxford University Press is a department of the University of Oxford.
It furthers the University's objective of excellence in research, scholarship,
and education by publishing worldwide in

Oxford New York

Auckland Bangkok Buenos Aires Cape Town Chennai
Dar es Salaam Delhi Hong Kong Istanbul Karachi Kolkata
Kuala Lumpur Madrid Melbourne Mexico City Mumbai Nairobi
São Paulo Shanghai Taipei Tokyo Toronto

Oxford is a registered trade mark of Oxford University Press
in the UK and in certain other countries

British Library Cataloguing in Publication Data

Data available

Library of Congress Cataloging in Publication Data

Mills, Janet.
Music in the school / Janet Mills.
p. cm.
ISBN 978-0-19-322303-5 (alk. paper)
1. Music—Instruction and study. 2. School music—Instruction and study. I. Title.
MT1.M63 2005
780'.71—dc22

3 5 7 9 10 8 6 4

Typeset by Hope Services (Abingdon) Ltd.
Printed in Great Britain on acid-free paper by
Biddles Ltd., King's Lynn, Norfolk

Foreword

'All children—and all adults—are musical'. Janet Mills threads this assertion, and supporting evidence, throughout this book. So why do some youngsters of school age conclude that they are 'unmusical'? How can every child express their musicality and acknowledge—and receive opportunities to fulfil—their musical potential? This book describes youngsters being supported or failed at school (in either case sometimes quite spectacularly) and suggests some ways in which music at school could be improved. The key is a music education that really is an education in music: in the author's words, 'this book is about putting the music back in music'.

Readers are left in no doubt as to the crucial role schools play in music education. But this book also sets schools in the context of wider education and life in general. Music in schools is seen to open out into wider possibilities which can benefit all youngsters, musically and educationally.

Schools share responsibility for youngsters' music education with others—including instrumental tutors, ensemble leaders, even carers, the youngsters themselves, and their peers. These 'others' may operate in settings including music centres, youth centres, the home, playgroups, and religious establishments.

In this 'other' music education world youngsters' learning might be clearly directed and closely supervised, self-generated and totally unsupervised, or somewhere in between. However, whatever the modes and degrees of teaching and learning, the musical engagement is marked typically by youngsters participating voluntarily with high degrees of motivation. Some youngsters, who do not show concentrated effort in any subject at school, may spend many hours on the equivalent of lessons and homework voluntarily!

On their first day at primary school every child brings through the school gates an individual musical background—cultural connections, interests (even passions), learning, knowledge, experiences, and skills. Teachers, with their incredible battery of specialist teaching skills and techniques, build on all this.

Aspects of a student's musical background may be revealed organically as a teacher delivers national curriculum objectives through music activities during lesson time. Teachers may also successfully make links between youngsters' music learning in and out of school, in a way that clarifies the purpose of music at school.

I believe that, whatever else they do, all schools must aim to excite youngsters about learning. And, whether or not it was intended, this book says much about the very nature of learning. The author comments on and provides illustrations of the deep and long-lasting impact of teacher expectations (whether high or low) on their students—the self-fulfilling prophecies, looking at issues such as motivation, choice, the different ways and settings in which people learn, and peer learning. Much of this book has relevance beyond music education, and beyond music teachers.

Music is different from some other subjects. Is there another taught subject where, from primary school through to higher education and beyond, it is almost certain that students will have some knowledge or skills that their teacher lacks? So, music teachers, irrespective of where or at what level they teach, must commit to being learners alongside their students.

This book draws its examples of teaching from all continents. It refers to a range of musical traditions: not only to western classical music. Further, the central messages—for example, the need to teach music musically—are undoubtedly universal. One gets a clear sense of a gamut of teaching practice (excellent, good, mediocre, and poor) well observed. I found it heart-warming to see an example of good practice cited from the school (now Queen Elizabeth High School, Hexham) I attended as a student. I remember, with fondness and thanks, being inspired and captivated by the musicianship and musical enthusiasms of my secondary school teacher, and how this teacher also encouraged and extended my musicianship and enthusiasms.

Among the observations of teaching that the author has made professionally, over many years in a variety of settings at home and abroad, Mills offers critical appraisal of her personal musical experiences. The whole provides a rich seam for learning. There are pertinent messages and useful food for thought, and 'theorizing' is directly related to practical example. The many examples of good practice offer grounds for optimism, and I hope that teachers will be able to find time to reflect on what they read.

But, back to where I started. Having asserted that we are all musical, Mills suggests that everyone has musical potential that substantially exceeds their actual musical attainment. Consider yourself and those around you—whether children or adults. Perhaps you think, as I do, that she may be right? In any event, we need to develop more even access to music for all youngsters. I am always at pains to stress in the work of my organization—Youth Music—that access to music opportunities for all should not mean operating to the lowest common denominator. We aim for high-quality, broad, engaging, purposeful, and enjoyable learning experiences for all, with high expectations of all.

The author draws our attention to much that perhaps we already know to be true, and addresses some complex issues in a refreshingly uncomplicated way. Significantly, the book encourages teachers to reflect on and critically appraise their work whenever they can. I suspect the author would expect this principle to be applied also to this book. Given its tenor, I am sure she would welcome feedback, reflect on it, and be pleased to debate the points robustly! You may not agree with everything in this book, but you will surely find it a useful springboard for consideration, reflection, and, hopefully, action.

Christina Coker
Chief Executive, Youth Music

Acknowledgements

This book owes much to the commitment, enthusiasm, and expertise of hundreds of teachers and headteachers, and thousands of students, whom I have met in over 800 schools. A few of them are named in its pages, but most are not, and I sincerely thank them all.

A large number of friends, colleagues, and relations, as well as my own teachers have, over the years, helped me to shape the ideas that are described here. Some of them are named in the text. The many others include Joan Arnold, Karen Brock, Pamela Burnard, Sue Cottrell, Leon Crickmore, Leonora Davies, Margaret Dickinson, Richard Hickman, Caroline Hunt, Colin Humphreys, Richard Jones, Philip King, David Marcou, Ione Mills, John Stephens, Stephen Tommey, John Westcombe, and John Witchell.

Margaret Barrett generously read one of the more lengthy chapters, and offered a wealth of much-needed advice. David Acheson painstakingly read and commented on the whole book.

My thanks to the teachers, students, and parents at the schools that contributed photographs for the cover of this book: Pashley Down Infant School in Eastbourne, Hamstead Hall School in Birmingham, and Exmouth Community College in Devon.

Finally, I would like to thank staff at Oxford University Press, in particular David Blackwell and Kristen Thorner, for their unremitting support of this project.

Contents

Figures and tables

Figures

Tables

Chapter 1

Introduction

I have to say, in the end, I think that all that matters in music education is that what we do is musical. I don't care what it is. I would applaud whatever was happening in a classroom provided that it was actually involving children in musical experience.

John Paynter, in W. Salaman, 'Personalities in World Music Education'
(1988)

Music in the school

I begin by restating a view about music in the school that is almost 20 years old—but which has, I believe, stood the test of time. John Paynter offers a picture of schools where students learn through direct engagement with music as musicians, for example performers, composers, or listeners. What could be better—more 'musical' in the sense 'of music'—than that?

I continue with a quotation that mercifully was not written about music in schools, but which conjures up a picture—at least for me—of what can happen to music in a school where it is no longer clear why the subject is taught, and where the word 'musical', if it is ever heard, is used differently:

everything in the room had stopped, like the watch and the clock, a long time ago . . . Without this arrest of everything, this standing still of all the pale decayed objects, not even the withered bridal dress on the collapsed form could have looked so like grave-clothes, or the long veil so like a shroud. (Charles Dickens, *Great Expectations*)

Pip, a boy of around 8, has been summoned to the presence of Miss Havisham, who cut herself off from the world on being jilted, as she dressed for her wedding, many years ago. Her room is a horrible living museum of the moment when she was last happy and fulfilled. The candles that light her room are replenished (or Pip would not be able to see her), and she must wander around a bit (as Pip tells us that one of her once-white stockings has become ragged through wear), but Miss Havisham carefully replaces her hairbrush and hand mirror in the exact places where they have lain since time stopped as she seeks to preserve a world that others may view, but not inhabit. Pip's evocative description of all this has, I would suggest, a resonance with how students could feel about lessons in which they may inspect music or its artefacts, as through the lid of a glass case, but are not permitted to do music: to engage with it, to act in a way that is musical.

This word 'musical' has caused, and still causes, a lot of problems in music education. It has many potential meanings, not all of them constructive educationally. I do not believe that 'musical' can usefully be used to describe people. If I ever believed that there were two groups of people—the 'musical' and the 'unmusical'—I rejected this notion a very long time ago, just as I have rejected the categorization of people into two groups called 'musicians' and 'non-musicians'. I accept that some people describe themselves occupationally as musicians—I would be mad not to accept this—but I do not think that it makes sense for this or for any other reason to talk about an opposite group of non-musicians, just as we do not typically speak of non-dentists, non-plumbers, non-gardeners, or non-headteachers. We all have potential as musicians, and even the most famous musicians among us have potential that remains untapped. And musical training does not always have a comprehensively improving effect. Some forms of training may actually interfere with the realization of our musical potential. Working in Japan, Hiromichi Mito (2002; 2004) has found that students training as western classical performers find it more difficult to learn songs aurally, and also that the students with absolute pitch find it more difficult to transpose on keyboard instruments.

No, when I use 'musical' in this book, other than when I explain further, I use it, as did John Paynter, simply to mean 'of music'. Thus, 'musical experience' in a classroom engages students—all students—in doing music: making it, creating it, responding to it. This means that classroom activities such as looking at a violin, looking at a picture of a violin, drawing a picture of a violin, learning to spell the word 'violin', or learning that the great violin composer J. S. Bach had 12 children—or that violins have four strings—are not musical experiences. Neither is it 'musical' to have music playing in the background, rather like wallpaper, as students do mathematics, or carry out science investigations, or move around the corridors or into assembly, or do drawing or writing that is unrelated to the music being played. And activities such as echoing rhythms, or learning about the time values of the different sorts of notes used in staff notation, are not musical experiences per se either—although they can, in some circumstances, be educationally helpful interludes within them.

Why is music taught in school?

The question 'why is music taught in school?' has at least two meanings: 'why do schools teach music?' and 'why should schools teach music?'

The question 'why do schools teach music?' can, if one wishes, be answered quite simply. Many schools have no option but to teach music. In England and Wales, for example, music is a compulsory subject of the national curriculum for all children aged 5–14 who attend maintained schools, that is the schools that many other countries describe as public schools, because they are run at public expense. So, in a sense, schools teach music because they have to.

This is not quite the negative reason for teaching music that it might at first seem. Once music became compulsory for all students in maintained schools, it could no longer be dismissed as a frippery, a subject only for children thought by someone to be particularly 'musical' (whatever was meant by this!) or something only for children who were not very good at other, seemingly more important, subjects. Until the Education Reform Act of 1988, the only subject that all maintained schools in England and Wales had to teach was religious education. When the Great Education Reform Bill 1987 (known informally as the GERBIL) was published, music made it into the list of ten statutory subjects, albeit at number 10. Music teachers should not have been surprised, as the subject clearly deserves to be in the top ten, if only because of the very high number of schools that were teaching it already. But music teachers have perhaps a tendency to expect to be downtrodden, and some even seem to relish the thought that they belong only somewhere in the twilight corner of school life, and there are many tales of how music made it into the GERBIL, supposedly against the odds. One hears, for example, that a famous musician happened to get into the same lift as a government minister while at Elizabeth House, the building near Waterloo Station that then housed the government Department for Education and Science,[1] so that the minister uttered the word 'music' by association when he went into his meeting on the lofty penthouse floor where many of the decisions that most affected education nationally were then taken. But just who this musician was depends on who is telling the tale, and the musicians who have, at some time or other, got the credit for saving the subject in this way could not all have fitted in the same lift at the same time.

---

[1] In 1987 the Department for Education and Science (DES) was the government department responsible for education in England and Wales. Subsequently the name of the government department responsible for education in England has changed through Department for Education (DfE), and Department for Education and Employment (DfEE) to Department for Education and Skills (DfES). During the same period, education in Wales has increasingly become a responsibility of the Welsh Assembly.

Whatever the reason for music entering the national curriculum, the subject that ministers received was not that which they had expected. Although music's role as an essentially practical subject for all—taught through performing, composing, and listening—had been affirmed for many years through publications such as John Paynter and Peter Aston's *Sound and Silence* (1970), and the government's own *Music from 5 to 16* (DES 1985) and national criteria for their new GCSE[2] music examination (DES and Welsh Office 1985), government ministers and their advisers seemed to expect that the children of the 1990s would be served up the theory of staff notation and 'appreciation' of easy-listening classical works of the ilk of Mozart's *Eine kleine Nachtmusik*, with some dated and occasionally jingoistic songs such as *Hearts of Oak* and *Men of Harlech* thrown in for good measure. In this, they harked back to their worst memories of the personal music education that had left many of them feeling that they were not very good at music, and proposed to recreate this music education anew for another generation. In 1991 the first draft of the new national curriculum for music—itself only a pale copy of the inspirational *Music from 5 to 16* published by the government six years earlier—caused uproar among ministers and their advisers with its seemingly liberal (i.e. musical) approach to music in the curriculum. Expectations of students as musicians diminished further when the National Curriculum Council[3] produced a 'peacemaker' revised version that spoke of offering something not too challenging (or musical) for 'pupils who do not have a practical aptitude for music' (NCC 1992: 16). One wonders who these pupils were, and how they were ever to show the extent of their 'practical aptitude for music', and develop it, if the national curriculum for music did not require them to at least 'have a go'.

The 'non-practical' option within music education did not come to pass. But its residue left a nasty stain on national policy for music education, partly through allowing policy shapers to speak of those who lack 'practical aptitude' without being greeted with the total opprobrium that they deserve. Ironically, the act of bringing music into the national curriculum had diminished notions of what was meant by good practice in music education.

---

[2] The General Certificate of Secondary Education (GCSE) is a national examination taken routinely by students aged 16 in England, Wales, and Northern Ireland, and which relates to individual subjects, e.g. GCSE mathematics, GCSE English, GCSE music.

[3] The National Curriculum Council (NCC) was the government agency responsible for defining the curriculum. It was superseded by the Schools Curriculum and Assessment Authority (SCAA), and then the Qualifications and Curriculum Authority (QCA). These latter two agencies also have responsibility for assessment.

While official expectations of music in schools have mellowed since those dark days, the forces of darkness—or perhaps they are the forces of silence—are still alive. There remain those with purchase on the national curriculum who seem to have had an impoverished personal music education, and to feel that it will do young people good to have a 'backbone-building' similar experience themselves. One sometimes gets the feeling that these people think of education as a matter of survival, rather than as a wonderful opportunity to blossom. Or that they view music as something that they have just found in an old shoebox after many years, or that died out with the Aztecs or the Romans, rather than as a living force that continues to drive and shape people's lives in so many ways, as it has throughout time. One gets the impression from these people that RnB, garage, fusion, Harrison Birtwistle—and even the figures of their youth such as Stephane Grappelli, Ravi Shankar, Stockhausen, Berio, and the Beatles—never existed.

Consequently, despite the fact that schools in many countries teach music partly because they have to, it still makes sense to consider the question 'why is music taught in school' in the second sense of 'why should music be taught in school?'

In 2002 I was asked, among others, by the International Society for Music Education to contribute an answer to this question. This is what I wrote:

Why teach music in school?
There is recorded music almost everywhere in everyday life, but so little music making, and so much misunderstanding of what music is all about. People think that they are 'not musical'. Or that to play an instrument you first have to learn to read music. Or that if they have tried to learn an instrument, but did not make too much progress, this was necessarily their fault. Or that you have to be Mozart to compose. Or that music teachers are only interested in classical music composed by men who are long dead.

Teaching music in school enables us to put all this right before it goes wrong. We build on the natural affinity for and joy in making music—including making up music—that all children bring to their first day at school, and help them on the early stages to achieving their full musical potential. We avoid dogmatic approaches to music teaching that constrain children, but rather guide them as they grow musically, and exceed our very high expectations of them. We make it easy for children to carry on thinking that making music is just as natural as speaking, reading and writing. We show children that there is much more to music than the 'Dance of the Sugar Plum Fairy' or 'Mary Had a Little Lamb'. We engage with the music of children's own culture, and also help them to broaden their musical perspectives. We help the children who become so passionate about music that they want a career in it to achieve their goals. And we also carry on showing all the other children that music can be a major force in their lives, if that is what they want.

We teach music in school primarily because we want children—all children—to grow as musicians. But music, also, improves the mind. While it is hard to catch the results of this in a scientific experiment, or to plan music teaching so that this will necessarily happen, no-one who has had the privilege of observing really good music teaching, and has watched children grow intellectually in front of them, can doubt that this is the case. It may be the raising of children's self-esteem through success in music making that helps them towards achievement more generally. It may be that enjoying music helps children to enjoy school more. It may be that chemical changes induced in the brain by music facilitate learning more generally. Or perhaps the thought experiments that musicians must carry out to improve their performing and composing help children to extend their thinking more generally. I don't much mind what the reason is, but am certain that it happens.

Music making is something that we can draw on to make the bad times in life more bearable. Sometimes this is just in little ways. But I know an elderly man who struggles to make himself understood in words through the fog of Parkinson's disease. The other day, he stood up from the dinner table, moved to the piano, and played the songs of his youth perfectly, and with such communication. I know a much younger man, an outstanding physicist, who has cystic fibrosis. When the frustrations of his life now, and his limited prospects, become too much, he sits down at the piano and improvises for hours and hours . . .

But music is mainly about good times, and making them more frequent and even better. Music is not a gift but a right. (Mills 2002)

This book

An entire book that was written in the style of this 'advocacy statement' would be a very heavy read. I have included it here because it is something that I believe, and it seems right to 'lay my cards on the table' in these early pages. It is a personal statement written as a consequence of what I have thought and done, so far, when involved in school music as a student, teacher, researcher, and inspector. And it underpins the whole of this book.

Chapter 2 is about change in music education. We consider how music in schools is changing for the better, and also some of the features of good practice that remain constant with time. Chapters 3 to 7 focus on teaching. They are, in a sense, an enormous chapter that has been subdivided. But Chapters 3–5 are essentially about what I see as good practice in all forms of music teaching, with Chapter 3 focusing on what it means to teach 'musically', Chapter 4 on creative engagement with music, and Chapter 5 on re-creative engagement in music. Chapter 6 is an additional chapter intended mainly for instrumental teachers, and Chapter 7 is mainly about bad practice in music teaching.

The decision to include examples of bad practice in this book was not taken lightly. There is much successful music taking place in many schools. This book promotes and spreads successful practice through publicizing it, discussing it, relating it to relevant findings from the vast research literature of music education, and sometimes by giving counter-examples: examples of practice that, for one reason or another, was not successful. Counter-examples are included simply because it is sometimes through considering something that has gone wrong that one can work out how to make it go right. There are very few, if any, schools where nothing ever goes wrong. Indeed, a school where nothing ever went wrong would almost certainly be one where nothing much went dramatically right, as teachers would not be taking the calculated risks with their teaching that leads to outstanding learning when they come off. The inclusion of counter-examples in the book is not intended as an indication that they are general, that there are serious problems with music in schools, or that there are large numbers of weak teachers in the system. I, for one, do not believe any of these to be the case.

Chapter 8 considers the notion of the 'musical student', and Chapter 9 the 'musical school'. Chapter 10 asks what music should be taught at school, and Chapter 11 considers what it means to make progress in music. Chapter 12 starts from the premise that students spend only a relatively small proportion of their waking hours at school, and asks whether there is more that schools could do to build on what students have learnt elsewhere. Chapter 13 asks whether music in school is as boring as it is sometimes made out to be, and considers what could be done about this. All the chapters draw, to some extent, on the findings of research: Chapter 14 concludes by asking more generally what teachers can learn from reading research in music education.

This is not a recipe book. Teachers will not find lesson plans or units of work that they can apply directly in schools, because such an approach could not lead to teaching of high quality that is tailored to the special qualities of the school, its students, its teachers, and its resources. If an analogy with food is appropriate at all, this book aims to provide food for thought. It is intended for teachers who teach students of any age, and to be of interest to those who are very well qualified in music, as well as those who have few, or no, such qualifications. It is written for all teachers, whether or not they see themselves as 'musicians'. It is for teachers who work in schools as instrumental teachers, and not just those who teach what I shall describe as 'class music'. It may also be of interest to those who work in the community. It seeks to help teachers teach music in a manner that is true to the nature of music and what musicians do, in other words to teach music musically.

Chapter 2

All change?

Their yearly trick of looking new
Is written down in rings of grain.

Philip Larkin, 'The Trees', from *High Windows*

Getting better

Music in schools has changed. Or has it?

Change happens even where there are no managerial or national initiatives. The music provision of individual schools can change almost continuously, as teachers refine and refresh what they do, as part of that never-ending quest to meet students' needs even more effectively.

But what of change on a larger scale?

Some things certainly have changed in the UK—the musical instruments that we use when teaching class music in primary or secondary schools, for example. Out have gone those blue-boxed tinkly glockenspiels with random dead notes, bouncy bars, and exploding beaters that we may remember from our time as students, or our early days of teaching. In have come computers and electronic keyboards that look—and on good days sound—as exciting as those that our students' pop idols play on television. Out have gone many of the untuned percussion instruments, bought to last (rather than to sound) from education catalogues, that are little more than toys, and shakers made from yoghurt pots partially filled with beans and other surplus cooking ingredients or garden residue. They have been replaced by maracas and cabasas—real instruments that are used in real life by real musicians playing real music—genuinely worth listening to, and that truly do sound different when students follow our requests to experiment with the effects of playing them in different ways.

The repertoire that we use is changing too, as we struggle to prise new music, not least the compositions that we are constantly encouraging our students to produce, in groups and individually, into a curriculum that is already bulging with material that we would not want to lose. There is less stylized 'school music'—music written literally for students to perform in schools—and much more of an attempt to link music in school with the music that is happening, now, outside school within and beyond popular music. Some teachers have introduced music drawn from their own lives, borrowed from the concert hall, the charts, or holidays overseas, into their teaching. This is not a new idea. Keith Swanwick's *Popular Music and the Teacher* (1968) and John Paynter and Peter Aston's *Sound and Silence* (1970) reflected the more enlightened music teaching of their time as they referred to music ranging from the Beatles' *Can't buy me love* and *Strawberry Fields forever* to Benjamin Britten's *Serenade for Tenor, Horn, and Strings* and Olivier Messiaen's *Et expecto resurrectionem mortuorum*.

There is hardly any—possibly no—music that is totally irrelevant to schools, provided that teachers act as advocates of the music, and provided also that the music is presented with due respect for cultural sensitivities, and in a way that enables students to make progress as musicians. But the music that teachers use in schools does need to be continually updated, so that music remains a living subject. And some variety in the repertoire that teachers use, whether students are to play it or listen to it, is helpful too. A school music repertoire that consisted only of charts music, or only of music that had been created in the last five years, would be as limiting and limited as one that consisted only of stylized 'school music', or the ballet music of Tchaikovsky, for example. It is only through having some basis for comparison that students come to understand what it is about a particular type of music that they know, or even like. One of the many functions of having music in school is that students become more aware of all the music that there is in the world. And undue focus on particular types of music can lead students to reject it in future. I recall a teacher who threatened his classes with having to listen to the music that he particularly enjoyed—church organ music—if they misbehaved. How sad, in the literal old-fashioned sense of the word.

There is now more singing, perhaps particularly in the early years of secondary schools. Few teachers in primary, secondary, or special schools would now select their naturally good singers for auditioned choirs, and ignore the needs of the other keen students who most need their help. Singing has, rightly, ceased to be a 'no go area' during the three or so years when boys', and to a lesser extent girls', voices are changing. More songs have been published that students, including boys, might want to sing. The singing that some students enjoy out of school, including karaoke, gospel, and singing along with one's pop idols, is welcomed in school. During the 1990s, secondary schools including the Duchess's County High School in Alnwick, Northumberland (see p. 50), and St Saviour's and St Olave's School in Southwark, London (see p. 188), each in its different way, effectively relaunched music at school through an emphasis on singing for everyone. At St Saviour's and St Olave's, the focus was on gospel singing that students had brought into school from the community. At Duchess's, singing was the core of the class curriculum. The voice became the students' main resource when they were performing and composing, and this led to the development of a successful choir, and larger numbers of students choosing to continue the subject once it became optional.

Many teachers have established singing as a normal musical activity that people do quite naturally, and this helps them to 'catch students singing' when performing, composing, or responding to music, and then build on what they have done. Singing is taught with pace and demand, and students receive feedback about how well they are doing, and how they might improve further. I am talking here about singing in schools that is the antithesis of what inspectors once described (DES 1985) as 'depersonalized sing songs'. I am talking about singing such as the following, at a mixed comprehensive school in Nottinghamshire:

The first 25 minutes of a lesson for 12-year-olds were based on *call and response*. The students and teacher stood in a circle. Each student, in turn, produced an individual clapped, and later sung or hummed, response to the teacher's call, and received feedback. Everyone had individual feedback that was conveyed through the teacher's body language, and everyone received verbal comment that was individual, or addressed to groups of students who had responded in similar ways. The continuous structure of *call and response* helped to move the lesson along, and made the students' work feel like music: the lesson did not feel like a test. The students were kept on their toes while others were responding partly through their interest in the piece of vocal music that was emerging, and also through the teacher's practice of targeting questions about other students' work at individuals, including any who showed signs that their attention might be wandering. The teacher's custom of returning to students who she thought had not responded as well as she thought they could, perhaps because they were nervous, helped students to feel satisfaction in their work, and also reduced any temptation to produce responses that met some minimal requirements, but were not students' best work. It also showed that the teacher was very knowledgeable about the skills of individual students. (Adapted from Mills 2000b: 64)

Of course, not everyone gets it quite right all the time. Back in 1995, I observed a lesson in which a class of 12-year-olds had been asked to listen to 'Nessun dorma' from Puccini's *Turandot* while following the musical score. It was not long after the aria had been chosen as the theme tune for the soccer World Cup, and many members of the class started to sing along with Luciano Pavarotti: happily, sensibly, and with attempts at Pavarotti's pronunciation and characteristic use of visual gesture. 'Be quiet,' snapped the teacher, 'I told you to listen.'

Few can have failed to spot the changes in the national framework within which music is taught in many countries of the world: Australia, Brazil, Japan,[1] South Africa, Sweden, the UK, and the USA[2] to name but a few. The newest, youngest, teachers entering the profession in England, for example, will have found that the national curriculum for music has been rewritten twice since they were last taught it, at the age of 14, and that it is now more markedly different from the curriculum in Wales, with its emphasis on Welsh music. The meaning of the phrase 'national curriculum' varies widely between countries, and ranges from the specification of a detailed chronological sequence of content at one extreme, to advisory guidelines at another. But it is now the norm for countries to make a statement about some aspects of how music is to be taught. Countries where not all children as yet have the opportunity to attend school, including Brazil[3] and South Africa,[4] are nevertheless making the development of policy for music in schools a priority.

All these changes are, in some sense, changes for the better. The greater use of real instruments in schools makes music more of a real subject. Examples of schools where students enjoy singing, and sing well, could not be but welcome. The replacement of a repertoire that could perhaps be described as 'school music' with real music cannot but promote the relevance of the subject. And even if one happens to think that some of the detailed changes made to the national framework for one's own country are not well informed (or that it would be nice for some students to follow their national curriculum all the way through, instead of it being changed twice or thrice during their school career, so that it can never be evaluated properly) the sheer fact that changes are made shows that national politicians value the place of music within education, and want it to be taught well.

---

[1] The Japanese national curriculum for music used to be based on playing, and knowing about, western classical music, but now students are expected to be more creative, and also to learn to play a Japanese traditional instrument (Murao & Wilkins 2001).

[2] Australia and the USA have set national expectations that they want all students to meet in music (McPherson & Dunbar-Hall 2001; Radocy 2001).

[3] For example, Sérgio Luiz Ferreira de Figueiredo (2002) is developing proposals for music to be taught to trainee primary teachers.

[4] In South Africa, research students are drafting units as part of a team project that runs alongside their individual doctoral projects. This approach is intended to ensure that ideas for the curriculum are researched thoroughly. The draft units will be submitted to a national committee for approval (van Niekerk 2002).

Continuing well

Some things do not change, and nor would one wish them to. They include the vision for music education of many of those who are most passionate about music in schools. When one trawls much of the vast music education literature of the past 80 years or so, music comes over as a subject with many successes in many schools, and that:

- is for all students, not just an elite. Writers recognize that there is no such person as an unmusical child, a child who it is not worth educating in music, just as there is no such person as a child without previous experience of music

- engages students in high-quality making of, and response to, music. In music one learns by doing the activities that musicians do—making and responding to music—performing, composing, and listening. In other words, one learns through, not about, music

- equips students with the skills and attitudes that they need to get as much as they want out of music as they move through life

- is, literally, a creative art. Music in schools requires students to be creative, and not just to implement the ideas of others

- is about sound, not symbol. Learning to read music, including staff notation or chord symbols, is simply that. Music is sound, and much of the music of the world takes place without anything being written down, just as much of the verbal communication in all areas of the world takes place orally and aurally

- does not need watering down, in order for it to be understood. It just needs, like everything else, to be taught well.

As examples of how some good ideas have been around for a long time, consider this chronological list:

1922 Walford Davies used the new technology of his time, the gramophone record, to teach children to compose melodies based on his ABC method of Adventure, Balance, and Completion (see Cox 1997).

1926 Walford Davies experimented on BBC Radio programmes with playing, and commenting on, melodies composed by children.

1931 The Hadow Report criticized the patronization of children through undue emphasis on listening to 'music that painted a picture', and rejected the use of 'artificial aids in the form of pictorial representations' when teaching children to read staff notation (Board of Education 1931).

1933 A Cambridgeshire report commented: 'It is undesirable to bury the notation under fanciful descriptions and elaborate pictures, such as notes dwelling in houses, or fairies and birds sitting on telegraph wires; small children prefer more normal treatment' (Cambridgeshire 1933: 73).

1935 Charles Lamp and Noel Keys disproved the supposed link between certain physical characteristics and the potential to play a particular musical instrument (e.g. that oboists require even teeth), and advised that children normally be allowed to play the instrument that they most wanted to play, rather than matched with instruments according to their physique (Lamp & Keys 1935).

1938 Carl Seashore, psychologist, argued against the notion that some children are innately unmusical: 'musical talent is not one thing, but a hierarchy of talents as varied, inter-related, and as dependent upon soil, environment and inherited traits as is the vegetation of the forest' (Seashore 1938: 288).

1952 Watkins Shaw wrote (Shaw 1952) that in school 'the child should be immersed in the best musical experience in the forms suited to his [*sic*] stage of development' (p. 17), of the need for 'something more than arises from the presence of a gramophone, music-ruled blackboard, portrait of a composer and wall chart of *The Instruments of the Orchestra*' (p. 18) and that 'It must be stressed that it is *sounds*, their reproduction and recognition, which is our concern, not the notes or symbols' (p. 35).

1982 John Paynter built on *Sound and Silence* when writing of music as a 'creative art' that requires 'creative thought, the exercise of imagination influenced by personal choice and preference' whether students are listening, creating, or interpreting music. On motivating students he wrote: 'Because most pupils already have an interest in music of one kind or another, a variety of musical activities are possible which are not dependent upon formal musical training. These are starting points, and appropriate training should then follow from identification of the pupil's musical interests' (Paynter 1982: xiii).

1985 Her Majesty's Inspectors of Schools (HM Inspectors) wrote: 'Music education should be mainly concerned with bringing children into contact with the musician's fundamental activities of performing, composing and listening' (DES 1985: 2).

Details of this last excerpt have not entirely stood the test of time. Young people as old as 16 are now rarely referred to as 'children'. And some musicians object to a distinction being drawn between 'performing' and 'composing', on the grounds that there are many forms of music-making—for example jazz—in which the same person or people both create and perform their music, sometimes concurrently. Kathy Primos (2001) puts this another way when she asserts that in sub-Saharan African music there is no search for correct reproduction of music, only for correct re-creation. However, a distinction between composing and performing is useful in forms of music-making, including western classical music, where some musicians—performers—have the role of interpreting music composed by others, or themselves on an earlier occasion, and so I use the terms 'performing' and 'composing' cautiously, and I hope carefully, in this book.

But while details of HM Inspectors' message may have dated, overall it remains strong, and very musical. Compare it, if you will, with the opening of the current version of the national curriculum for music in England:

The importance of music
Music is a powerful, unique form of communication that can change the way pupils feel, think and act. It brings together intellect and feeling and enables personal expression, reflection and emotional development. As an integral part of culture, past and present, it helps pupils understand themselves and relate to others, forging links between the home, school and the wider world. The teaching of music develops pupils' ability to listen and appreciate a wide variety of music and to make judgements about musical quality. It encourages active involvement in different forms of amateur music making, both individual and communal, developing a sense of group identity and togetherness. It also increases self-discipline and creativity, aesthetic sensitivity and fulfilment. (DfEE & QCA 1999: 14)

Yes, yes, who could possibly want to disagree with any of this? But, when compared with the words of HM Inspectors in 1985, isn't the 1999 statement a little low on MUSIC? Isn't the importance of music being argued primarily in terms of its extra-musical value? Wouldn't most of these sentences work just as well if we crossed out 'music' and wrote 'English' or 'writing' or even 'French' or 'Latin'? I, for one, would be delighted if students emerged from my music lessons able to speak, read, write, count, think, or relate better than when they came in, but that is not why I teach them music. I teach them music because, like the HM Inspectors and the earlier writers I quoted, I want them to have the experience of being a musician: creating, interpreting, and responding to music; joining in performances that everyone feels proud of; feeling 'musical'; being moved by music; understanding how some music is put together; waking up in the morning with music playing in their heads; sometimes turning off background music because it draws them in so much that they cannot concentrate on what they are supposed to be doing; wanting to listen to new music that they have never heard before, as well as their old favourites; wanting to think about the role of music in, and beyond, their own culture . . .

This book is about putting the music back in music. Having music teaching that is primarily about music is good for teachers as well as students. Teachers who plan their teaching while focused on the musical reasons for teaching music, and the musical skills, knowledge, and understanding that students are developing, are better placed to teach music effectively. They can see some sort of developmental line, something to do with students' musical growth, that runs from the teaching that they plan for their youngest students, to their older students and beyond. This developmental line could, perhaps, be loosely envisaged as the trunk of a tree. I think of the trunk of a tree here, rather than a plastic clothes-post, for example, because the trunk is living, and has biology, sap, and growth rings that the clothes-post lacks. Branches that sprout from the trunk provide further musical enrichment, and various forms of extra-musical development. They intertwine, and have sub-branches, but move essentially upward, loosely following the line of the trunk in this respect, and helping to stabilize it.

As I look through my window at the trees outside, I see that my analogy is starting to break down. My apple trees do not have an unambiguous trunk towards the top and, of course, no tree goes upwards for ever. Perhaps I am talking about a cross between a tree and that beanstalk that Jack went up in the fairy tale, only without the giant at the top . . .

But my point is that a music teacher who sees their business primarily as music has a sense of direction to their work, and the planning of their work, that a music teacher who sees their work as meeting lots of other professionals' extra-musical objectives inevitably lacks. However, it is a sense of direction, with lots of opportunities, choices, and challenges along the way, not a strait-jacket. It provides music teachers with a basis for enjoying their work, and allows them to be thoroughly—and appropriately—convinced that they are individually doing something educationally worthwhile: something distinctive that an English, French, or Latin teacher could not do just as effectively.

And this leads us to the subject of the next chapter: teaching music musically.

Chapter 3

Teaching music musically

Alan, aged six, moves stealthily across the classroom. He is the Wolf creeping out of the deep, dark forest. As he creeps, he makes music: a pattern of mysterious taps and scraping sounds which tell us that the Wolf and the forest are sinister and fearful. No-one has instructed him: Alan chose the drum himself and decided for himself how the Wolf's music should go. As he creeps slowly across the room, he is lost in the world of his imagination, intensified by the music he is making.

J. Paynter & P. Aston, *Sound and Silence* (1970)

Teaching musically

John Paynter and Peter Aston began *Sound and Silence* (1970), a landmark book that continues to change the way that teachers and student teachers think about music and music education through its emphases on music-making and contemporary music, with this evocative description of one child's music-making. The account of Alan's music-making—his composing—is a reminder of the music that young children have inside them, just waiting to come out, if only they are given the opportunity. We have probably all seen something like this at some time or other, in our own children or other relations, our friends' children, or the young people we teach. This particular example of Alan's music emerged as a piece of music-theatre. Given another context, a different place in which to work, or an alternative range of resources to choose from, it might have been a song, an instrumental piece without movement, or a mixed instrumental and vocal piece.

In her article 'Say It Till a Song Comes', Coral Davies (1986) described some of the spontaneous songs, frequently influenced by known songs, that children from the age of 3 had sung for her. One 3-year-old based her song very obviously on *The big ship sails through the alley-alley-o*; other children buried the known songs that they were adapting more deeply. Margaret Barrett, working in Australia (Barrett 2002*a*; 2002*b*), has collected, documented, and analysed the spontaneous compositions of many children aged 4 to 5 years, and has considered how these spontaneous compositions, and children's thinking about them, develop as they get older. Her work, as we shall see (p. 158), challenges the view of some psychologists that children's musical development takes place in a straight line, or in clearly defined stages. Bertil Sundin, working in Sweden in 1960 (Sundin 1998), collected the spontaneous songs of children aged 3–6, and rated the 'creativity' shown through these songs. When he returned a few months later, to listen to the children again, he found that the creativity of the children whose songs had previously been less creative had increased: and attributed this to the influence of hearing their peers sing.

Esther Mang, working in Canada with girls from the age of 18 months, reported how some children who had learnt to distinguish between singing and speaking when vocalizing sometimes made imaginative use of both singing and speaking when communicating through what she describes as *contextual intermediate vocalization*. In particular, there was Amber, aged nearly 5:

Amber was reading a book on *Peter Rabbit*. She delivered the story in an animated voice with speech inflections noticeably different from the ones she used in her normal conversations. At the point in the story where Peter Rabbit met Winnie-the-Pooh, Amber shifted abruptly to sing a song, *Winnie the Pooh*. After singing several phrases, Amber continued to tell the story. To build up climax and anticipation, Amber slowed down her speech and whispered 'a . . . big . . . black . . . wolf' in long sounds; to keep the intensity, Amber continued to whisper as she described how the big black wolf chased Peter Rabbit. When she described how Peter Rabbit climbed a tree to escape, she raised her voice gradually to the peak of her vocal register. Amber slowed down her speech to convey a gloomy mood as she described how the wolf cried because he could not climb the tree. She rounded off the story by stating 'The End', and switched to look for songs in her folder.

Thereafter, Amber sang two verses of *The Wheels on the Bus*, as she was going through her music scores collection. In the second verse, she sang in a high, piercing sound to imitate baby cries. However, without a pause, Amber suddenly switched back to the 'story-telling' mode and introduced the character of a bumble bee into her story. Again without a pause, she inserted a *learned song* fragment about bees in the story-telling. This *spontaneous* song then emerged into a *pot-pourri* song, which included some fragments of a song about fishing. The singing sequence was sung slower and slower until it gradually integrated seamlessly with another section of story-telling. Amber again returned to the excerpt describing how the big black wolf ate up other animals. This and the earlier segment on a big black wolf were not from the story book which Amber was reading. Since Amber was familiar with Prokofiev's *Peter and the Wolf*, she might have been trying to incorporate the story of this instrumental work into her *nursery musical*. (Mang 2001: 118–19)

Amber was roughly the age by which children must enter school in England. She knew many songs, sang them well, and moved between them seamlessly.

She alternated between speaking and singing deliberately, for dramatic effect. She had already undergone a lot of musical development. How sad if she arrived at school and had a teacher who taught her as though she were an empty bucket waiting to be filled, or who expected less of her, as a musician, than she could do already.

Not all children are like Amber when they arrive at school. Some will have developed musically in different ways. Others may have fewer overt signs of musicianship. But they are all, through virtue of being alive and interacting with their culture for up to 5 years, far from empty buckets when it comes to music.

Musical class teaching welcomes all students with their existing musical skills, experiences, and interests, whatever these may be, and finds ways of helping students to build on all this: to move forward as musicians, without needing to leave behind what they already know, understand, can do, and were moved by. The teachers are motivated by wanting students to learn. They know that there is no such thing as a 'child with no previous experience in music'. They want their teaching to complement the musical learning that all students continue to do out of school. They want students to finally emerge from school as competent and confident musicians with the skills and attitudes that they need to get as much as they want out of music as they move through life.

Implicitly or explicitly, teachers plan their teaching (the next lesson, the next term, or a course that lasts several years) by asking themselves a sequence of questions of roughly the following form:

- Where are the students now? (What do I know about their knowledge, understanding, skills, interests, attitudes, etc.? Is there more that I need to know, perhaps with respect to particular individuals, and if so how can I find this out?)
- What, musically, do I want them to learn next? (Why of all the possible directions that we could go in, do I want them to learn this next? What do I think that I am going to want them to learn after this, and why?)
- How am I going to teach them this? (How will I present the learning in a musical context that does not lead students to forget, or reject as childish, the music that they can already do? How will I enable the students to learn from each other, as well as from me? How can I cater for students' individual learning styles?)
- How will I know that I have taught them this? (Can I rely on my eyes and ears to do this, or might I need to ask them some questions, give them another task that will show whether or not they can apply what I hope they have learnt?)

- How will they know that they have learnt this? (Am I going to tell them about my intentions—possibly even write them up and ask them to copy them down—and, if not, why not?)
- How will I know if they have also learnt something else? (How am I going to remain alert to the possibility of students learning something constructive other than what I intended, and how will I build on this?)

Teachers, of course, often return to at least some of these questions during lessons, as well as between them.

I have said that musical teaching builds on students' musical achievements. But it is also possible to consider it in terms of what teachers do—along the lines of what a psychologist might refer to as teachers' *behaviour*. Teachers who are teaching musically draw in students with their differing enthusiasms and backgrounds, and leave each of them at least slightly better for having been to a lesson. They teach through music (not just about music): students spend lessons making music, listening to music, and reflecting on music. The teachers understand that all forms of notation are only a means to an end, that many ends do not require notation, and that some ends would be compromised by it. They have high expectations of their students: they organize lessons so that the sky is the limit, and do not oversimplify their teaching material. Their lessons are ones that they, personally, would quite like to attend. They are observant of the response of their class, and continually fine-tune their lessons to maximize the benefit to students, adjusting their expectations upwards, where this is appropriate.

I have said that it is possible to think of effective teaching in terms of students' learning, and teachers' behaviour. I do not think that it is constructive to try to think of it in terms of the *content* of lessons. A lesson that is a success in the hands of the teacher who planned it can be disastrous when carried out, as faithfully as possible, by another teacher who has not been part of the debate about what the lesson is for. Schemes of work that have been published recently have often sought to work round this through careful statements of what the students are intended to learn. However, lessons planned by others will still only be successful if the teacher has worked through, for themselves, questions such as those listed above. Only the other week, I visited a secondary-school music department where two teachers were teaching classes from the same year group, in adjacent classrooms, using the same written lesson plan. The lesson related to the interpretation of a simple grid score with three independent parts (Fig. 1). The students interpreted the score using their hands as percussion instruments.

	1	2	3	4	5	6	7	8	9	10	11	12
Part 1	X		X		X	X		X			X	X
Part 2	X	X	X		X	X	X			X		X
Part 3	X			X				X				

Fig. 1 A simple grid score

Despite the simplicity of the material, the lesson taught by the teacher who had planned the lesson was magical. The students had chosen three subtly different timbres for the three parts, and the teacher had pointed out how the three parts fitted together. The players of each part sat together so that they, and the teacher, could see (as well as hear) that they were playing at exactly the same time, and get back on track quickly if something went wrong. The performances were conducted, with total commitment, by the teacher—assisted by a student who sat by him, and who was charged with spotting whether any of the other students failed to give the conductor eye contact, or were not playing at exactly the right moment. The students were engaged, and smiling. They were motivated by the enthusiasm and high expectations of the teacher, the efforts being made by their peers to play precisely and consistently, and the pleasure of hearing a piece that they understood 'come out right'. The lesson exuded music, and musical learning in the forms of enhanced listening skills, enhanced performing skills, and the satisfaction that comes from having played something, as a team, very well.

The other lesson was proving less fulfilling for the students and the teacher. The teacher was a fine musician who was trying extremely hard to implement the lesson plan given to her by the colleague working in the adjacent classroom. But she had not seen the musical potential of the material she was using. She thought that the exercise was just about having students play at the right time, and had not shown them how the parts fitted together, or asked them to think about timbre: all the students were just making whatever clapping sound they wished. Consequently, the students were not aware of anything interesting to listen to, thought that the exercise was beneath them, and were not concentrating. The piece was performed five times, each time slightly worse than the time before . . .

Here is another example of something going wrong because it is the content, rather than the student's learning, that has been planned. A professional orchestral musician writes of the 'education' work in primary schools that he must undertake as part of his contract: 'What is the point in trying to force a musician . . . to sit in a school hall singing about rainbows and shaking a maraca—and being called a dinosaur if he doesn't?' (Musicians Union 2000: 14). Clearly there is no point at all. Singing songs about rainbows (or anything else for that matter) or playing maracas (which go in pairs) makes sense only if there is some educational point to this activity: if it is the means to the end of students learning something worthwhile. Our professional musician appears to have been asked to help teach a lesson that someone else has planned, without being told its purpose. What a missed opportunity!

Starting well

Let us return to the happier experiences of Amber, Alan, and the children who worked with Coral Davies, Margaret Barrett, and Bertil Sundin. How can a teacher who is meeting a class for the first time teach them so as to build on their achievements? How can a teacher organize a first lesson in order to find out something of the music that students are bringing with them, and also so that students have a worthwhile musical experience marked by high expectations, enjoyment, and individualized learning? This may sound quite a tall order! But one teacher taught a first music lesson this way:

This was the 5-year-olds' second full day at school. The teacher led them in a song about Goldilocks and the Three Bears. They had to match the loudness of their singing to the size of the bear that they were singing about: to sing at three different dynamic levels. Over the space of no more than 20 minutes, they learnt to do this well and consistently, and showed that they had understood through talking about the song using vocabulary including loud, soft, softer, high and low. Although the teacher had focused on dynamics, the children's pitching of the melody improved too.

The teacher had skilfully chosen a song based on a story that many of the children knew already: these children already understood its 'threeishness', and the others picked this up quickly and without the need for verbal explanation because of the models being provided by the teacher and their peers. The teacher taught them how to apply 'threeishness' to the loudness of their singing voices, and they made progress with learning how to control their voices to do this. She checked their learning, and helped them to consolidate it through talk using simple musical terminology. She did not intervene when the children used 'soft' rather than the 'quiet' preferred by the writers of the national curriculum in England (on the grounds that children may confuse texture with dynamics), as the children were not confused, and were using 'soft' in a manner consistent with its use by musicians. But she did intervene when one child used 'low' vernacularly, to mean 'soft/quiet', and explained and demonstrated 'low' as the opposite of 'high', which the child then applied correctly in his singing. As the learning about dynamics was presented in the musical context of a song, the children also improved their pitching of its melody. There was something for everyone in this lesson, no matter how much music they had done before. Nobody was held back, and the teacher began to learn about individual children's musical strengths and areas for development.

Another recently arrived class of 5-year-olds made an equally promising, but different, start to their music education at school:

The teacher taught the children two short action songs: she just sang them several times and the children picked them up with ease. The teacher matched the tone quality of her voice to the mood of the lyrics, pitched accurately, and sang with good articulation, and so the children copied her and did all this too.

Next the children went on a 'lion hunt' with their teacher. This involved copying repeating rhythmic speech/action patterns as the class 'walked through the short grass', 'walked through the long grass' and so forth. The 'lion hunt' took many of the children to the limits of their ability (because they could copy some patterns accurately immediately but others only with practice or approximately) in circumstances where it did not matter to a child if something went a bit wrong. The 'lion hunt' allowed the teacher to make a visual diagnosis of some children's individual rhythmic strengths, and their areas for development.

Like the first teacher, this one provided her class with real musical activity, and helped them to improve their response. She used visual information to make a start at assessing the individual strengths and weaknesses that are difficult to pick out aurally when a whole class is singing together. Of course, it does not follow that children who have difficulty picking up a visual pattern during the 'lion hunt' will necessarily have difficulty with aural patterns when singing and playing instruments, but it is worth taking a closer look at these individuals, and seeing how they get on.

Not all teachers are so successful in their attempts to guide and promote young children's musical development:

Some 4-year-olds had chosen to work with the untuned percussion instruments that were freely available in their nursery class. Working as individuals, they experimented sensitively with ways of playing the instruments, listening carefully to each sound before trying to repeat it, or to play another sound. They were totally engrossed in their work.

A teacher joined the children. She immediately organised them so that one child 'conducted', and the others were to synchronise their instrument movements with his 'beat'. An absorbing aural activity had been replaced with a banal visual one, and the children soon looked bored. When the teacher left the group, the children returned their instruments to the storage trolley, and dispersed.

The teacher did not stop to study what the children were doing before giving them something else to do and, entirely accidentally, lowered the challenge of their work.

A related problem sometimes arises when students change school. Here is an example of a very first lesson at secondary school that was offered to a class of 11-year-olds:

Once the students were seated, the teacher began the lesson with: 'I am just going to ask you some questions, to see which of you are musical.' She then asked who did what at primary school. Who played the violin, played the recorder, played the triangle and so on. She wrote down what the pupils said. Eventually, the teacher worked her way through playing and singing to composing. 'I don't suppose any of you have done any composing,' she said. Four pupils put up their hands, but the teacher had already started writing, and did not see them. (Adapted from Mills 1996b: 9)

There are so many things wrong with this lesson that it is impossible to do them all justice here. They include the notions of a first music lesson at secondary school that contained no music; that some students might not be 'musical'; that if this was the case it could be ascertained through asking the students questions; that it would be good to tell students in their first lesson at a new school (or at all) that they were 'not musical'. Then there were the equating of the opportunity to have instrumental lessons with being 'musical'; the negative presentation of the question about composing; the assumption that students with experience of composing would recognize that as the technical term for what they had been doing; the failure to notice the students who, despite the odds, nevertheless still disclosed that they had composed . . . This was not a promising start to the students' secondary-school music career.

A different, but possibly equal, kind of damage can be done to students through the *no keyboards before Christmas* approach to the early stages of secondary-school music:

Extreme versions of this approach are founded on the belief that students' natural reaction on being given a musical instrument is to try to break it. The teachers seem to see the students rather like young horses that need to be broken in, and not as young musicians eager to explore the musical possibilities of instruments that were not available in their primary school. What actually happens is that the specialist resources of the school are withheld until the students have become so bored that they are no longer likely to appreciate them. Meanwhile, the pupils are set activities that barely pass for music, are less demanding and motivating than those usually encountered at primary school, and are not appropriate use of time that the school has allocated to the national curriculum in music. Particularly popular taming activities include projects on the instruments of the orchestra, in which few instruments are seen or heard, and opportunities to listen again to primary favourites such as *Peter and the Wolf, Carnival of the Animals* or *The Sorceror's Apprentice* (with *Fantasia* video). Students may also be given some staff notation to copy out, with the promise of being allowed to play it on a keyboard when they have finished. Only they never do finish. Or if they do, what they have written is so illegible that nobody could possibly play it. The melodies CABBAGE and BAGGAGE [see Fig. 2] are frequently introduced into *no keyboards before Christmas* lessons. But the students do not get to hear what they sound like: they just decode the staff notation to produce words. (Adapted from Mills 1996b: 11–12)

CABBAGE and BAGGAGE typically appear in these lessons simply because they are examples of relatively long words that only use the letters A–G, and not

Fig. 2 The melodies 'Cabbage' and 'Baggage'

because of any aesthetic qualities of the melodic motifs that they generate. The speciousness of CABBAGE/BAGGAGE activities was illustrated at a national music education conference when I showed a slide of them written in staff notation, asked the delegates to join me in singing them, and then asked if anyone knew their names. It was a full two minutes before anyone recognized either of them, and spotted the joke.

Students' early lessons at secondary school can be much more constructive, as the following example of a lesson taught in a school in Dudley, near Birmingham, shows:

This was the 11-year-olds' second music lesson at a new school. They sang four songs, and were taught to sing them more effectively. The standard of the singing at the start of the lesson was quite low, but everyone was taking part, and so the teacher had something on which to build. The teacher used the class's shared knowledge of the songs to improve students' ability to internalise music. Students who had done some extra work at lunchtime played a phrase from any of the songs on an instrument, and the other students had to say which song it came from, describe its location in the song, and say which words were sung to it. (Adapted from Mills 2000*b*: 64)

This was a school in a town that had grown up around a pit that was long closed, where students' rate of attendance at school was very low, and where it was difficult to persuade students that it was worth coming to school, or planning a career, because of high rates of unemployment locally that had persisted for more than a generation. The music teacher wanted to show students that their education is continuous, and has direction and purpose. He was determined to get the learning of new students off to a cracking start, and to present music as a subject where everyone could achieve together, and well.

This teacher had avoided the 'backwards slip' suffered by the students starting at the other secondary schools mentioned so far in this chapter. Although it was only the second week of term, the students were working to the limits of their ability, and clearly enjoying stretching and twisting their memories as they worked, as speedily as they could, to locate a phrase that one of their peers had played on an instrument. Because the teacher worked with songs that students had already memorized, they did not need written copies of the lyrics, and so the students with limited literacy were not needlessly held back from making progress in music. Through deploying students who had learnt to play phrases of the songs on tuned percussion instruments at lunchtime, typically by ear, the teacher showed everyone that the extra music that they can do through returning to the music room at lunchtime or after school, or by joining one of the school ensembles, is linked to work in class, rather than being the province of a musical elite. The students' next challenge, which would begin in their third lesson, was to work in groups to compose instrumental pieces that would serve as a link between two of the songs, so that the songs could eventually be performed in a continuous sequence.

The teacher could work in this demanding way because there were four especially composed songs that everyone knew, in exactly the same version. In other words, the students and teacher already had a shared memorized repertoire. So the secondary teacher did not have the usual problem of either having to teach new songs to students still nervous of each other's company, or choosing songs that everyone seemed to know, only to find out that students from different schools knew frustratingly differing versions. This was because the secondary school had agreed with its primary schools to work on a published primary/secondary transition curriculum that began in the students' last few weeks at primary school, and led into the first term at secondary school. Called *Moving On* (Dudley LEA 1996) this curriculum was developed by local primary and secondary teachers, including the secondary teacher whose teaching is described above. At its core were four musically contrasting songs, each about a mode of transport, and each written by a secondary teacher. The students from the secondary school's main primary schools had all learnt the four songs, and the small number of students from other primary schools had learnt the songs rapidly from everyone else, when they were sung during an 'induction' visit to the secondary school during the previous term.

Time moves on, and so have many of the teachers who were involved in developing *Moving On*. Different materials have been developed to promote continuity in the curriculum that students follow when they transfer from primary to secondary school in Dudley. I think that this is very encouraging. Were the original materials still in use, they would have become little more than a published scheme of work. The involvement of new teachers in developing materials will help to keep them alive.

I wonder what John Paynter and Peter Aston's 'Alan' is doing now. He will, I guess, turn 40 soon. Did he receive a school music education that built on his Wolf experience at the age of 6? Or was his creative and holistic approach to music curtailed by a teacher who taught him as though he was an empty bucket to be filled, either when he was at primary or secondary school? Or did he have some of those narrow sort of instrumental lessons that discourage you from doing anything except playing the notes on a printed page for years on end? Is he a fulfilled musician—not necessarily a professional one—who still loves making music, or a narrowly trained instrumentalist who wishes that someone had taught him to play by ear and improvise? Or did he give it all up years ago, and now consider himself to be 'tone-deaf' or 'unmusical'? Does he remember being the Wolf? I do hope so.

Music teachers

In 1994 there were many primary schools where teachers believed that class music lessons taught by class teachers were necessarily inferior to those taught by music specialists . . . Since 1994 more schools have become aware that good class teaching and poor specialist teaching both exist . . . (Ofsted 1999: 132)[1]

Who has been doing this 'musical' teaching that I have been describing?

So far in this book, I have avoided referring to any teachers as 'specialists'. I take the view that schools should deploy teachers to teach class music in much the same way as they deploy teachers to teach any other subject. Thus music in secondary schools should normally be taught by music graduates who specialized in music during their teacher training. And the deployment of teachers for music in primary schools should also follow that of other subjects. If a primary school has a culture of 'teacher swops' in later years, so that older students are prepared for secondary school through learning from more than one teacher, and so that teachers can play to their strengths—and there happens to be a teacher who is so good at teaching music that they can do this effectively with a class that they know less well than their own—then it may make sense for music to be included in this arrangement. But if the culture of the school is that class teachers teach everything—a model that reflects and reinforces the ability of all students to do all subjects—then it can damage students' image of themselves as musicians if some special arrangements are made for music.

Categorization of primary teachers as 'specialists' and 'generalists', as in the unfortunately entitled booklet *Using Subject Specialist Teachers to Promote High Standards at Key Stage 2* (Ofsted 1997), frequently carries the implicit assumption that a specialist is necessarily better at teaching than a generalist, and yet it may not be at all clear what the writer means by these terms, and hence what is being compared. For some, a specialist is a teacher who has music qualifications—for example a music degree—that a generalist lacks. For others, specialists are marked out by only teaching music—whether or not they have any qualifications in music. For a few (e.g. MacDonald *et al.* 2002), specialists are thought to plan lessons that are more specialized in some

---

[1] The Office for Standards in Education (Ofsted) is a non-ministerial department of the UK government that was established in 1992. It is responsible for the inspection of schools in England, and HM Inspectors of Schools now form part of its staff.

(not always defined) way than those taught by generalists. Whichever way one defines a specialist, it does not follow that their teaching will necessarily be superior to that of other people. Good teaching leads to students learning. That can happen whether or not the teacher has a music degree, and whether or not the teacher also teaches other subjects. When Ofsted compared the quality of music lessons taught in primary schools by children's own class teacher with those taught by someone else (Mills 1994a), they found no difference. A year later, Ofsted observed that:

many music specialists have not revised the curriculum they offer . . . to reflect [the national curriculum], and overemphasise the use of staff notation, which is not required . . . or singing at the expense of composing and appraising. The highest standards . . . are often found in lessons taught jointly by a music specialist and the class teacher, or when teachers who work for part of their time as music specialists are teaching their own class. (Ofsted 1995: 18)

More recently, Susan O'Neill and I (2002) investigated the quality of provision in music for 11-year-olds in ten primary schools. We used the term 'quality of provision', like Ofsted, to relate to the quality of teaching (as observed), curricular and extracurricular opportunities, and resources made available to the 11-year-olds. After a consultant had visited the schools to rate their music provision, we divided the schools into three groups accordingly— high, medium, or low—and found at least one teacher deployed as a specialist in each of these groups. So, having a teacher who is deployed as a specialist can be excellent news, but may not be. The school where the provision was best turned out to have a teacher who is a music graduate, and also a well-rounded musician—and who was teaching her own class. So she knew them well, and was confident to work with them in a wide range of musical activities. Clearly, having a teacher who is a music graduate and also your class teacher is an ideal combination that could not possibly be provided for all primary students— unless all primary teachers had to take a degree in music (and mathematics and English and . . .)! But primary students can sometimes be served better by a teacher who knows them well, rather than a teacher who knows music well, but does not know them at all. Even outstanding primary music teachers tend to become a little less effective when they work with a class other than their own.

Some of the finest music teachers that I have observed, particularly, but not only, in primary schools, have no qualifications in music, and teach many subjects—in some cases the whole of the primary curriculum. They may never have learned to play an instrument, and they may not read staff notation well, or at all. What they bring to their music teaching is their ability, typically developed in other subjects, to diagnose where students are, and work out ways of helping them to learn, frequently coupled with a degree of humility about their music skills that leaves them continually questioning how well their students are learning, and whether there are approaches that would enable them to learn more rapidly. They also often bring particular musical skills, interests, and knowledge that are additional to those of the teacher in charge of music at the school, and that enrich the music curriculum of the school. When teachers with little formal training in music teach it, their problem is often confidence, rather than competence (Barrett 1994; Mills 1989). When I work as an inspector in schools, such teachers sometimes try to apologize to me for their teaching before they have even begun, and then the most wonderful lesson unfolds as they focus on the students, closely observe what the students can do and what they cannot do yet, and use a range of skills developed in other subjects to help the students make progress.

Teachers who do not see themselves as musicians often greatly overestimate the range of musical skills—in particular instrumental skills—that music graduates possess. I realized this on my very first day as a teacher, when I got into conversation with a French teacher at my secondary school. He asked me when the school might have an orchestra, and I spoke of starting a violin and viola class when I could get some instruments, and also of enquiring whether the local education authority might be able to send some instrumental teachers to the school to teach other instruments. He was genuinely surprised, as he had assumed that any music graduate would be able to play, and hence teach, every instrument that a student in school might wish to learn.

Jo Glover and Susan Young, when writing of music for children aged 7–11, take a firm line on the need for more than one teacher to be involved in teaching music in any school. They point out that in a single primary school:

staff musical strengths and interests may include opera, travel, and world musics, guitar playing and folk groups, several orchestral instruments, choral singing, musicals, and dance ranging from tap to Arabic dance and salsa.

They continue:

Schools are often under-using this kind of whole-staff potential, preferring to rely on the skills of one specialist teacher than draw on those of all staff. Yet however well trained and broad in interests, one teacher presents only one musical personality. Making the most of what each staff member is able to contribute allows for a wider range of working styles in music. It is not acceptable for schools to offer only a single, narrowly defined musical direction for all pupils. (Glover & Young 1999: 6–7)

This point applies as much in secondary schools as in primary schools. However broad and deep the musical knowledge, skills, and interests of the single music teacher who comprises the music department in many secondary schools, it would be helpful for their students to be able to draw also on the musical enthusiasms of other teachers.

I recently visited a large secondary school where the art and design department of five teachers had organized the curriculum for students aged 14–16 so that, for particular pieces of coursework, individual students could work with—in effect consult with—whichever teacher had most of the specialist skills that they needed. More of this could happen in music. While students may have the opportunity to work with an instrumental teacher in addition to their class teacher, they are rarely able to consult more than one teacher about their informal music-making, compositions, and improvisations, or experiences of listening to music, for example. And yet secondary schools are as full as primary schools of teachers who sing in choirs, play in bands, and travel the globe in their holidays, collecting, and becoming absorbed by, new musical experiences as they go. While these teachers may not have the qualifications and range of skills needed to teach class music all year round, they may be able to share their musicianship through extracurricular activities, through occasional team teaching with a music teacher, or through carefully organized, and very occasional, exchanges of teachers for different subjects for perhaps just one or two lessons. I greatly valued the skills of an Irish ceilidh band who taught subjects other than music at the first school where I worked, and whose extracurricular contributions to the school greatly enhanced its relevance to the community. I experimented in team teaching with a drama teacher at the second school where I worked, and felt that our combined classes benefited from drawing on our collective music and drama skills when creating and refining music-theatre compositions. In both these schools, in consultation with English or history teachers, I planned music lessons that were intended to complement work being undertaken at the time in English or history. A history group had been studying the Tudors: we performed Elizabethan music, and I felt that the students' knowledge of the context of the Elizabethan music was much greater than it would have been had I attempted to provide the history rapidly myself. An English group composed music to complement a poem they had been studying: they knew much more about its structure and significance than they could possibly have learnt from me.

While successful class music teaching by teachers with little formal training in the subject is found more frequently in primary schools, it can occur also in secondary schools. I have seen superb music lessons taught by secondary senior managers—including headteachers—who are skilled mathematics, science, or English teachers, for example, and who are helping out an over-stretched music department by teaching a few lessons of music each week under the guidance of an effective head of music. Senior managers who are skilled teachers know how to manage—orchestrate—lessons so that the students learn much what they would have learnt from the head of music, but without the senior manager needing to pretend to demonstrate musical skills that they do not possess. There are many occasions, in subjects other than music, when teachers ask students to take an individual role in a lesson, rather than always taking it themselves. They ask students to read out loud, sketch a graph on the board, or bowl in cricket, for educational reasons. In music it need not always be the teacher who sings the starting note, plays the keyboard accompaniment, or counts people in, for example, although teachers do need to know when these musical roles are being fulfilled adequately, and to offer advice that will, where necessary, help students to fulfil them more adequately in future.

What is crucial is that students engage in music. And this is the focus of the next chapter.

Chapter 4

Creating, interpreting, and responding to music

By working directly with the raw materials of music, young people can best discover something of its nature—its vitality, its evocative power and the range of its expressive qualities.

HM Inspectors of Schools, *Music from 5 to 16* (DES 1985)

All musical activity—listening, making, and interpreting—requires creative thought; the exercise of imagination influenced by personal choice and preference.

John Paynter, *Music in the Secondary Curriculum* (1982)

The prime requisite is that the child should be immersed in the best musical experience in the forms suited to [his or her] stage of development . . . These activities in themselves will involve skills of a progressive order: but the activities will not be a sugar-coating on the pill of acquiring skill. They will be sufficiently worth while in themselves to dignify the task of acquiring it.

Watkins Shaw, *Music in the Primary School* (1952)

Engaging with music

These quotations from several decades ago remind us that there is nothing new about the idea of students doing music at school by engaging directly with it. But, of course, the ways in which today's students engage in music at school need to be appropriate to the twenty-first century.

In Chapter 2 (p. 15) I listed some aspects of being a musician that I want students—all students—to experience:

- ◆ creating, interpreting, and responding to music
- ◆ joining in performances that everyone feels proud of
- ◆ feeling 'musical'

- being moved by music
- understanding how some music is put together
- waking up in the morning with music playing in their heads
- sometimes turning off background music because it draws them in so much that they cannot concentrate on what they are supposed to be doing
- wanting to listen to new music that they have never heard before, as well as their old favourites
- wanting to think about the role of music in, and beyond, their own culture.

Here I expand on this. The first item of the list is overarching. Joining in performances and feeling proud of them are among the outcomes of creating, interpreting, and responding to music. So are feeling 'musical', being moved by music, understanding how some music is put together, and so forth.

The present chapter—Chapter 4—focuses on the overarching item of creating, interpreting, and responding to music, and emphasizes composition. The following chapter—Chapter 5—turns to the outcomes: joining in performances, and so forth.

I have already suggested (see p. 2) some activities that have been known to take place in lessons called music lessons, but which are not musical. Here are some more. Learning information about music (such as that 'B' is located on the third line of the treble stave) or about musicians (such as that Django Reinhardt, the great jazz guitarist, lost some fingers in a caravan fire) is not the same as learning through doing music. And activities that some teachers describe as 'warm-ups', and which are intended to lead to musical activity, are worthwhile only if that musical activity takes place. For example, the game *Pass the Tambourine*, in which students try to pass a tambourine round a circle without making a sound, is not music, because the students are not perform-ing or composing, and they are not listening to music. However, *Pass the Tambourine* can help students to develop the motor skills that they need to play the tambourine well, and can teach them to listen closely for quiet sounds, and so it could become worthwhile if it led immediately to music-making using a tambourine, or work on some very quiet music, for example. Similarly, the information about Django Reinhardt's tragic loss of fingers could become rel-evant were it linked to some work on how this influenced his technique as a jazz guitarist—including his development of lightning fast two-finger runs—and this point was applied to show how compositions or improvisations can take particular techniques as their starting point, and how this influences their sound. And learning that 'B' is located on the middle line of the treble stave would be relevant to a young composer who has created a piece that could readily be notated using staff notation, and wants to have a go at writing it down so that they can remember it, or so that a friend can learn it, for example.

So-called 'warm-ups' of the sorts that are not needed are a problem too. Time is so precious in all subjects, but perhaps particularly in music because the time-based nature of the medium means that pieces cannot be played, or listened to, on 'fast forward'. There are no parallels to scanning or skimming of text, or 'fast fire numerical computation' in music. I recently spent a day at the Barbican in London, watching large groups of primary-school students give performances intended to celebrate their achievements in special projects that focus on instrumental tuition. There was some magical playing. Performances that remain particularly in my memory include a whole class jazz project from Portsmouth that had begun with everyone learning to play harmonica before they progressed to other instruments, and the djembe drumming of two primary schools and a special school in rural Devon. And then there were the massed orchestral strings of a primary school in Haringey, London, whose performance was reminiscent of the Tower Hamlets Strings Scheme of 20 years ago only, importantly, recreated for the new millennium through the use of updated repertoire, through the linking of music and movement during performance, and through the way that the students and teachers looked—well—happier and more confident than when some students did similar work in the 1980s.

But some other participants in the day had much of their time wasted, musically speaking. Students who had travelled for miles with their shiny new instruments hardly got to play them, because the majority of their time on stage was occupied by 'warm-ups', for example singing (on one note) simple rhythms written on flashcards, that just were not needed as preliminaries to their instrumental work. Perhaps there had been a time, earlier in the students' musical development when a very small amount of this activity was helpful, but it had passed, and the 'warm-ups' had degenerated into rituals that simply delayed worthwhile music-making, and which could leave the young people with some strange ideas about what musicians do, and what learning an instrument is all about. And, at one point, a teacher was asked by the organizers to get on stage and lead the entire Barbican audience in singing the one-note rhythms, while the cameras panned round and caught groups of us on a big screen, although we were not being 'warmed-up' for any more worthwhile musical activity . . .

At the end of a musical lesson or musical activity a teacher can always answer the following two questions with answers other than 'none' or 'I do not know':

- What music (for example, composing, performing, or listening) did the students do?

- What music did the students learn?

They can sometimes also answer a third question:

• What else (other than music) did the students learn?

The answers to this last question might relate to social or personal skills, the application of concentration—or the skills needed to pass a tambourine to a friend without making a noise.

Of course, if students are to learn through music, then giving them one-off lessons that provide an opportunity to perform, compose, or listen is not enough: students need a series of lessons that build one on another. Lessons that are repeats—for example because they ask the same, or similar, easy questions about a recorded piece of music, say the 'Waltz of the Flowers' from Tchaikovsky's *Nutcracker Suite*—do not help students to make progress. Neither does giving them a few opportunities to play a particular instrument, perhaps drum kit, and then failing to enable students to follow this up, for example through practice at lunchtime, or through the offer of lessons that continue well into the future, if a student wishes.

In this respect the introduction, 20 years ago, of GCSE as the standard examination taken by 16-year-olds in England, Wales, and Northern Ireland has been one of the most significant developments in the history of UK music education over the last century. GCSE replaced the O level[1] examinations that had been introduced initially for students in selective grammar schools, and the CSE examinations that were intended originally for students in secondary modern schools—and each of which had music syllabuses that needed a good dusting—with a single examination that was open to students of all abilities, and markedly more musical in approach. All the marks available had to be allocated to listening, performing, or composing activities, with at least 25% of the marks going to each of these headings. The proportion of students continuing to study music until age 16 quickly doubled (from around 3% to around 6%). At the time, there was no national curriculum in any part of the UK: the specification of GCSE music—the national examination to be taken typically by 16-year-olds still studying the subject—signalled clearly to secondary schools, and also primary schools, where their music courses for younger students should lead.

GCSE music gave credibility to ideas that were still regarded as experimental in some circles. Although it was 15 years since the publication of *Sound and Silence*, 60 years since Walford Davies had tried to teach children to compose melodies using gramophone records, and many distinguished music teachers,

---

[1] O level was an abbreviation of Ordinary Level General Certificate of Education. CSE was the Certificate of Secondary Education. A levels, Advanced Level General Certificates of Education, still exist as academic examinations routinely taken by 18-year-olds.

including Peter Maxwell Davies, Murray Schafer, George Self, and Robert Walker, had long since introduced composing into their curriculum, much of the music education taking place in schools was confined to playing, singing, listening, and dull music-free writing activities that were sometimes misleadingly called 'music appreciation'. GCSE brought music closer to art, with its long history of engaging students in actually making art. GCSE music insisted that 'a music education must be a coherent experience of listening, performing and composing' (DES and Welsh Office 1985: 2). The 'three essential activities' of listening, performing, and composing were to be taught together, although it was accepted that it might be expedient for them sometimes to be assessed separately. And GCSE opened up music examinations to students who had received all their music education in class: the writers insisted that 'it must be possible for candidates who have received no instrumental tuition outside the GCSE course to achieve high grades in the examination'.

Many GCSE teachers had little personal experience of composing, and were daunted by the prospect of teaching it to students. In the shadow of GCSE, large numbers of courses were held, and materials published, that addressed composing out of its context of performing and listening. It was not long before most schools were teaching GCSE music using separate 'composing' and 'listening' lessons, that were frequently taught by different teachers in the larger schools that had more than one music teacher. Performing was typically taught by a third set of teachers: instrumental teachers working in the school, or students' private instrumental teachers if they had them. The 'coherence' of composing, performing, and listening was quickly shattered in the GCSE classes of many secondary schools.

In this context, it is not surprising that composing also had a rocky start in the lower years of many secondary schools, and in many primary schools. The introduction of GCSE had been driven by teachers who had composing in their classrooms and, despite the support provided by the excellent national publication *Music from 5 to 16* (DES 1985), there were not sufficient of these teachers to ensure that the others learnt what they needed to know in order to teach composing. Schools that had looked to BBC radio and television to provide many of the resources that they used for teaching music looked to them again, and sometimes did not find the help that they sought. The format of the programmes stayed much the same, but bits of 'composing' were added in, frequently in ways that understandably left teachers feeling uneasy.

Some readers may recall, from their days as teacher or student, that many of the songs included in the BBC radio programmes of the time had lyrics that were quite sophisticated. A song for primary children that cropped up frequently, known as *The Miller of Dee*, was based on Isaac Bickerstaffe's poem *There was a jolly miller* that begins:

There was a jolly miller once lived on the River Dee.
He danced and sang from morn till night, no lark so blithe as he.
And this the burden of his song, forever more shall be:
'I care for nobody, no, not I, if nobody cares for me!'

Teachers were already taxed by needing to use time in music lessons to explain repeatedly to children what 'no lark so blithe as he' meant, and what exactly was the 'burden' of a song. If the booklet that accompanied the series of radio programmes included a suggestion such as 'now go and compose your own music about the Miller of Dee', teachers would be likely to overlook it, particularly if they were not helped with considering what the students were to learn, how the work was to be organized, or what the teacher might say to the students about their work when they had done it. I am not suggesting that it is easy to teach composing over the radio. The problem was illustrated by a radio broadcast of the time, in which the presenter said 'And now, children, it is your turn to compose a piece about [something or other—perhaps it was spring]' and then returned after silence of perhaps only 30 seconds (but which felt like hours) to say 'well done!' But I cannot help feeling that if Walford Davies had still been available, he would have had some good ideas, such as broadcasts for teachers (rather than for children) in which children's compositions were introduced, performed, and discussed, perhaps alongside the children's own comments about what they were trying to do and how well they thought they had done it—with a view to deciding what the children might be taught next.

Some bizarre practices developed. I recall a primary school where, on the strength of some very expensive training provided for teachers by distinguished music graduates, 11-year-olds were 'composing' by asking a line of eight students, each holding a card containing a crotchet or a pair of quavers, to stand in a different order: the rhythms so produced were not even performed, let alone evaluated! I recall a host of secondary schools where students 'composed' directly onto manuscript paper—without hearing a sound—and then took their compositions out to the teachers to be played. As most of the students had very little understanding of the conventions of staff notation, their 'compositions' were, typically, unplayable.

Some of these bizarre practices remain. There is a 'standard' secondary-school lesson, still seen from time to time, that runs along the following lines:

1. Teacher begins lesson at the board with questions to students about what some symbols of staff notation (typically just crotchets, quaver pairs, bar

lines, and perhaps a minim, a crotchet rest, or the odd time signature) look like. The only sounds are verbal: no music, not even clapping, is heard.

2. Teacher writes up some rhythms on the board for the class to clap together. The results bear little resemblance to what the teacher has written.

3. The class are asked to 'compose' in their manuscript books. No talking or clapping is allowed.

4. Students who finish their compositions to the satisfaction of the teacher may play them on a keyboard.

A class of 11-year-olds I observed receiving this lesson quite recently is part of a school where nearly all the students are Muslim or Hindu, and so the cultural relevance of the teacher's heavy focus on staff notation is perhaps particularly questionable. Only three students made it through to the keyboards, and they did not play their compositions: they played extracts from Lloyd Webber musicals with independent left-hand and right-hand parts, either by ear or from memory. Few of the others bothered to attempt the 'compositions'. Some of the clapping that took place under 2 above was deliberately disruptive: I could see students waiting for the teacher to turn towards the board before adding an irritating anonymous extra clap at the end of six crotchets given.

The environment in which the class was working also left something to be desired. The school was rightly committed to improving students' reading and writing in English, and insisted that all classrooms included a display of books. However, the music department had interpreted this instruction with a display consisting of *Carols for Choirs 1, Hymns Ancient and Modern*, two volumes on the lives of composers from (as I recall) Mendelssohn to Ravel, sundry mutilated copies of a classroom text called *Enjoying Music*, and a booklet that accompanied a series of radio broadcasts that took place in 1961. I am not kidding!

Composing

The above teacher's notion of composing is a far cry from that which spawned *Sound and Silence*. The title of the book reflects a definition of composing given by the American composer John Cage: 'The material of music is sound and silence. Integrating these is composing' (Cage 1962: 62). Cage uses the term 'integrating' carefully: to mean 'making whole'. Making sound and silence 'whole' is clearly something that requires judgement, thought, and decision-making. This relates closely to what John Paynter has written about composing, by professionals or children, as a process of selection and rejection. It ties in with what Gary McPherson and Peter Dunbar-Hall (2001) report is the principle whereby composing takes place in schools in Australia: namely that composing is a process of 'continual rethinking and reworking'.

John Paynter sees composing in groups—a practical necessity in many educational situations—as a way of organizing students that enhances, rather than dilutes, their learning:

Fundamentally, [composing in groups] is about setting up problems for oneself, taking decisions that will answer those problems and having the satisfaction of having answered them. Gradually, over the years, I felt that there was a lot of educational value in this method. (Salaman 1988: 29)

Children are capable of a great deal as composers, if enough is expected of them, and if the tasks that they are set are not so narrow as to constrain them. Where young children initiate their own instrumental compositions, these are often guided by the layout of the instrument(s) they use: in the words of Jo Glover (1998)—*music made as played*. Thus, a composition for rainmaker might consist of it being tipped in one direction, until the 'swishing' sound ends, and then being tipped through 180° until there is silence. A composition for tambourine might begin with it being played in several different ways (shaken in different directions, tapped, rolled), not all of which necessarily sound very different to adult ears. A composition for xylophone might begin with an initially even scale from the bottom of the instrument to the top, and back down again. If a glockenspiel has two 'decks' of notes, then a scale up and down one deck may be followed by a scale up and down (or down and up) the other. Patterns, for example based on a few notes from the glockenspiel scale, may be introduced. It can sometimes be difficult to work out whether the composers are being guided by the sounds that they are making, or the visual shapes and muscular sensations that flow from playing the instrument, or a mixture of the two. But play an audio recording of one of these compositions to the rest of a class, and someone can usually show everyone else how it was played. This suggests that children, as listeners, can make sense of the aural aspects of their peers' work when that is what is presented to them. Susan Young (1995) suggests that 'listening' to and understanding the music of early childhood is multi-sensorial, requiring teachers (as well as students) to use their eyes as well as ears. I agree, but think that there are circumstances in which teachers can use their 'mind's eye', like the children listening to the audio recording above, rather than needing to look literally.

Of course, not all young children compose in the same way. Seemingly random experiment on a tuned instrument may lead to a 'moment of recognition' as a child realizes that they have picked out a melodic fragment that they recognize—perhaps the opening four notes of *Happy birthday*—and an attempt to continue this melody will turn gradually into an improvisation.

And, of course, many children left to their own devices will not compose in the same way all the time, but from time to time will oscillate between working from the known, working from the unknown, and various combinations of these modes.

The compositions that children produce when teachers give them specific tasks can, of course, be quite different from those that they initiate on their own. Working in Italy, Gabriella Baldi and Johannella Tafuri (2000; Baldi *et al.* 2002) asked students aged 9 or 10, at a primary school where music is not taught, each to improvise six short pieces for which six different stimuli were given. Without being asked, the students all used beginnings and endings that could be related to the classical and popular music in their environment. In a subsequent investigation, the researchers found that many students of similar age, and with similar lack of formal musical experience, could also structure the middle sections of their compositions. Middle sections were described as 'unorganized' if they:

- were obviously exploratory, consisting of notes played one by one, and hesitantly or irregularly
- consisted of many sounds played very quickly with two beaters without an obvious rhythmic or melodic pattern: a reflection of pleasure in motor activity coupled with sound
- consisted of only one note that was repeated without rhythmic patterns.

'Organized' middle sections developed melodic or rhythmic ideas such as motifs through variation or sequence, had a tonal or modal centre, or were structured using clear phrases, for example.

If students can do all this if only we give them the chance, how can we help them to improve? Or to put it another way, what might one mean by 'making progress with composing'? Historically, teachers were sometimes reluctant to discuss the musical details of younger children's compositions with them, on the grounds that children's compositions are just 'what they feel'. John Paynter points out that feelings are activities of the mind, and encourages us to be less timid:

Even the simplest intuitive piece made up by a very young child is recognised as music only because it is heard as music: that is as a *process* which starts, goes on, and stops and in which sounds follow one another or are combined in various ways. Spontaneous and natural though the music may be, there are points where things change: some things happen that are not heard again; some things go on for a short time and others for much longer; some passages are *progressive*, so that we feel the energy and forward 'drive' of the music, others are *recessive* in effect, the music calming or becoming quieter or slower until it seems to want to stop of its own accord. These things are the result of decisions—not necessarily conscious decisions but decisions nonetheless—

taken by whoever makes up the music, and the precise moments when changes occur are crucial to its success. Since . . . all musical expression, simple or complex and of whatever style or cultural background, behaves like this, we could conclude that the surest way to help pupils to get better at composing is to encourage them to think about the essentially *musical* process, not as abstract rules, but directly in relation to what they themselves create. (Paynter 2000: 7)

He points out that, with composing, the teacher 'cannot even begin [to respond] until students bring something which they have made', and continues:

when anyone has tried putting sounds together and is pleased with the results, enough to remember them, then the teacher can start to teach—mainly by asking questions about what is presented. It may be no more than a brief melodic pattern or a progression of chords discovered, remembered and rehearsed until fluent. It does not have to be notated, and even if there were only two notes the teacher could ask, 'Why did you put that note there and the other one there?' We are not imparting received techniques because what is presented to us did not exist until the pupil(s) invented it. Of course, there are bound to have been influences—all the music they have ever heard, and their musical preferences: what they think of as 'music'—but even if it is derivative, what they produce is *what they have made*, and to do that they had to take decisions. By focusing on those decisions, and by pressing students to discover as much as possible about why they have made the music as it is ('I just like it like that' is not good enough!), we start them on the path of asking the questions that every composer must ask about every piece: 'Where are these musical thoughts leading? What are the possibilities? Why should I choose that path rather than any other? How do I know when this piece is completed?' (Paynter 2000: 8)

John Paynter provides suggestions concerning the questions that we might ask students about their compositions:

As soon as the performance concludes we must be ready to comment. For example, we might ask, 'How do you feel about [this tune/this rhythm pattern/those particular instruments]—do we hear enough of it/them so that we can really enjoy what happens? Or is it over too soon? How would you describe the *character* of this music?—serious?—solemn?—light-hearted?—does it need more—or less—time? Do you think you've got it right? Shall we get tired of it if it goes on too long? What about the beginning? Should that music go on longer so that we really get to know what it's about? Does it change too suddenly to something different? Or does it take too long to get anywhere? Are you sure about the beginning/ending? Why is it like that? Listen to yourselves as you play what you've made: do you think the important things happen when they should? How can we tell? We have to try to feel when it sounds right. Why do you think *that* sounds right? What could you do differently? Would that be better? Why?' And so on. These questions should be directed at the composers. Other members of the class learn from that discussion. (Paynter 2000: 21)

I think that it is also useful for students—the ones whose composition is being considered and the ones who are listening on this occasion—to ask some of the questions. And it can be appropriate for both students and teachers to occasionally make suggestions, provided that it is clear that all the ideas being offered can be rejected, and provided also that the suggestions are not so numerous or so complex as to endanger the composers' recall of their piece. In a lesson for 10- and 11-year-olds that I observed at Meadow Vale Primary School in Bracknell, taught by the composer Roxanna Panufnik and their teacher, Mary Sefton, some of the listening students followed the lead of the adults in asking questions and making suggestions:

Although the compositions were not complete they were securely formed: when asked by [Roxanna Panufnik], the pupils could take their compositions to pieces and perform the individual parts, change the parts in accordance with [her] suggestions, and then reassemble the piece by playing all the revised parts together. Some of the [listening] pupils' suggestions showed that they were learning to dissect and reassemble compositions with their ears and eyes, and talk about what they could hear and see: they would comment on the way that an individual was playing, and then suggest an often subtle change that they believed would improve the overall effect of the piece. (Mills 1998a: 66)

There are at least three verbal modes in which teachers can respond to students' compositions: questioning, suggesting, and encouraging. Teachers do not listen to students' compositions only when the students have said that they want some support: teachers frequently like to monitor the work of each group of students at least once each lesson, particularly when, as is often the case in secondary schools, students are working in several different rooms. Sometimes a teacher will listen to the students' work, and their account of what they are going to do next, judge that suggestions or further questions would simply interfere, be encouraging, and leave the students to try out their ideas.

Teachers can also respond to students' compositions by working alongside them musically, for example:

Students age 13 at Queen Elizabeth High School, Hexham, worked on compositions that used voice and acoustic instruments alongside their own computer backing tracks. They used software written by their teacher to edit their tracks by moving, cutting, copying and overlaying blocks of sound. The teacher worked alongside the students as a musician. He sang, played, made suggestions and asked questions that helped students continually to raise their musical sights. The students caught the teacher's enthusiasm, and his very high expectations for the musical quality of his and their work. (Adapted from Mills & Murray 2000: 133)

Eventually compositions become complete, or as complete as they can be at that moment in time: once the composers have made a recording or record of their work, so that they can refer back to it, and noted any 'action points' that they could take account of in their later work, they are ready to move on. When listening to students' work, we are nearly always alert to ways in which we could help them make even more progress. But this progress will not necessarily be accomplished through further revision of the same piece. Mozart did not continually revise the symphony he wrote at the age of 8! He did the best he could with it right then and moved on, showing his progress through the music that he wrote later. Sometimes, the most appropriate response to a composition is simply the suggestion that the piece is now complete, followed by the offer of another stimulus for a new piece of work.

This stimulus will be the starting point for musical thinking. It is possible that it will relate to a visual or verbal idea. But, in the words of John Paynter:

> it is important to ensure that students do not think they are being asked to make music about pyramids, volcanoes, or the 'story' of a haiku. These literary ideas are no more than starting points for musical thinking, and the intention is that they should stimulate ideas about structure and procedure. This needs emphasising. The widespread notion that music in some way portrays visual and verbal ideas hampers musical education by focusing on non-musical matters. At the same time we have to recognise the value, to composers, of literary and visual stimulus. (Paynter 1992: 104)

It is also important that students' progress as composers is not impeded by unduly dogged insistence that they react to other sorts of stimuli. In secondary schools in particular, teachers sometimes organize lessons—'get the students going'—by giving them a list of musical ingredients that their compositions should contain. Perhaps the composition will begin with a rhythmic ostinato supporting a melody based on a particular set of notes, there will be a middle section with a contrasting ostinato and a different set of notes, and then the first section will return as the closing third section. Or perhaps they are to programme the 12-bar blues into their keyboards, and then 'fix' a composition by improvising over it. Fine. Well, fine as far as it goes . . . Unduly scrupulous attention to the teacher's instructions could—for no good musical reason—limit composers from developing compositions markedly more inspiring or inspired than the teacher had envisaged. Of course, students should not normally expect to deviate from the ostinato idea, for example, casually, or because they cannot be bothered to remember what an ostinato is, devise one, or concentrate sufficiently to repeat it accurately. But what if the students decide—perhaps by capitalizing on a mistake—that it would work better to bring the first ostinato back in variation in the last section of the piece, or to let the second ostinato develop after it has been established, or to use more or fewer notes than they had been asked to use in their melodies, or to build their melodies from ostinati and combine them in the last section? Couldn't—possibly shouldn't—students be able to ask the teacher if they wish, for musical reasons that they would explain, to deviate from what they have been asked to do? Wouldn't this help them to develop more autonomy as musicians, and to behave a little more like professional composers? Of course professional composers sometimes have to work to a very tight brief, for example when matching the duration of a piece exactly to that required for an advertisement or film sequence. But students in school are often expected to work under several different types of constraints at the same time.

Imagine the young Beethoven in conversation with a fictitious teacher:

TEACHER: I want you to write a symphony. Symphonies always begin with the tonic chord in root position.

BEETHOVEN: I want to start mine with a dominant seventh chord.

TEACHER: You can't.

And related to this, who will be the arbiter when it comes to deciding whether those two ostinati are 'contrasting'? For whom are the students creating the piece: themselves or the teacher? Is it 'good' to feel that you need to make your ostinati so grossly different that you are absolutely certain that your teacher will spot that they are different? Is it 'bad' to make your ostinati only subtly different so that your audience has to—well—listen?

But, I hear some readers gasp, doesn't this partial passing of responsibility from the teacher to the students conflict with what happens in numeracy and literacy, for example, these days—where students are expected to complete highly focused exercises that are designed to build up their skills? Not in my view. Students develop these skills in literacy and numeracy so that they can apply them in the 'real stuff'. Composing is part of the 'real stuff' in music.

Coherence

This chapter is about creating, interpreting, and responding to music, but I have written mainly about activities that focus on creating—or composing—music. What of the coherence of composing, performing, and listening that was sought when GCSE was established?

In *Music in the Primary School* I wrote of composing, performing, and listening as interrelated activities that could nevertheless be thought of as a sequence of creative process:

$$composing \longrightarrow performing \longrightarrow listening$$

I suggested that the interrelation can be thought of in two main ways:

First, much music making involves musicians in doing two, or even three, of these activities simultaneously. When listening to music, we may respond by performing, for example clapping in time with the beat. When performing, we listen to what we are playing. When composing, we often try out ideas by performing them, and make judgments about them as a result of listening. Second, the three activities have a common factor: they are all creative. Creativity is not just an attribute of composers. Performers are not automatons concerned exclusively with accuracy; their interpretation of a composition reflects their personal style. Listeners are not just pieces of blotting paper; they have differing, personal responses to the same performance.

and that the sequence of creative process could be entered at any of three stages:

At the first stage . . . we have composers, who devise music. They may also, simultaneously, perform and listen. At the second stage we have performers, who interpret music which is already composed. They may also be listening. At the third stage we find listeners, who listen to the performance of others. They are not, at that moment, either composing or performing. (Mills 1991e: 9)

I still find this a helpful way of thinking about the coherence of performing, composing, and listening. There are, of course, forms of music-making where it is difficult to distinguish between the performers and composers, and others where it may be pointless even to try to do so. Take jazz, for example. While a group of musicians who originate some repertoire are clearly composers, what are they when they interpret a jazz standard? I do not think that the answer that one reaches by considering this question matters much, although the debate is an interesting one. I have proposed a sequence, not a set of categories, and the jazz musicians playing a jazz standard are clearly somewhere to the left of the listeners. They might well refer to themselves, as I have already referred to them, as 'musicians' rather than as 'performers' or 'composers', and so it may be helpful to extend my diagram:

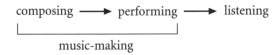

Many successful music projects in schools move seamlessly to and fro across this sequence. *Rana Temporaria*, a project that Peter Roadknight (2000) devised to use when 11-year-olds first arrive at St Richard's Catholic College, Bexhill-on-Sea, is a case in point. It was inspired by his shopping trip to Telford Shopping Centre, in Shropshire, where a large Time Machine has been built to entertain shoppers. Rana Temporaria is a huge fibreglass frog that sits atop the Time Machine and who, on the hour, blows bubbles, has beautiful leaves fanning out from behind him, and performs breathtaking music. The students do not get to visit the shopping centre, which must be almost 200 miles from Bexhill, but there is 'a postcard showing the clock, a video tape showing how the machine evolved from concept to reality, and a CD of the music that accompanies the bubble blowing bit'. By the end of their first lesson the students have joined in Rana's song, first by naturally singing along with the CD, and later with a piano accompaniment, and finally with no accompaniment. As they return for their second music lesson, a week later, they sometimes spontaneously sing the song. As the project develops, over several weeks, students listen to the CD regularly, gradually focusing more of their attention on Rana's song, sing it, analyse it, and create a poem of their own as a basis for composition, and perform their compositions in small groups and as individuals. Careful teaching ensures that students learn to compose, by ear, only melodies that they can sing.

Other, equally worthwhile, activities may focus on performing and listening, but deal with both of them creatively and imaginatively:

A lesson for 12-year-olds at Robertsbridge Community College, East Sussex, focused on the sound track to *Waterworld*. The students learnt to play a melody on keyboards, and then used the transpose facility as they played it with the sound track. Next, the students gave their full attention to the film, which was replayed on wide-screen TV with quad surround sound. Focused questioning by the teacher kept the students listening to the sound track as they watched the film, and helped them to think about the relationship between what they were seeing and the sound track. They evaluated the effect of particular voices, background sounds, sound effects, changes in mood, and panning front to back, for example. The teacher shared his knowledge about some of the technical aspects of adding music to film. (Adapted from Mills & Murray 2000: 133–4.)

And this leads us towards Chapter 5, which begins by considering performance.

Chapter 5

Making music

There are two musics . . . the music one listens to, the music one plays. These two musics are totally different arts, each with its own history, its own sociology, its own aesthetics . . . the same composer can be minor if you listen . . . tremendous if you play.

Roland Barthes, *Image—Music—Text* (1977)

This chapter continues the discussion of aspects of musicianship that students can develop in school, and turns to lessons that focus on performing and listening. While performing is not, in my view, the *raison d'être* of music education that some commentators consider it to be, it is an important facet of it, and it is here that we begin.

Performances that everyone feels proud of

Yes, performing and performance are important. As is taking part in performances of which one feels proud. Back in 1994 Tim Brighouse, then the Chief Education Officer for Birmingham Local Education Authority, pledged—as part of a major effort to improve standards in schools generally—that all children in Birmingham primary schools would have the opportunity to take part in a public arts performance by the age of 7, and again by the age of 11. In 1996 he added a pledge that, by the age of 14, each student in a Birmingham secondary school would have the opportunity to be involved in an artistic performance or physical activity, involving the community (Birmingham City Council 1996a; 1996b). Tim Brighouse believes, as do many other people, that being involved in memorable music performances does much more than raise young people's standards in music. But the focus of this chapter is the musical dimension of performance.

Performing is a fundamental activity of musicians: all musicians including western classical musicians, South Asian classical musicians, rock musicians, jazz musicians, folk musicians, or specialists in electronic music. While schools cannot hope to cover all forms of music performance equally (whatever this means), and may wish to specialize in aspects of performance according to the strengths of teachers and the interests of students, it is healthy for students to come into contact with a wide range of performance practice over time. It is inevitable that not all the performing that takes place in schools will have the musical or personal significance to students of the public events described above. But there is a limit to what is acceptable as performance in school, and some activities that are currently billed as musical performance in schools fall below this. Singing lackadaisically with a backing track while one's teacher looks bored, marks, or knits, is not performance. Neither is several years spent beneath headphones, working one's way through many volumes of five-finger melodies. Neither is counting 1 2 3 4 1 2 3 . . . and shaking a single, cracked, maraca on every '2' and '4' without thinking what it sounds like, and how this fits with the rest of the piece. Neither is learning to pass a tambourine round a circle of children without making a sound. Neither is using computer software to assemble a grid of visual images that represent sounds, printing them out, and sticking the printout on the wall . . .

Earlier (Chapter 2) I mentioned the Duchess's County High School in Alnwick, Northumberland, which, in the late 1990s, became quite well known for its singing (Mills 1998a). What marked this school out from others that are known for their singing was that it was the classroom work, rather than the choir, that was the initial cause of its reputation—although the school also developed a fine choir in due course. Duchess's is a school for students aged 13–18, and so students enter it in mid-adolescence, when the boys' voices (and to a lesser extent the girls' voices) are changing. While some other teachers might have thought this was a problem, and made only a half-hearted attempt at organizing singing in class, the school's then director of music, George Adamson, made singing the centre of the music curriculum, with some very impressive results. There was nothing half-hearted about the singing at Duchess's. Mixed classes of 13-year-olds entered the music room and moved straight into a horseshoe formation, ready to sing, rather than sitting at desks. Lessons began with a vocal warm-up, and then went straight into learning or working on songs. The students were moved between parts without fuss, during lessons if need be, so that the material that they were asked to sing best fitted their changing voices. Everyone sang, and sang with commitment. And if George Adamson judged that a student needed particular help, was not concentrating, or was doing something particularly well that he wanted others to hear, they would sing solo on request without fuss, just as they would respond to the request of a teacher in another subject, mathematics for example, that they say what answer they had got to a problem, or explain the process that they had used.

How did George Adamson do this? Basically, he showed through the demanding and confident way in which he organized his lessons, and through his body language, that he believed that the students could sing well, with the result that they did so. I never heard him plead with a student to sing, or feed students the thought that singing might be embarrassing, or something which one might choose not to do. How could one do other than sing, and sing to the best of one's ability, in these circumstances? George Adamson's own role model as a singer, and that of the sixth formers who often came into lessons to sing with the classes of 13-year-olds, also helped to portray singing as something that adults do.

But what did the students think? George Adamson once asked students to give their views on singing for homework. The response below was typical:

Singing in my opinion is the second most important musical skill after listening. It can be used for composing and expressing feeling, tone and all the things that musical instruments can do and more, just with our voices. It has been said that the most versatile instrument is the human voice. It can be as haunting and melodic as the pan-pipes and as loud and clashing as rock and roll. Singing is an ideal way of expressing all feelings in a way that cannot be achieved from any musical instruments. To sing well all you must do is let yourself get into the music, feel the pulse of the music and then let go. Singing well leaves me with a sense of well-being that comes from knowing that you have done as well as you can have done and enjoying getting into the music.

The boy who wrote this seems to have learnt a great deal about what music is through his experience of singing. And the standard of his writing here is higher than one might have expected given the teaching group in which he had been placed for English, thus suggesting that the 'sense of well-being' and self-esteem to which he refers are also helping his achievement more generally.

Of course, not everyone was quite so persuaded, or so comfortable with what was happening. But, even where students were more ambivalent and a little self-conscious, they still sang well and got to know music better accordingly. A girl wrote about how she had learnt more about her preferences for music, and showed that she had listened to what her teacher had told her about singing solo not being a problem—even if she did not quite believe him yet:

I quite like singing, not all songs though. I can't sing very high, but I can't sing very low either, sort of in between. I like singing *Let it be* and *Love is all around* more than *Stome omeme o mali!* I don't know why exactly. Maybe because the people who wrote *Love is all around* and *Let it be* are people I've heard of, and that I already liked these songs before we sang them in school. I don't think I'd like singing in front of people that I don't know, but it would probably be worse in front of people that I do know. Singing on your own should be just like singing with a few other people, except if you had a few people singing with you, you would have someone to back you up, and make you feel more confident.

It is interesting that this girl has implicitly accepted her teacher's policy of choosing some songs that she likes, but also attempting to broaden her experience and taste: she does not expect to sing the songs that she most likes all the time.

Undue emphasis on performance can be counter-productive. Keith Swanwick has commented that, in American middle and high schools where the music curriculum for some students consists of four timetabled band rehearsals each week, 'students tend to get a limited view of what music is and how it functions' (Swanwick 1999: 102). It is easy to see how a curriculum that consists of performance could shrink in on itself until it ceased to be creative or imaginative, and failed to involve students in musical activity away from the instruments or voice in which they specialize. Lessons could degenerate into junior versions of the rehearsals of choirs or orchestras attended by professional musicians, but without students having the opportunities to develop some of the broader skills that professional musicians possess. Students with differing learning styles would be unlikely to have their different needs met.

Improving performance

Teaching students to improve their performance simply by going into rehearsal mode, finding the fastest speed—tempo—at which everyone can play a section, and then gradually winching up the speed, only works occasionally in class. It is just one strategy of many that are available. It can be successful if the 'fastest tempo at which everyone can play' is close to the ideal tempo, everyone is concentrating, everyone has the motivation to want to play the section faster, and the teacher exudes confidence that the faster tempo can be achieved. In these circumstances, the most able players pick up the teacher's new tempo instantly, and this gives other players some 'working music' to join in with. Otherwise, 'the fastest tempo at which everyone can play' can become slower and slower, as students lose concentration or motivation, or find that the instrumental or vocal techniques that they use at normal tempi no longer work. Once the motivation goes, or the most able players lose confidence that they can carry out the teacher's instructions, the whole class may make progress at the speed of the student who finds the work most difficult, or who is concentrating least. In other words, the performance soon becomes worse than it was to begin with, or disintegrates totally.

This teacher used another strategy:

Everyone in the class (of 12-year-olds) was learning to play *In the Mood* (melody and chords) on keyboard. The teacher wanted them to play it much faster and more fluently, without feeling that they needed to read it from staff notation, checking more or less every note before they moved on. He also wanted more swing. He started the lesson with the class singing *In the Mood* to his piano accompaniment. Techniques including sharing the melody between two groups that were expected to stand to sing, and sit when they were silent, ensured the concentration of the class, and encouraged them to think of the melody as phrases, not just notes. Next, he asked the class to repeat what they had just done, but singing along with a commercial recording of *In the Mood*, which was much faster. They did. Finally, he asked them to go to the keyboards and play *In the Mood* as they had just sung it, singing along in their heads or out loud if they wished. This worked extremely well. (Adapted from Mills 2000*b*: 65)

The teacher utilized singing to give the students a mental model of *In the Mood* that they could use to guide instrumental performances, and replay at different tempos, and taught them to 'chunk' the music so that their fingers and eyes did not fall behind this mental model. And it worked! Which was very motivating for all concerned. The students had learnt something about learning that they could apply in other circumstances: not just how to play *In the Mood* faster. And they had also learnt a way of using singing as a means to an end, and not just as an end in itself.

Tânia Lisboa might have described the teacher's strategy as 'multi-modal', because one mode—singing—was used to help the students in another mode: playing keyboard. She developed a similar approach with three students to whom she was giving individual lessons on cello. She experimented with different ways of teaching them to play a new piece, and found that it worked best to teach the students to sing the piece during several lessons, before show-ing them the written music, and before asking them to play the piece on a cello. Tânia Lisboa suggests that this is because the cellists had a mental representa-tion of the piece before they started to play it: they already knew what it should sound like, and so were free to think about expression. The cellists' instru-mental interpretation of the piece mirrored the way that they had sung it: they played it in phrases, rather than 'note-by-note'. Because of the multi-modal approach, the awkward stage of learning to play a piece, when instrumentalists struggle with their understanding of staff notation and their technical difficul-ties as they work out what a piece should sound like, had been avoided (Lisboa 2002).

This is not unlike one of the beneficial effects that some western classical performers find from listening to recordings of pieces that they are learning, but find technically difficult. It is not that these individuals necessarily need to listen to a recording to work out 'how the piece goes': they can typically use the staff notation to do that. Nor do they listen to the recordings so that they can copy someone else's interpretation of a piece, and avoid having to work out how to interpret it for themselves. But because they are complete performances, the recordings model the piece structured in units longer than individual notes, such as phrases and sections: listening to them enables the performers to move on from thinking of pieces only as a series of notes, one after the other, each with what can seem like a considerable probability of being played 'wrong'.

Applying skills learnt in one type of musical activity more generally can help students to perform too. In schools where the music curriculum is broad, and students are taught to plan, and reflect on, the ways that they learn, these sorts of applications can become a way of life. During the 1990s, Ernesford Grange School and Community College, in Coventry, developed into this sort of rich musical environment. When students arrived at the school, at the age of 11, they often quickly formed into girl bands, boy bands, and mixed bands that had weekly lessons from rock tutors, provided by the local education authority performing arts service, who taught them as a band, rather than individuals, and expected them to develop all their own repertoire. Cover versions were not allowed! The curriculum and range of ensembles provided by the school music teachers were equally strong, but also more diverse, and it became usual for students to play drums in a band, and compose, perform, and listen at the cutting edge of the twentieth-century avant garde, for example, in their class music lessons. Far from being passive recipients of this rich and diverse musical experience, the students cultivated it, and actively applied what they had learnt in one musical sphere to another. By 1999, inspired by models including the Spice Girls, some band members were taking lessons from a classical teacher to improve their singing, and many of them had joined the school choir, which sang a mainly classical repertoire.

Feeling 'musical'

Music in school is not just for those who may make music their career, or as a breeding ground for able musicians (whatever this means), with other young people gradually falling by the wayside as they find out, or are told, that they are 'not good enough'. Music lessons introduce all students to the power and value of music by engaging them in creating, interpreting, and responding to music, and by helping them to make progress.

I believe that there is no such thing as a 'non-musician'. I believe this so strongly that I wrote about it in the first chapter of this book. Graham Welch (2001) agrees, and writes of the whole of humankind being 'programmed' for music. We do not talk about 'non-historians' or 'non-artists'—why should we talk about students as 'non-musicians'?

Students who are confident in their musical ability—who have what psychologists refer to as self-efficacy (Bandura 1997) across a range of musical activities—are more likely to be motivated, and so more likely to be successful.

Motivation is 'an integral part of learning that assists students to acquire the range of behaviours that will provide them with the best chance of reaching their full potential' (O'Neill & McPherson 2002: 31).

I return to the subject of 'feeling musical' in Chapter 8 (The musical student).

Being moved by music

Perhaps you could think of a performance in school that has moved you. I can think of many. I recall a 5-year-old in an English lesson who spontaneously stood up and sang a verse of a nursery rhyme, beautifully in tune and with fantastic communication, to his class—who were as surprised as I was. Then there was the primary-school assembly when all 200 children chorused 'Yes!' on being told the number of the hymn to be sung that day—and then put their all into singing it. Then there were the countless steel bands that play complex music superbly from memory, and who continually remind me how little we expect of young people's memories in many of the things that we ask them to do at school. Then there were the secondary-school clarinettists with quite distressingly challenging personal lives whose troubles seemed to vanish as they focused on playing the most wonderful jazz. Then there was the rehearsal at a specialist music school when the tiny 11-year-old leader of a string quartet took a repeat section in a Haydn movement down to such a quiet and controlled *pianissimo*, which everyone followed minutely, that even their teacher—a hardened world-class chamber musician—was almost moved to tears. I could go on . . .

I am writing here about an adult—me—being moved by music. I cannot be sure that the children making the music that moved me were moved themselves, although something like that was certainly going on in the primary-school assembly. Child musicians can move us, as a function of their youth and music, without necessarily being moved themselves. If music made by adult musicians moves us because the adult musicians are moved themselves, and communicating this to us through the music, which is something that some psychologists believe (see Persson 2001), then children are different. But, actually, I believe that there is much more to this matter with adult performers too. A performer who is too caught up in a performance cannot fully control it. Listeners can be moved by performances that were not moving their performers at all, at that moment in time. Listeners build 'being moved' for themselves—through engagement with the actual music, and through association with experiences of listening to music (perhaps particularly music that is similar in some way) on earlier occasions.

Being moved by music as a listener is part of understanding its 'evocative power' (DES 1985). Clearly, one cannot guarantee that all children will be moved by music while they are at school. (Music and movement classes have rather different aims!) But creating conditions where students can give music their full attention, whether they are in an audience, or performing, or working with their friends on a composition, can help. Never being able to listen to a piece of music without someone, possibly the teacher, interrupting the experience by saying something, does not help. Neither does trying to perform or compose with one's friends in the same room as other, understandably noisy, groups. The DfEE (1997) has produced some very helpful guidance on music accommodation in secondary schools that would be useful reading for all school architects, including those working on primary and special school buildings. When John Sloboda (1989) asked 70 adults to recall any incidents from their first ten years that were in any way connected with music, all the memories of positive emotions were associated with musical surroundings that were also positive or, at worst, neutral.

One cannot understand the 'evocative power' of music if one is not paying attention to it. John Paynter writes of differences in how audiences listen in theatres and concert halls. Referring to observations made by the American composer William Schuman, he comments:

In the theatre, as the lights are dimmed, people sit up in their seats and lean forward attentively, eager to see from which side of the stage the actors will enter and anxious not to miss the opening lines of dialogue. But in the concert hall, as the conductor lifts his baton, the audience tend to sink back into their seats, waiting for the music to drift over them! (Paynter 1997: 6)

Contrast that with the total attention to music and musicians that one typically sees at pop concerts. In school, students can be taught to give all music the attention that adults give it at pop concerts, rather than at many classical music concerts. Once listeners are concentrating, they are in a position to be able to hear what music is all about—as sound in time—rather than as a wash of sound perhaps loosely linked to a story or visual image that is thought to have inspired the composer.

While the relationship between music and emotion is a popular subject for psychological research (see Juslin & Sloboda 2001), much of this work has focused on adults, whose experience, as I have already argued, may differ from that of children. However, research into the out of school 'everyday' listening of adolescents (North et al. 2000) found that more girls than boys referred to emotion in relation to music listening, and also that boys were more likely to listen alone than girls. This leaves us with tantalizing questions including whether adolescent boys may listen alone to obtain the emotionality that their masculine identity prevents them from acknowledging when they are with their peers, and also whether it might be constructive, during the adolescent years, to organize listening more frequently as an individual, rather than a whole class, activity. Teachers may find it worthwhile to experiment with using new resources, including the school intranet and the Internet access that many students have at home and at school, to offer listening as an individual activity from time to time.

Understanding how some music is put together

We learn, by making music, how it is put together. This principle is fundamental to both *Sound and Silence* and *Sound and Structure* (Paynter & Aston 1970; Paynter 1992) and reflected in many of the curricular developments that followed these books. Three brief extracts from *Sound and Structure* give a flavour of how varied, challenging, and above all musical this approach to learning how music is put together can be.

Project 4: Fingers are great inspirers (p. 54)

Musical instruments themselves inspire musical ideas, not only by the quality of the sounds they produce but also by the way that they are constructed and played. The outward appearance of an instrument often seems to invite you to place your fingers on it in a way that will produce interesting arrangements of sounds.

For example, the harp's strings suggest long sweeping movements across them—and that is perhaps one of the commonest and most characteristic uses of the harp in orchestral music. A whole piece of music for solo harp could be made from a series of those *glissandi.*

Assignment 1

For guitarists. The guitar seems to invite broken chords: one hand holding down three or four strings against the frets while the other plucks them separately, one after another. Choose a fingering pattern for any chord (or make up a new one) and then, keeping that hand shape, move it, fret by fret, up and down the finger-board, plucking the strings individually or strumming gently across them. Include one or more open strings to produce a series of different chords, some of which will probably sound unusual. Develop this into a short piece of music that contrasts the different kinds of chord obtained . . .

Project 4 taps into Jo Glover's *music made as played*: compositions that are guided by the layout of the instrument. All the work outlined in Assignment 1 could be carried out by a guitarist of any age or stage. Teachers will judge the best way of explaining it to any younger guitarists without the verbal literacy skills needed to read and follow the instructions for themselves: I would be inclined to instruct a student in playing a very simple chord, such as E minor, in front of the whole class. Ironically, guitarists who have been playing chords conventionally for many years may find it harder to break away from what they are accustomed to doing, in order to carry out this assignment. They may find it helpful to work initially with a student who does not play guitar as mentor.

Clearly, this assignment could be adapted for other instruments. In *Sound and Structure*, John Paynter provides further assignments for violinists (who build up their piece from left-hand glides—*glissandi*), and keyboard players (who work with melodic motifs guided by their hand shape). Teachers may see links between students' pieces and well-known pieces of music. For example, J. S. Bach's famous Prelude in C, from the *Well-Tempered Clavier*, is based on the repeated use of similar hand patterns. These assignments could be used by instrumental teachers, as well as class teachers.

Project 8 starts at the other end from usual when building a piece of music. Instead of starting with a motif, perhaps a melodic motif, and working it up into a large piece, students begin with an idea for the large piece—in this case an Egyptian pyramid with its square base and four triangular faces—and work out a way of building it. Working this way round from time to time can be very instructive.

Again this is a project that could be undertaken by students of differing age and experience. Teachers would adjust the way that they explained the task according to the age of the students, but they would not need to reduce its musical demand for younger students. In primary schools, it might be possible to time this project to coincide with the students studying 3D shapes in mathematics, or when thinking about the Egyptian pyramids might be relevant to what they were doing in history or geography. This could bring increased understanding of the stimulus to their music-making, and it is possible that thinking about pyramids for musical purposes, perhaps by considering how one might look from inside or to a steeplejack (pyramidjack?) perched on top, or rotating a pyramid in one's mind, might help some students develop their mathematical thinking. Teachers will research their stimulus as thoroughly as possible. Music teachers who inadvertently teach students half-baked geography, history, or mathematics, for example, rightly cause just as much irritation to their subject colleagues as music teachers feel when teachers of other subjects appear to undermine them, perhaps by using recorded music for mood control, instead of as a focus for attention.

Project 8: Re-inventing the grammar (pp. 97–8)

It is one thing to invent a musical idea, but quite another to make it go on in time to become a substantial and coherent piece of music. As an alternative to starting from a musical idea which is a tiny cell—or perhaps just the first phrase of a melody—and developing that by extending it, expanding it and decorating it in various ways, you can begin with an overall view of the way the music will work. This is rather like inventing the grammar for a language; deciding how the various parts will function together, and then inventing the words to fulfil those functions.

Assignment 1

Devise a way of making a piece of music that will 'work' like a pyramid, i.e. not a piece of music about pyramids, but a method of putting musical sounds together that resembles as closely as possible the way in which stones were put together to make the ancient Egyptian pyramids.

Think about the structure. It is built of individual blocks; its base has four corners and is the most extensive area. As it grows higher, the area of each successive layer diminishes until there is only one stone at the top. At the same time all the lower layers remain in place.

When you have thought of a way of making this idea work with sounds, experiment to find the most suitable musical sounds to use as building blocks for your musical pyramid. Using the sounds you have chosen, invent a short musical motif to build with. You then have a number of possibilities for working with this figure, for instance:

(i) building up a complex texture gradually (figure by figure; instrument by instrument; layer by layer; corner-stones first, then fill in the rest of the layer)

(ii) using all the instruments, with the same figure or different versions of it, all together so that the structure is created in one go and simply 'stands' there

The first option could make it easier to maintain the musical interest because it is a process that goes on. But is there some way in which the second possibility could also be made to go on in time and be interesting to listen to even though the pyramid is (in a sense) 'complete' right from the start? (NB it does have four sides.)

Note the emphasis in Assignment 1 on building a piece of music that sounds interesting. This continues through other published assignments, not reproduced here, that begin with ideas including geological strata, a volcano, and a delta. As ever, these 'literary' ideas are just starting points for musical thinking, which stimulate musical ideas about structure and procedure: students are specifically not invited to imitate the sounds of volcanoes, nor to attempt the impossible task of converting visual images into sound. In one of the assignments students devise a theory for selecting the notes that they will use—the sound-world of their music—and think about the implications of this for their choice of instruments and voices.

The following project explicitly has something in it for everyone: experienced instrumentalists and singers, as well as students who do not see themselves as instrumentalists or singers. It does not need further comment here.

Project 9: New ears (pp. 117–18)

Tradition can be something of a liability. So much that is valuable and stimulating has been received from the past that just to be aware of those achievements can be daunting, and may hinder new ways of thinking about things. Then again, familiarity can breed contempt, but it also tends to confirm assumptions. We have all heard so many good tunes that we may take it for granted that music, to be called music at all, has to be tuneful— or, at least, melodic.

Similarly, it is very easy to associate particular instruments with certain kinds of music, and that strengthens our convictions about what is or is not 'beautiful' and 'musical' sound. It is easy to imagine a harpist playing calm, unruffled music with lots of gentle sweeps across the strings; even when harp music is fast and energetic it still has that same 'beautiful' quality. Could this instrument ever produce an ugly sound?

Yet, if we had never heard the familiar instruments being played—if we came upon them unexpectedly and with no preconceptions—we might discover many unusual ways of playing them; and we'd listen to their sounds with new ears.

Assignment 1

For individual players using their own musical instruments. Think of ways of making musical sounds as different as possible from those normally expected from the instrument. Make a piece of music using only those unexpected sounds.

Assignment 2

For four string players (preferably the conventional string quartet). Listen to a number of Classical and early Romantic string quartets (e.g. by Haydn, Mozart, Schubert, Mendelssohn). Make a note of features that are characteristic of the string quartet sound. Think of ways in which those features could deliberately be avoided (i.e. ways of playing the instruments that would prevent the players from making the conventional sounds). Using these controls, make a piece which has an overall *new* 'string quartet sound', unlike anything that could have been composed in the eighteenth or nineteenth century.

Assignment 3

Make up the most unlikely combination you can think of with any three instruments available to you. Improvise together (to discover the musical possibilities), and then compose a piece of music for this unusual sound.

Assignment 4

Make up a melody that is not 'tuneful'.

Assignment 5

Make up a piece of music for drums that is not 'rhythmic'.

Assignment 6

Make a piece for any combination of strings, wind and keyboards in which every instrument is treated as a percussion instrument.

Assignment 7

Make a piece for singers in which the voices are always used like percussion instruments—except at one point only, where they produce the kind of sound usually expected of them.

Waking up in the morning with music playing in their heads

I do not mean this literally—or perhaps I do? If you have worked at learning pieces of music until you can replay them in your head, either in their entirety or from any point that you choose, and possibly even discovering something new about a piece as you replay it in this way ('I did not know that the horns were playing there . . .'), you will know how seemingly infinite the mind is in this respect. Playing with music in your mind—carrying out thought experiments to change melodies, or improve them, or to work out new ways of combining them—is part of composing, and part of the mental rehearsal that many performers undertake. In *Rana Temporaria*, which I have already mentioned (p. 46), Peter Roadknight teaches his new students the first stages of being able to do music in their head:

> [the students] have internalised the four notes to such a degree that they can use singing to help them to compose. This is liberating. They can now compose at home, on the bus, in the dinner queue. They can compose anywhere, and they do not have to be glued to a keyboard. Composition and singing become partners. (Roadknight 2000: 7)

Four notes are only a start, but they are an important start. In *Rana Temporaria* they are the four (D E F♯ B) from which Rana's song is built; others can follow as further songs are learnt.

Teaching students to use their mental skills more in music can be great fun for everyone. Try asking a class, or group, of students to start singing or playing a melody that they know well, sing or play a particular phrase in their head, and then come in again on the next one. Initially, they may be all over the place. As they get better, remove the visual cues that they may be, rightly, taking from each other by asking them to turn round so that they cannot see each other, try longer phrases, and vary the task in other ways. With brief periods of regular practice, students can build up their skills rapidly—and surprise themselves as much as their teacher as they do so.

Sometimes turning off background music because it draws them in so much that they cannot concentrate on what they are supposed to be doing

Most young people experience music for much of their waking lives, but they frequently experience it passively, often using it as a backdrop for other activity. Through music in school, we can show young people that there is more to music than this: that music is worth listening to actively and with engagement, and also worth performing and composing. We could not stop young people listening to music passively in their own time—even if we thought that it might be appropriate for us to seek to do this—but we can introduce them to complementary musical activities that will engage them in music through being of high quality and interest.

Wanting to listen to new music that they have never heard before, as well as their old favourites; wanting to think about the role of music in, and beyond, their own culture

While listening to old favourites is clearly an important, as well as enjoyable, way of spending time, I would argue that one of the functions of education is to introduce students to new ideas and new material, including music that they would not come across in their everyday listening. Adults sometimes think that children will find it even more difficult than they do to listen to music that is out of the ordinary in some respect. Actually, this is not the case. Young children are particularly open-minded as listeners. More than 30 years ago, Sam Taylor (1973) found that the music of some relatively spiky twentieth-century composers— Hindemith, Stravinsky, Schoenberg—was more popular among children than adults might expect, but less popular among 11-year-olds than 7-year-olds. It is likely that he would have found something similar had he included music other than western classical music in the material that he played to children. It is never too early to start widening the range of music to which children listen. Music does not have to be appreciated in terms of the music that went before, or the music that originated closer to home. Children can appreciate music intuitively on its own terms. John Paynter considers that adults should try to do this too:

So often today's concert audiences seem to need the reassurance of programme notes before they listen to even the most familiar works, which suggests that there is a widely held assumption that music has to be 'translated' to be understood. But far from being *opposed* to reason, every art object and every art event is reason. A poem or a piece of music is not a record of its creator's thoughts: it is *thought* itself, made independent of its creator by its presentation (the act of making it present) and interacting with the thought of those who participate in it or receive it in various ways. (Paynter 1999: 102)

Of course, schools are about understanding, as well as listening to, music. I have said above that it is by doing music that one comes to understand how it is made. In Australia, students who include music in the Higher School Certificate taken at the age of 18 have to submit compositions that show understanding of the musical practices of the previous 25 years. In addition, the compositions of students in junior high schools routinely draw on what they have learnt through listening to the music of contemporary Australian composers. When investigating the role of music within and beyond their own culture, students are encouraged to interview musicians and other artists: the use of secondary sources, such as books, is discouraged (McPherson & Dunbar-Hall 2001). These are approaches to helping students extend their understanding of music.

Chapter 6

Teaching instruments musically

the periodical Ta-ta-ta-taa of the trumpeters sounding their various ingenious calls for watch-setting, stables, feed, boot-and-saddle, parade, and so on . . . made her think how clever her friend the trumpet-major must be to teach his pupils to play those pretty little tunes so well.

Anne, the miller's daughter, admires the pedagogical skills of
John Loveday in Thomas Hardy, *The Trumpet-Major*

Over the ages, in real life and not only in literature, instrumental (including vocal) teachers have often been noticed and admired. They also require some special mention here. While previous chapters have related to all forms of music teaching, including instrumental teaching, the present chapter focuses on some aspects of instrumental teaching that differ from class teaching:

- **an emphasis on performance**   In instrumental teaching there is greater focus on performing music, rather than composing it or listening to it, and correspondingly greater attention to interpreting music, rather than creating it and responding to it

- **the instrumental curriculum and the school**   The instrumental curriculum is, typically, additional to a broader music curriculum that students follow in school, and instrumental teachers have to find a way of helping students to make sense of this situation, despite often visiting each of their schools for only a few hours a week

- **the optional instrumental curriculum**   Not all students take instrumental lessons, and the ones that do sometimes decide after a while that they want to give up

- **the autonomy of instrumental teachers**   Instrumental teachers in the UK have greater autonomy than class teachers when it comes to shaping their teaching. While they often like to organize their teaching so that it leads towards graded music performance examinations[1] they do not have to do this, and they are not required to follow a national curriculum.

This chapter develops these four differences.

An emphasis on performance

'Why do people go to recitals? Partly to be amazed by the pole vaulting, but also because they hope the performer will break their heart.' (A concert pianist, London: December 2001)

'But if my children were encouraged to use their imagination and intellect, surely it would take them longer to get through their music grades?' (A parent, Oxford: December 2001)

A problem

Performance can be wonderful. But it is also much misunderstood. The pianist reminds us of the impact—magic even—of live musical performance. He speaks of western classical music that is played at recitals, but what he says could apply to almost any music. He is talking about aspects of performance that come partly from what a composer has written, and partly from what a performer has done to bring the writing alive, but his message could apply also where the performer is the composer as well, where the music has never been written down, or where music is improvised by one or more musicians. A performance can amaze us and move us. How better to give this to children than by teaching them to be performers? And students who opt to take instrumental lessons are saying that they want a taste of this, a chance to do more performing of a particular type than they would do otherwise.

The parent reminds us of what can go wrong when the matter of 'teaching children to be performers' is misunderstood. He sees examination certificates, rather than performances, as the goal of performance training, and limits his view of the process that his offspring should go through accordingly. He sees the instrumental lesson as something that should help his children assemble what they need to the standard required by examiners, and the use of their imagination or intellect as fripperies that would slow this down. I think that it would also be safe to say that he sees performance as something that relates only to western classical music.

---

[1] Graded performance examinations for different instruments are run by UK examination boards including the Associated Board of the Royal Schools of Music and Trinity Guildhall. The basic system runs from Grade 1 to Grade 8, and the overall standards of the different grades have been agreed between the examination boards and are linked to the National Qualifications Framework.

My conversation with this parent followed the broad drift of many conversations with other parents over the years. On learning that I work in music, the parent had told me that one of his children was not hurtling through her grades at quite the dizzying speed of the others because she spends some of her practice time on improvisation. What could he, as a parent who is interested in music but, in his view, *not musical*, do about this? The piano teacher had suggested that his daughter was not as musical as his, more focused, other children—and had hinted that she should give up lessons—but the parent would like her to carry on, at least for a while, even if she was not going to reach the high standards of her brothers.

As usual in such conversations, I observed that it is healthy and musical to want to apply one's new musical skills imaginatively and intelligently, and that perhaps the piano teacher could be urged to capitalize on these strengths of his daughter's approach. Perhaps the parent raised this thought with the piano teacher and she took some action; perhaps he didn't or she didn't. Whatever the outcome, at the time of our conversation, the parent—and possibly also the piano teacher—shared some misconceptions about performance and how it is made. Even within the realm of western classical music, the re-creation that is performance requires much more than the ability to play the right notes in the right order. Performances that are not quite note-perfect may occasionally be preferred to ones that are, if the trade-off is a higher degree of expression and communication. Performers find ways of playing pieces that make sense, and which communicate much more than a string of notes to their audience. To do this, they draw on resources that are not found on the printed score, and which they develop through intellectual and imaginative engagement with music, and through experience.

It is never too early to start to develop and build upon a student's intellectual and imaginative engagement with music. When we watch a young child at play with musical—or sound-making—materials, we can see that this engagement comes naturally. Children frequently focus intently as they experiment with different ways of making sounds, different ways of making different sounds, different ways of assembling sounds into patterns or motifs, and as they try to repeat or re-create sounds, patterns, or motifs that they made earlier. This natural engagement can be drawn into education, and developed through composing, listening, and musical approaches to performing. Instrumental teaching that is no more than repetitive drill or that consists, in effect, of a list of instructions to follow, switches it off.

We should not worry that thinking about expression while learning to play accurately is too difficult for children. They have formidable musical potential that remains untapped. Children in Japan work within the western and

Japanese tonal schemes in their class musical lessons, without confusing them, and sometimes fuse the tonal schemes when devising playground games (Murao & Wilkins 2001). Surely, this is much more difficult.

Clearly, there is no single 'right' way of performing, or interpreting, any piece of music, although there may be limits, or 'bounds' to what is acceptable in particular cultural circumstances. A professional performer's unusually mournful and slow performance of the first movement of Beethoven's so-called 'Moonlight' Sonata, say, might be deemed 'tedious' in a recital at a country house, 'daring' in the Purcell Room, 'well-judged' at a memorial service, 'innovative' on a CD, and not really noticed as part of a film score. Examinations and competitions are occasions when performers—and their teachers—worry particularly about what their audience want, rather than what they would like to give them. And yet examiners and adjudicators, as perform-ers themselves, may be open to a wide range of interpretations and styles. The cellist Lowri Blake, who also works widely as an examiner, explains:

A so-called romanticising of Bach cannot be dismissed: it may be superlatively good technically, and wonderfully communicated, but not 'authentic'. How far is that the student's own choice, his teacher's, or a complete lack of awareness of twenty-first century baroque practice? Or, perhaps this is a truly innovative student developing a whole new concept of fashion and stylistic practice—it must be considered on all its merits![2]

Lowri Blake is speaking of students at a conservatoire. We need to set younger students on this path of playing expressively, and not only accurately. Expression is not the same as licence: we can encourage—teach—children to play expressively without reducing our expectations of their technique, listening skills, or ability to vary their timbre, play strictly in time, or follow a conductor's beat. In fact, playing expressively requires greater control of all these than playing robotically. Mick Jagger made this point informally: 'Its alright letting yourself go, as long as you can let yourself back' (Green 1982). If we do not facilitate expressive playing through our teaching, then the only stu-dents who become expressive players will be survivors, rather than successes, of our teaching.

A piano teacher once spoke to me of one of the many higher education stu-dents who she had taken on after they had been learning with other teachers for several years: 'Alice is so musical. Whatever she plays—even scales—there is always something special about how it sounds.' Perhaps playing expressively and communicatively did come easier to Alice than to her, equally technically competent, peers. But perhaps it was more that Alice's musicality had somehow

---

[2] Conference for instrumental professors at the Royal College of Music, London, in 2002.

survived some regimented and potentially stifling piano teaching that she had received from her previous teachers. Alice was a singer. She loved singing, particularly musicals and Gilbert and Sullivan, and she put her all into it. She carried this over into her piano playing. I sometimes heard her humming as she practised piano, and perhaps she sang in her head for much of the time that she played. She carried the phrasing that came naturally to her as a singer into her piano playing. It seemed that everything that she played on piano was a *Song without Words* to her. In Tânia Lisboa's terms (see p. 53) she was working multi-modally. I feel sure that her peers could have been taught to work multi-modally too or, better still, could have been taught piano in a way that kept alive the musicality that they had brought to their very first piano lesson.

How can we keep this musicality alive when giving lessons on piano, or on other instruments? In lots of ways. We can draw students' attention to the high-quality performances that they produce from their very first lesson, even if we suspect that their quality may have arisen partly fortuitously, or if students find it difficult to repeat them. We can organize special projects, perhaps related to *New ears* or *Fingers are great inspirers* from *Sound and Structure* (see pp. 57 & 60), that challenge students to listen to, and use, the sounds that they can already make in different ways. We can make improvising a routine part of lessons, and a routine part of practice. We can sing as we teach, and encourage students to join us. Above all, we can organize instrumental lessons so as to destroy the myth that students have to spend years getting things 'right' before starting to 'express themselves'. *Leave your imagination and initiative at the door, all ye who enter here* . . . We may want to focus on accuracy and control in instrumental lessons, but they are not our only concern. We can organize instrumental lessons so that students make music as they develop their technique.

This approach can start with the very first instrumental lesson. It simply is not the case that students need to spend whole lessons on amusical preliminary activities such as learning how to assemble their instrument, clapping rhythms, or learning to read music before they start to make music, of some carefully chosen sort, on their instrument.

I recently observed a 7-year-old's first ever keyboard lesson. This was scheduled to last a mere 15 minutes, and the teacher had to use some of that time to collect the student from her very distant classroom. He used the time well. When the teacher and student arrived at the keyboard teaching room they already had a professional relationship, and the teacher knew what sort of keyboard the student had at home, and that she had 'just been playing around on it' so far. The student sat down at the keyboard immediately, ready to play. The teacher taught her a right-hand five-note eight-bar melody by ear, then showed her how it fitted with a three-chord autochord accompaniment and taught her that, and finally taught her to also add an autorhythm. The student left her first lesson with a worthwhile memorized piece that she could work on, including by playing it to her friends and family, during the week.

The teacher showed me this memorized piece written out at the beginning of a tutor book that he has prepared, for use with his own students. He planned to give a copy to the student I saw, and show her the memorized piece written down, two or three weeks later: 'when this will no longer get in the way'. Playing a piece that she already knew, while following it written down, would form her introduction to staff notation.

This student is being introduced to staff notation musically, in a way that shows that staff notation can be used to record a piece of music that is complete in someone's head, whether or not it has ever been played to an audience. The strengths of this approach also include its similarity with the way that young children learn the relationship between writing and oral language. Children often learn to spot words that are important to them—such as their name in birthday cards or on birthday cakes—long before anyone has taught them how to work out what a written word says from its individual letters.

Below, we have an example of how not to organize a first lesson:

So enthusiastic were the 7-year-olds that they seemed to float into their lesson, their eyes and faces ablaze. They gravitated towards the shiny new violin cases at the side of the room. 'Don't touch those', the teacher said. By the end of the lesson, the children had learnt to open their case, take the violin out, and put it back 'properly', without making a sound.

And don't tell me that this happened because the students were being taught in a group! I have seen initial group lessons on many instruments that were just as musically exciting as the keyboard lesson described above. And, sadly, I have also recently seen a first violin lesson for just one student, in which he was only shown how to hold his bow. I have to say that he was able to hold it very nicely by the end of the lesson. But how was he going to remember how to hold it over the next week, until his next lesson, given that he could not judge whether he was holding it well or not through the sound that he made, because he was not making any sound at all? And what was he going to show his friends and family that he had learnt when he got home? And perhaps an unkind brother or sister might even laugh at him for being so pleased that he could hold a bow but not make any sound? And how long was he going to remain keen on playing the violin if he was not actually allowed to play it? If it really does make sense to teach a student how to told a bow before you have taught them how to hold the violin across which they are to draw their bow (and I am not convinced of this!) what would be wrong with the teacher also getting the violin out of its case, tuning it, and showing the student how to hold it 'banjo style' and pluck open strings to play the opening of *Twinkle twinkle little star* using three different starting notes, for example? (Fig. 3) A daring teacher might also show students how to use the first finger of their left hand to stop the 'next' note needed for *Twinkle twinkle*, and might well find that students came to their next lesson able to play the three following notes as well. Or with a melody that they had composed using the notes that they had learnt so far . . .

Fig. 3   Opening of *Twinkle twinkle little star* on the violin

Practice and memorization

'Practice makes perfect', or so we are told. Instrumental teachers typically encourage students to practise. Inexperienced students sometimes find this a chore. Some students who practise a lot do not succeed. Some very competent musicians appear not to practise. The link between practice and perfection is clearly complex.

According to the psychological theory of expertise, which encompasses music, and also fields as diverse as chess and skiing (see Ericsson & Smith 1991), expertise is the result of sufficient 'deliberate practice' over an extended period of study. Fuelled partly by the development of expertise theory, over the last few years there has been considerable research into instrumental practice. Much of the first research focused on the quantity of practice, often measured in terms of thousands of hours, rather than its content and quality. While this is of interest descriptively (because it tells people who are not performers something of what it is to learn to be a performer), it is of little use educationally, because it does not help us, as teachers, to enable students to make better progress. Thousands of hours—even tens of thousands of hours—of the 'wrong' practice will clearly not turn a novice performer into an expert performer. 'Lots of practice' is a symptom, rather than a cause, of learning to be a performer.

More recent research has considered also the quality of practice, particularly when musicians are preparing performances that they will give from memory. Some of this has focused on the way that performers often divide pieces into short segments that are combined as the piece is learnt. When Aaron Williamon and Elizabeth Valentine (2000) analysed the practising of 22 young instrumentalists (see Fig. 4)—all pianists working on one of four pieces by J. S. Bach chosen by the researchers to match their standard of playing—they found that the pianists whose final performances were more successful had

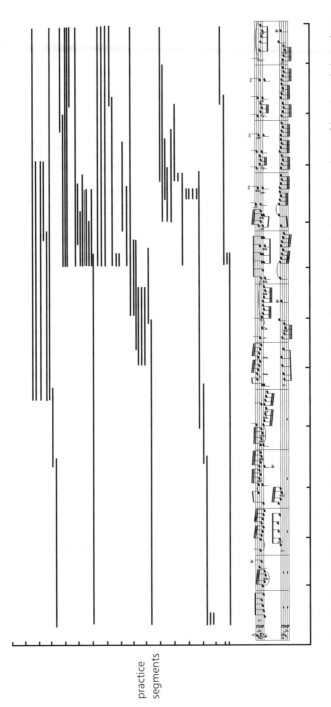

Fig. 4 A pianist practises Bach's Fugue in D minor. After playing bars 1–8, the pianist repeats a beat of bar 8, and then plays bars 8–11, and so forth (Williamon & Valentine 2000)

practice
segments

started to work on longer segments earlier. This applied whether the pianists were elementary or advanced.

Does this mean that we should teach students to play longer segments of pieces earlier in their practice? The answer is both 'yes' and 'no'. Students who are able to play longer segments earlier can spend more time building up, consciously or subconsciously, the aspects of their performance that lie deeper than the accuracy of individual notes or individual bars. Their final performances are likely to be more mature, more 'considered', and better memorized. But in order to be able to play longer segments of pieces, students need to have eradicated the performance difficulties that cause them to stumble. So one of the messages of this research is that students should be taught to organize their practice so that these difficulties are eradicated speedily, and then to take the opportunity to practise longer segments as soon as possible.

The researchers also analysed the total time that the student pianists spent practising. Unsurprisingly, those working on the most advanced—and longest—piece did most practice. However, the advanced players also practised more economically: they required much less practice time 'per beat' than the beginners. They had learnt to work more efficiently. Related to this were the strategies that they used for memorization. While the starts and stops during the early stages of pianists' practice related mainly to bars that they found difficult, the more effective memorizers soon mastered these bars and stopped strategically, according to the way that they had divided the piece into segments. And in due course they did not need to stop at all, but still moved from playing the whole piece to playing segments of it from time to time, thus providing themselves with further 'copies' as insurance against memory loss. The division of pieces into segments was not always related to what musicologists might view to be the formal structure of the piece, but worked for the pianists concerned (Williamon & Valentine 2002).

How did the pianists who produced the better performances of Bach pieces learn to practise more effectively? And how did they learn to memorize? Were they taught, or did they just find out? And, if the latter, would they be able to explain what they had found out to their own students, should they become teachers? The findings of a study by Roger Chaffin and Gabriela Imreh (2001) suggest that musicians who do practise effectively may not always be entirely aware of their strategies. A concert pianist—Gabriela Imreh—recorded her practice as she learned the *Presto* of the *Italian Concerto* by J. S. Bach for performance, commenting on what she was doing as she worked. Her remarks were not in total agreement with data resulting from the analysis of her practice sessions. In particular, while she had suggested that her early practice sessions were spent attending to fingering, technical difficulties, and 'familiar patterns of notes', before moving to sessions where she also considered dynamics, analysis of her actual practice revealed that she had been working on dynamics from the beginning.

This is interesting. Here we have an expert performer who works musically with the piece that she is learning from the very beginning, a procedure that is, in my experience of observing expert performers, characteristic. And yet, this is not what she thinks that she does. Is this, one might ask rhetorically, because the dictum 'sort out the notes and then add the expression', which I have suggested we should not build into the long-term development of novices into experts, and which is applied here to the shorter term process by which an expert learns a piece, is so ingrained?

Are some instrumental teachers telling their students to sort out the notes first and add the expression later, in effect because this is what their teachers said to them? And when they were students did they nevertheless play musically at all times, either because they picked this up subconsciously from their teacher, or because it came naturally? And are their demonstrations for their present students mechanical: embodiments of sorting out the notes and adding the music later? And, to refer back to the parent who was worried about his improvising daughter (p. 66), might this tie in with the idea that using one's intellect and imagination gets in the way of success in performance examinations?

I began this section of the chapter by objecting to the view of a parent who saw the construction of an instrumental performance as a linear process rather as a child might build a tall tower from building bricks, by placing one on top of the other. I end it, in a sense, where I began. Almost all the research to which I have referred has been limited to western classical music. Even so, it is clear that the re-creation that is performance requires much more than linear activity if, as the concert pianist might put it, hearts are to be broken and hurdles jumped. And it is not just a matter of thinking of expression before, or after, one has got the notes right. Tânia Lisboa's research reminds us that where our intellect and imagination are already engaged, learning the notes may become less of a problem.

The instrumental curriculum and the school

The instrumental curriculum is, typically, additional to a broader music curriculum that students are following in school, and instrumental teachers have to find a way of helping students to make sense of this situation, despite often visiting each of their schools for only a few hours a week—or not at all if they are a private teacher. Instrumental teaching has to relate more to students' whole musical lives, and teachers' whole musical lives than would 'a string of individuals passing through, as if visiting the dentist' (Swanwick 1999: 106).

It is easy, but dangerous, to think of the music curriculum, in the broadest sense of the word, as divided into separate 'boxes'. Instrumental tuition forms one box, school music forms another, and the informal music-making that students carry out on their own at home or with their friends is a third box, and so on. An instrumental teacher might feel that their box contains all the constituent parts of a graded performance examination—perhaps scales, pieces, and studies, sight-reading and ear tests, and so forth. A school teacher might think just in terms of the requirements of the national curriculum, GCSE or A level. Trying to divide music into boxes can make things appear easier for teachers, because they only have to concern themselves with their own box. But it is rarely in students' interests for their learning to be so compartmentalized. It typically leads to diminished expectations of what they are able to achieve. Teachers may entirely overlook the skills and understanding that students have developed in another box, and either teach them again or assume that students are not capable of developing them. Students quickly learn the bounds of what particular teachers expect, or do not expect, them to do—this is part of induction into an educational system—and may not show a teacher that they have a musical life that lies outside the box that surrounds the ambit of the teacher.

A particular conversation with eight children aged 8 and 9 comes to mind here. It was one of those schools that propels itself to the forefront of my mind when I bristle with anger on reading (yet again) in a newspaper that children today do not want to learn, or that school teaching is an easy job because of the long holidays. The school is a maze of dark steep stairs and dark narrow corridors under leaky roofs. It is set in a derelict industrial landscape intersected by several busy roads of speeding 'through traffic'. It does not have a supply of money from its community that it can use to help improve its buildings or environment: nearly all its students are entitled to take free school meals, and many of them are refugees. The school had fallen on hard times educationally, and was working phenomenally hard to try to improve itself. It was making a good shot at teaching the children everything that it should be teaching them, including numeracy, literacy, and the national curriculum in music—including composing.

The children had just had a cornet lesson from a visiting instrumental teacher. In many respects, it was a very good cornet lesson: the children had worked hard, had fun, and emerged from the lesson playing their cornets better than when they arrived. The teacher had told the children at the start of the lesson what he intended they should achieve by the end of it, this was ambitious, they had achieved it, and he had ensured that they knew that they had achieved it. But it was one of those box-bound cornet lessons. There were no obvious links with the music that the children do in their class lessons, at home, or in the community. The teacher operated as though the children only did music during their cornet lessons, and when they were at home practising the cornet pieces that he had given them.

The children had rumbled this. When I asked whether they ever composed on their cornets, they explained—somewhat sheepishly in the first instance—that during cornet lessons they played the music that they had been given, but that when they were at home practising they made up their own cornet tunes. In a sense, they had brought together composing from school music, and cornet playing from their instrumental lessons, in their private musical lives. I asked them whether they ever played their cornet compositions to their cornet teacher, or to their school teacher. Of course not. The children clearly thought that I must have come from another planet to be even asking this question. They patiently explained again about only playing the music that one is given during cornet lessons, and then added that one does not bring compositions to class music lessons either—the composing that one does there has to be in response to ideas from the teacher. All this was said without trace of cynicism.

Just think how much more progress the children could make, musically, if the education system in which they found themselves helped them to bring together their music education in class music, in their cornet lessons, when they are playing their cornets at home, and so on. No teacher can know everything about the richness of children's individual musical lives. But teachers can give children opportunities to talk about, and to show, the music that they do out of school, and try to build on this. Instrumental teachers can liaise with schoolteachers about the content of their curriculum. And they can give children some composing tasks to carry out during their practice time at home, and listen to the compositions that they have made at home on their own, from time to time.

In some local education authority music services, composing is a routine part of the instrumental curriculum. Teachers may set students practice tasks such as composing a melody based on a scale that they are learning, or composing a study or exercise that will help them to consolidate a new technique, and then make time in the next lesson to listen to the students' compositions, and work with them on improving them. Students may be encouraged to share their instrumental compositions with class teachers, and to keep any notes on their compositions, or any scores that they write, in the folders where they store the work completed during class music lessons.

Pat Gane (1996) developed ways of helping instrumental teachers to integrate their curriculum with the national curriculum, even though students may start instrumental lessons at widely differing ages, and show different rates of progress in becoming instrumentalists. She suggested ten 'instrumental levels' based on a notional student who starts instrumental lessons at age 7–8, achieves level 4 (roughly equivalent to Grade 2–3 in a performance examination but broader in scope) on leaving primary school at age 11, and who achieves level 7 (roughly equivalent to Grade 4) on completing the national curriculum in music at the age of 14. She defines five 'areas of learning' for the instrumental curriculum:

♦ performing/playing
♦ composing/improvising
♦ listening/aural
♦ appraising understanding
♦ personal development

and offers sample programmes of study and linked assessment profiles for a notional student, Warren Black, who began the violin aged 7 in September 1995, and who reached level 6 by July 2001. Warren and his teacher, Mantovani, completed an assessment profile each July, and two of the sections (the general section and the section relating to composing/improvising) from July 1998, when Warren was level 3 and age 10, are as follows (Gane 1996: 59):

Table 1 Extracts from the assessment form of a 10-year-old

Composing/Improvising	Teacher's comments
Makes up simple Question and Answer phrases in keys G, D, A, C, e, a;* devises simple accompanying ostinati and riffs; makes up simple musical ideas e.g. on a given mood or idea; uses symbols to achieve a planned effect; can use some musical elements expressively: melody/rhythm/dynamics and simple texture; uses simple structural ideas e.g. repetition, contrast, question and answer.	Improvising is good, some excellent, for instance the jazz riffs you made up for our blues arrangement; composing is hampered by your tendency to accept your first go; try and refine ideas a bit more.
	Student's comments
	I liked the jazz piece; I don't like writing music down much because it takes too long

General notes

Well done, Warren: I am really pleased with your progress this year; you deserved your merit in the Grade 2 examination; you are much more comfortable with your work now; you have been a good member of the string club and played in class composition projects too I believe; you seem a lot happier with the change of group this year; next term you are ready to begin level 4 work; I will keep you in the same group for one term and then perhaps move you to another one.

Pat Gane's work relates, of course, to the 1995 version of the national curriculum for England (DfE 1995), but the ideas that it contains have the flexibility to be applied to any version of a national curriculum that encompasses composing, performing, and listening, including the current curriculum in England.

* G, D, A, C major; E, A minor.

A Common Approach 2002 (FMS *et al.* 2002*a*), a published instrumental/ vocal curriculum framework that reflects the distilled thoughts of hundreds of instrumental teachers in the UK, has taken even further ideas that are similar to Pat Gane's. 'Creating, developing, and interpreting musical ideas' is one of six interrelated areas of musical experience that teachers are encouraged to integrate into their day-to-day and longer-term planning. From their earliest lessons, students learning string instruments, for example, are taught to improvise and compose on their instrument, as shown in Table 2:

Table 2 Example from Programme Study 1 of *A Common Approach 2002: Strings* (FMS *et al.* 2002*b*: 9)

Possible teaching activities*	Points to note
Ask students to explore different ways of making musical sounds on the instrument in response to an imaginative or pictorial idea.	The teacher can promote pupils' confidence by:
Help pupils to make up short and simple rhythmic/ melodic patterns from suggested musical starting points, e.g. two or three selected notes, ostinati. Abstract or pictorial ideas could also be used.	◆ demonstrating how to experiment with musical ideas ◆ providing step-by-step assistance with models, patterns and procedures
Repeat the process, selecting and discarding musical ideas for musical coherence.	◆ emphasizing the open-ended nature of the activity—all outcomes are valued and enjoyed.
Lead pupils in a discussion about the musical effect of their improvisations.	
Play 'Follow my Leader': a pupil plays three or four notes, then the next pupil plays three or four more, starting on the last note of the first player, and so on.	
Ask pupils to compose short pieces from a given starting point, e.g. a story, poem, theme, picture, or one of the musical techniques suggested above. Discuss the outcomes. Initially, this could consist of asking pupils to write down their improvisations as an aid to memory, perhaps using their own forms of shorthand as a precursor to staff notation.	Through composing, pupils are able to explore the music from the inside. Composing is valid in its own right, but it can also be used to develop performing skills, knowledge and understanding. Productive links with general classroom work should be made wherever possible.
Provide opportunities for pupils to perform their compositions to others.	It may be necessary to store pupils' ideas for them since their creative imagination may run ahead of their ability to write down their ideas, at least where staff notation is concerned.
Encourage pupils to use their instruments in creative activities in the classroom, applying technical skills already acquired.	

* Instrumental teachers should harness the composing interests of pupils whenever it is appropriate. This may be as an integral part of the instrumental curriculum, or to support the pupils in other areas of the national curriculum.

By the time that string students have reached the most advanced stage of *A Common Approach 2002*, the possibilities for teaching activities include those shown in Table 3.

It is possible to think of many music projects which involve the creative use of instrumental skills, have potential benefits for instrumentalists as performers and creators of music, and that could be led either by instrumental teachers or by school teachers. *Fingers are great inspirers* (see p. 57), Project 4 from John Paynter's *Sound and Structure* (1992), in which musical instruments themselves inspire musical ideas by the ways in which they seem to be asking to be played, is a case in point. Pieces of music for individual instruments can be built from *glissandi* on a harp or trombone, by moving chord shapes up and down the neck of a guitar, or by hitting a suspended cymbal in different places, with different strokes or mallets, and with different methods of damping sounds. There is scope to build these ideas into pieces for mixed instruments that begin, perhaps, with each instrument stating its ideas, and move, via combination of these ideas, to the development of one instrument's ideas by another instrument.

Table 3 Extracts from Programme Study 5 of *A Common Approach 2002: Strings* (FMS *et al.* 2002b: 57, 59)

Possible teaching activities	Points to note
Continue to link improvisations to repertoire being studied, e.g. pupils improvise a short piece in the baroque or romantic styles.	Improvisation provides an obvious and enjoyable way of exploring musical devices and conventions. It often provides the groundwork for more extended compositions. These advanced improvisations can be as challenging for the teacher as the pupil!
Teach a well-known jazz standard, e.g. 'I Got Rhythm': • play pupils a recording of the piece • familiarize them with the 32-bar AABA form and teach them the chords and melody. Play it with them as a pupil/teacher duo, swapping roles • demonstrate how to embellish the melody freely and encourage pupils to do the same when their turn comes • finally, ask them to improvise over the chords, making fewer references to the orginal melody.	
Ask pupils to compose pieces for more than one instrument, e.g. string quartet, solo string instrument and piano . . .	Pupils can use techniques associated with pieces being learnt. These may include contrapuntal textures and more complex structures, and can involve a higher level of technical difficulty for the performer . . . Encourage pupils to exploit the idiomatic potential of instruments.

New ears (see p. 60), Project 9 from *Sound and Structure*, challenges instrumentalists to identify their preconceptions about music—for example that music is melodic, or that specific instruments usually use only a small, prescribed, range of all the sounds that they are capable of producing—and deliberately try to override these preconceptions as they compose music that is new in some way.

I suggested that such projects could be led either by instrumental teachers or schoolteachers. They could also involve students who are not learning to play an instrument, and could include teachers, including music teachers, among the participants.

Here is an example of a short project that was led by a primary class teacher:

Two [9-year-old] pupils who had recently started cello lessons had brought their instruments to the lesson. The teacher organised them to provide a demonstration of *high*, *low*, *higher* and *lower* on cellos. Next, there was demonstration and discussion of steps and leaps on cellos. This led to a composing activity. In pairs, the pupils composed question and answer phrases, thinking about their use of *steps*, *leaps*, *high*, *low*, *higher* and *lower*. The teacher circulated round the pairs, helping them to develop their ideas. The lesson ended with detailed appraisal, discussion and development of two compositions in front of the class.

During this lesson, the pupils appeared to grow musically in front of your eyes. They already had reasonable skills in playing tuned percussion with two mallets, and they understood that *high* and *low* are relative terms, that what is *high* for a cello might be *low* for a violin. The teacher elicited demonstrations from pupils, and used them constructively when instructing the whole class. She encouraged pupils to lengthen their *questions*. She developed their verbal analysis of their peers' compositions. She expected pupils to remember their compositions, and repeat them so that others could analyse what they were doing. There were no short cuts, such as 'safe' use of pentatonic scales, or giving some pupils untuned instruments. The teacher's expectations were very high, and proved to be realistic.' (Mills 1998*a*: 65)

The optional instrumental curriculum

Instrumental lessons are optional, and students have the option of giving them up, as well as continuing them. In the past, giving up was sometimes viewed as entirely negative—as 'wastage' (Mawbey 1973). Certainly, it is a waste when students decide to give up instrumental lessons because the lessons that they have had were unsatisfactory in some way, perhaps because the teacher was not very well organized, or was not sensitive to students' interests, and styles of learning. However, 'wastage' was usually viewed as the students' fault, and considerable efforts were made to select instrumental students who were thought to have 'stickability'. I find the notion that 'stickability' is a virtue that applies in all circumstances a somewhat troubling one. I would prefer children to learn to be critical about what it is that they wish to stick with. The desire to 'stick' with instrumental lessons can—ideally does—result from the very high quality of the experience that is being offered through them.

Gary McPherson (2000) found that, among a sample of 133 children in Australia, students who told an interviewer, before they started lessons, that they intended to play for many years, were more likely to still be playing nine months later. Yes, but was this cause or effect? The children did not volunteer that they were going to learn for many years: they were asked. Could the split-second decision about how to answer this question, if one has not thought about it before, help to determine how long one continues lessons? I find this a fascinating, but rather worrying, thought. It suggests that, as teachers, we need to be careful not to put ideas into children's heads that could lead them to lower their expectations of themselves.

Having hobbies, and exchanging them for new hobbies, is part of growing up. Children should be able to give up instrumental lessons, with dignity, simply because their interests have changed. When children give up collecting stamps, or roller blading, for example, they are not typically viewed as 'failures', or 'letting their teacher/parents down' even though both these activities, like learning to play an instrument, require some financial investment and are ones that some people continue well into adulthood. Moreover, a child who is allowed to give up learning an instrument with dignity may be better disposed to look back on their experience with pleasure, and to apply their skills by taking up another instrument, or looking favourably on the wishes of their own children to learn an instrument, at a later stage.

Some instrumental teachers believe that students who are not making good progress should be 'counselled out' of continuing instrumental lessons. Susan Hallam (1998) writes of 'sensitively negotiating children giving up playing'. I am not sure why one should do this. The sheer fact that a student is enjoying the lessons may be a good enough reason for them to continue with them. We do not suggest that a young person stops taking tennis coaching when it is clear that they are not going to make Wimbledon, or stops going to a voluntary painting class on Saturdays for fun because their teacher thinks they will not get a Grade A* in art and design at GCSE. Why should instrumental lessons be any different?

I recall a girl, aged 12, whose cello lesson I observed. She had been learning for five years, but was still playing very simple pieces. At the end of the lesson, the teacher set her exactly the same homework task that she had had the previous week, as he did not think that she had made enough progress to try a new piece—or even try a new way of playing the same piece. I looked back through her book and discovered that the teacher had actually set precisely the same homework task for the last six lessons! Yet this student persisted with her lessons, and showed signs of enjoyment during them. I feel sure that had the student been better, and more imaginatively, taught, she would have made more progress. But, even without the progress, she showed pleasure in simply playing cello, and working with a teacher on playing cello.

I recall another girl, with some embarrassment. Lois started at secondary school on the same day that I began my teaching career, and I taught her once a week for three years. I remember her well as a student who tried hard, and who did not find music very easy, but who stayed behind after lessons on several occasions to ask me questions that she had been too shy to ask in class, and to tell me that she was taking piano lessons, and what she was playing. However, she did not get involved in any of the many music activities that I ran at lunchtime and after school, and it did not occur to me that music was a special part of her life. Six years after I had left her school, she somehow found out where I was working—more than 200 miles away—and wrote thanking me for getting her interested in music, explaining that playing piano was the activity that had sustained her through two years of serious illness after she left school. Now, unlike the cello teacher above, I never taught her in a group of fewer than 28 students. But I feel sure that I could have done more for her musically had I spotted how motivated she was.

The autonomy of instrumental teachers

What shapes instrumental teaching?

Matt, age 13, plays guitar. Yes, he used to take guitar lessons, but they cost £160 a year, and were a waste of money, because he feels that he did not learn anything. He refers to his former guitar teacher as 'the man with the book'.

Matt's guitar lessons seem to have been shaped by the tutor book that his teacher chose for them to work through. Matt clearly had very little respect for this approach. It was probably a notation-centred tutor book, whereas Matt was interested in playing MUSIC. Matt feels that he made progress more rapidly once his lessons ended, since when he has learnt by playing alone, or with his friends.

What should shape instrumental lessons? In 2001, 134 instrumental teachers working for eight local education authorities in England agreed to complete a questionnaire about instrumental teaching. These teachers mainly had several years' experience of teaching successfully in schools. Jan Smith and I wanted to know:

- what teachers believe makes instrumental teaching effective in schools
- what teachers believe makes instrumental teaching effective when students go on to study music in higher education

- how this all relates to factors including teachers' recollections of the instrumental lessons they received at school and in higher education, the courses that they have attended, and the lessons that they remember as 'special' from when they were students (Mills & Smith 2003).

Many of the teachers wrote at length, and gave us a great deal of very high-quality material when responding to our questions. First, we asked them to write about the 'hallmarks' of effective instrumental teaching in schools, and effective instrumental teaching in higher education. It soon became clear that many teachers consider that the hallmarks of effective teaching in schools are different from those in higher education. For example, three teachers' responses were as shown in Table 4. Note, for example, how two teachers refer to students having 'fun' when writing about effective teaching in schools, but none use this word when referring to effective teaching in higher education. The images of instrumental teachers that come to mind when I read Teacher A, B, and C's writing about schools are quite different from those that result from their writing about higher education.

We found this difference more generally within the responses of the 134 teachers. We coded the hallmarks that 134 teachers had identified, and then ranked them according to the total number of teachers who mentioned them. The table shows the 'top ten' hallmarks of effective teaching in schools, and effective teaching in higher education. Teachers believe that effective teaching in schools and higher education shares six hallmarks:

- *the teacher is knowledgeable.* Clearly, a teacher needs to be able to play the instrument that they are teaching, play it well, know what they do to play it well, and know some other ways—that may be more suited to one or more of their students—in which the instrument can be played well. There are some rare examples of students who become successful performers despite initially having a teacher who is not a good player, perhaps because the teacher is caring and encouraging and provides an environment in which a child's musical talent may be developed (Kemp & Mills 2002). For example, a clarinet student at the Royal College of Music recently told me that his first clarinet teacher, from whom he learnt for several years, had 'failed Grade 3'. But it takes a rare commitment to music, and a considerable amount of luck, to survive teaching that is quite as unknowledgeable as that. It may be no coincidence that the clarinettist who is now at the RCM joined a band when he had been learning clarinet for only a few weeks, and played alongside young musicians with more technical accomplishment than his teacher.

Table 4 Three teachers' hallmarks of effective instrumental teaching at school and in higher education

	School	Higher Education
Teacher A	Trying to lay the foundations for good technique and habits, while trying to keep lessons fun and interesting. Pupils should enjoy playing but expect to work hard, practise regularly at home and be shown how to do it (Do we show pupils how to practise enough?). They should learn to play fluently and expressively and have opportunities to perform solos, play in small groups, and in larger orchestras.	The development of a good technique as a means to play musically and expressively. To encourage exploration and initiative but give clear guidance on how to work and what is expected. To play and perform as much as possible in different sorts of music - solo, ensemble, orchestra, other.
Teacher B	Enthusiasm. Able to relate to children. Sensitive to individual needs. Use of popular tunes. Encouragement.	Technique. Variety and breadth of styles. Encourage individual interpretation.
Teacher C	Being approachable, communicating well. Making lessons fun. Giving good descriptive teaching both for technical and musical ideas. Allowing the pupil some autonomy in the way their lesson goes – e.g. would you like to play top or bottom in the duet? – What do you feel needs most attention in this piece? Teaching with humour. Also, play and response work is brilliant for keeping people responsive and aurally switched on.	Giving good background to the style / character of a piece. Clear, easily understood technique teaching that enables the pupil to take off with their own musical ideas. Supporting the pupil and giving positive support when they experiment musically.

- *the teacher is a good communicator.* The issues here include that teaching needs to be presented in a manner that is appropriate to students' age. Harald Jørgensen (2001) investigated whether starting to learn an instrument at a young age ultimately led students to achieve higher standards, and discovered that an early start was advantageous only if one was lucky enough to choose a teacher who is skilled socially and musically. Many teachers are effective at explaining material to younger students. They have learnt to build relationships between what they want to teach children, and what the children already know. They do not underestimate the enormous potential of children as learners, and so do not 'dumb down'—oversimplify—their teaching to the point that it makes little sense, and children feel patronized. They learn the routines through which children are accustomed to being managed by teachers at school, and so do not misinterpret children's uncertainty about what the teacher wants them to do as naughtiness, or inability to concentrate. When the instrumental teaching services run by local education authorities were first inspected, inspectors found that instrumental teachers who are qualified to work as class music teachers were more likely to communicate effectively in ways such as these (Mills 2000*a*).

- *the teaching is matched to what the students need.* This means that students are presented with challenges that build on their learning, are attainable, and feel worthwhile. In class lessons in all subjects, it is now very common for teachers to explain at the beginning of each lesson what students are intended to learn, and to review with students at the end of each lesson whether or not the 'learning objectives' have been achieved. Some instrumental teachers do this too, and this can help to build bridges between class music and instrumental music, and encourage students to focus on the progress that they are making. An example of one of the more mundane learning objectives for a lesson for some violinists might be 'to learn to play two octaves of the scale of G major, slurred, with two notes to a bow'.

In seeking to match their teaching to the musical needs of students, many teachers try to provide much more than instrumental skills through their instrumental lessons. Doris da Costa (1994) argues that it can be helpful to support instrumental lessons with classes for listening to music recordings. *A Common Approach 2002* (FMS *et al.* 2002*a*), includes 'out of lesson listening' in addition to the composition and improvisation that have already been referred to (see p. 78). Fred Seddon and Susan O'Neill (2001) found that, even when instrumental students had not composed as part of their instrumental lessons, their compositions had higher 'technical complexity' than those of students who had not taken instrumental lessons. In addition, the students who had taken instrumental lessons tended to give higher self-evaluations for 'how good their composition sounded'.

The teacher's learning strategies need to be matched to the students too. We do not all learn in the same way, or in the same way all the time. Siw Nielsen (1999) has investigated the learning strategies used by pipe organ students in higher education, and argues for 'strategies to direct attention to the task at hand' and 'strategies to secure efficient use of time' to be taught more extensively in instrumental music at school, in the same way as they are taught in other subjects including mathematics and reading.

Matched teaching is not the same as teaching that suggests that there is only one correct solution to a problem with technique or performance. Teachers who teach in this way may argue that students need to be able to 'control' a piece before they can 'shape' it. They often appear to be very knowledgeable, and are sometimes very popular with their students, and their students' parents. However, they do not help students to develop their autonomy as learners, or to understand the extensive range of approaches that may be used to interpret a piece of music, or solve the technical problems implied by particular interpretations. If the approach of 'first get the notes right and then add the expression' ever had its day, this has now passed.

♦ *the teacher is positive, and praises students.* Where the music provision in a school is weak, students may feel that their teachers do not praise them adequately for work done well. Being positive with students, and praising them when appropriate, is important at all stages of instrumental teaching, but perhaps particularly when students are going through periods of potentially disruptive transition, such as moving from primary school to secondary school. While secondary schools can provide students with wonderful educational opportunities that could not possibly be available in primary schools, because of their smaller size, the sheer fact of changing school can lead students to reappraise their commitment to instrumental lessons. There is more homework at secondary school, the journey to school often takes longer, there are new friendships to be built, it may take a few weeks for the secondary school to set up a timetable for instrumental teaching, and the instrumental teacher available at secondary school may be someone whom students have not met previously. The *Young People and Music Participation Project*, which included 1,209 students in their last year at 36 primary schools (O'Neill 2002), and which tracked many of them through to the end of their first year at secondary school, reported that the students who continued instrumental lessons often had greater confidence in their ability, and an instrumental teacher who communicated belief in the students' potential to do well at music.

- *the teacher provides plenty of opportunities for students to perform.* Students opt for instrumental lessons because they want to play an instrument. The teachers who answered the questionnaire recognized this by endorsing lessons where students have plenty of time to make music—and where issues, including some technical problems that need to be resolved through talk, or away from the instrument, are dealt with very efficiently. The teachers also approved of lessons where students are allowed to play whole sections—or even whole pieces—for detailed appraisal: students are not stopped routinely every time that something goes wrong.

- *the teacher gives plenty of attention to the development of instrumental technique.* Teachers felt strongly that there was no place for teaching that overlooks the development of a good technique. Technique needs to be considered dynamically, with students and teachers routinely diagnosing the student's technical problems and working out ways of solving them in a manner that is appropriate to students' physique. Part of this is the adjustment of technique as students grow. A right arm position that works well for a violinist who has just acquired a full-size bow, for example, may work less well when they have grown another six inches taller.

Interestingly, there are four hallmarks of effective teaching in schools that teachers mention less frequently in respect of higher education—see Table 5:

- *the teacher is enthusiastic.* Enthusiasm is infectious: enthusiastic teaching helps to sustain the enthusiasm that students brought to their first instrumental lesson, even at stages when they feel that progress is hard won.

- *the teacher is inspiring.* Teachers wrote of trying to inspire students through their own playing, and their own love of playing, and music in general.

- *the teacher is patient.* Teachers wrote of needing to be able to draw on a range of learning strategies, in order to help students make progress—to try different ways of helping students to learn if they are not successful initially.

- *lessons are fun for students.* The role of fun in instrumental lessons has sometimes been underestimated in the past—but the teachers who completed our questionnaire were clear that fun is essential. Fun lessons build on students' interest and enthusiasm. They are worth attending. It is interesting that the teachers mentioned 'fun' much less frequently in respect of higher education. Perhaps this was because they assume that students in higher education will bring their own 'fun' to instrumental lessons even if the teacher does not, or that instrumental lessons in higher education are always fun? The need to inject fun—as well as plenty of music—into lessons for students of school age forms part of the training as instrumental teachers that many students at music college receive. For example, fun is a central theme of

Spelrum, a textbook used widely in Sweden and also in some other countries. The author, Robert Schenck, draws a parallel between what he wanted his 13-year-old daughter to gain from her hobby of horse riding, and what he would want her to gain from learning an instrument: 'Naturally I hoped that my daughter would learn to ride well, make friends, experience the trials and tribulations of dealing with live and powerful animals, and get fresh air and exercise. But what was it all worth, what would she learn, and how long would she keep it up, if she wasn't enjoying herself? Above all, I wanted her to have fun!' (Schenck 2000: 4).

Table 5   The 'top ten' hallmarks of effective teaching at school and in higher education

Ranking at school level	Hallmark	Ranking at HE level
1	Enthusiastic teacher*	(11)
2	Knowledgeable teacher	1
3.5	Communicative teacher	9.5
3.5	Fun for pupils*	(21.5)
5.5	Teaching matched to pupils	9.5
5.5	Praise/positive teacher	3
7	Performance opportunities	6
8	Technical focus	2
9.5	Inspirational teacher*	(15.5)
9.5	Patient teacher*	(29.5)
-	Development of individual voice	4
(11.5)	Wide repertoire	5
-	Teacher gives career advice	7
(21)	Teacher has high expectations	8

* Hallmarks that are in the 'top ten' for schools, but not HE.

It is difficult to see why these four hallmarks would not also be advantageous in instrumental lessons that take place in higher education.

There are also four hallmarks of effective teaching in higher education that teachers mention less frequently in respect of schools:

◆ the teacher develops students' individual voice

◆ the teacher teaches a wide repertoire of music

◆ the teacher has high expectations of students

◆ the teacher offers students advice about the development of their careers.

It would be wrong, however, to suggest that the first three of these, in particular, are not relevant to instrumental lessons in schools. A teacher with low musical expectations of students may assume that they will give up—with the result that they probably will! Or they may be unaware how much application even young students are expected to show in other subjects at school, for example in English and mathematics, and consequently not challenge them in their instrumental lessons. A wide repertoire of music is as important in school as in higher education, and built into the schemes of work used by several of the local education authority music services where the teachers work, with students learning to play popular melodies, songs from the shows, melodies from around the world, and specially composed music as well as arrangements of the classics. The development of musical autonomy, which encompasses the development of students' individual voice, is a theme throughout *A Common Approach 2002*, to which some of the teachers who took part in our survey contributed.

One explanation is that the teachers listed these three qualities less frequently because they are so widespread that they do not differentiate effective teaching from less effective teaching.

Another explanation relates to the different levels of experience from which instrumental teachers write about effective instrumental teaching in schools, and effective instrumental teaching in higher education. The teachers have all been trained to give instrumental lessons in schools. They have all been trained by the music services for which they work, and many of them also have Qualified Teacher Status (QTS), usually gained via a Postgraduate Certificate of Education, taken over a year on completion of a degree in music. However, training to teach instruments in higher education is much less widely spread, and so teachers must draw more heavily on their own experiences of being taught.

We asked teachers to write about the strengths and weaknesses of the instrumental teaching that they received at school and in higher education, and to comment on whether they thought that their approach to teaching had been influenced by the ways in which they were taught. Most thought that it had. Some teachers wrote only about trying to emulate the strengths of the teaching they had received, while others wrote only about trying to avoid the weaknesses, and a third group wrote on both of these subjects. Many teachers were keen to point out that they did not blindly teach students as they had been taught.

But one finding was that many teachers are still influenced, now, by the 'special' music lessons that they had when they were students. These lessons often had a sense of 'revelation' as teachers (when students) suddenly learnt something that helped them to move their playing into a new gear.

One teacher's special lesson was a 'masterclass' where she realized how much she could learn from watching her peers play, and analysing what they did well and what they could do even better, and noticing how the 'master' taking the session helped each student to make progress. This teacher now encourages children to comment on each other's playing, and suggest improvements, in many of her group lessons. What she found out about learning from one's peers is related to the observations of Janet Ritterman (2000) that former students of the Royal College of Music, describing their time there, frequently refer unprompted to what they have learnt about performance from contact with other students. This led Janet Ritterman to consider whether:

◆ the types of peer learning to which these students refer could be formalized, and if so how?

◆ the attitudes and approaches that students develop in relation to peer learning and performance might help to inform their studies in other areas of the curriculum.

Another teacher's special lesson taught her to listen more closely to her playing. Until then, she had not listened to her own playing much, because she was so busy trying to play the right notes at the right time. Her tutor played to her, one note at a time, and did not move on until he was told all about that one note: whether it was in tune, whether it was too loud, whether it sounded warm enough, and so on. When the teacher applied this to her own playing, she soon learnt to play with a much better sound, and much better tuning, than she had ever done before. So this teacher often includes short activities—or games—based on close listening in her lessons.

This close relationship between the special lessons that teachers recalled and their hallmarks may be related to what psychologists refer to as 'peak experience'. Although this term was initially used (e.g. Maslow 1954) in the 1950s to refer to the most wonderful experience of someone's life, it has more recently been used, for example by John Sloboda (2002), in reference to specific fields. Thus one might speak of a peak experience in music or, as here, a peak experience of being taught music.

One sometimes hears the anecdotal assertion that instrumental teachers simply teach as they were taught. Clearly, this is a myth, at least in the context of local education authority music services. Teachers appear to analyse the strengths and weaknesses of their various teachers and create their own teaching method that draws heavily also on other influences, including any initial training that they have received, and the in-service training provided formally by their employer and informally—for example through conversation with other teachers. However if, as it appears, a teacher's peak experience of being taught has a strong influence on their teaching style, it may be helpful for teachers to work on recalling their peak experience and analysing what made it so significant to them as learners. It may also be helpful for teachers to have the opportunity to recapture or update their peak experience, by getting involved in musical activities where they are taught, as well as teach.

One teacher's special lesson was rather different from the positive experiences described above. She was studying three instruments at music college—let us say that they were flute, violin, and piano—and her flute teacher complained that the student had not done enough flute practice since her previous lesson, and tried to order her to give up the violin. The student took umbrage at this, stormed out of the lesson, gave up the flute immediately, and says that she has never regretted this decision. Clearly, however, 'special' lessons of such negativity would rarely have such seemingly positive outcomes.

Chapter 7

How not to teach music musically

Singing master then sit on stool of skool piano as if he could pla it
. . . Fotherington-tomas hand round books full of minims crotchets
etc which have been made into beetles by boys mischievous
fingers dear dear wot will they be up to next. Master than sa
Number 56 hearts of oak class sing mightily and windows burst all
over the skool.

The fictional student Molesworth in Willans and Searle,
Down with Skool!

It is difficult to believe that anyone actually *tries* to teach music unmusically.
Why should they want to do that? So what is it that sometimes stops hard-
working thinking committed music teachers from teaching musically: through
musical activity in a way that leads students—all students—to make progress
as musicians? What is it that leads teachers to—well—lose the plot? I guess that
most of us feel that we have occasionally lost the plot when teaching, for
example that we have started to focus on routines, i.e. lists of actions that we
will take, rather than the students, their learning, and music. But what is it that
leads some teachers sometimes to lose the plot more generically or comprehensively? Over the years, through reflection on my own teaching as well as on
other people's, I have come to the conclusion that the factors include:

* published schemes of work
* bandwagons
* dogma
* not daring to be different
* the difficulty of analysing one's own teaching
* the difficulty of analysing one's own musical development
* underexpectation of students' musical development.

Published schemes of work

Commercial schemes are now much more freely available in the UK, and in many other English-speaking countries, than was the case until recently. In addition, in England, the Qualifications and Curriculum Authority (QCA 2000) has published schemes that are intended to help teachers implement the national curriculum. Of course, published schemes of work are not necessarily a bad thing per se. Reading them may give teachers—perhaps particularly those who are the only music teacher in a school—new ideas that help them to keep their teaching alive, and teachers may occasionally find lessons that they want to adopt wholesale, thus saving themselves time. The problem arises when teachers do not think through why they are teaching a particular lesson, in terms of what the students are intended to learn. When asked about the role of re-creation in musical performance, the cellist Pablo Casals once observed: 'Every year the leaves of the trees reappear with the spring, but they are different every time' (Corredor 1956). Lessons are like that too. They need to be re-created each time that they are taught. A lesson that was written for another class in another school will not necessarily work well elsewhere, and I rather suspect that some of the lessons described in some published schemes of work have actually not been taught anywhere! Which takes me to another point: some literal following of unsuitable material in published schemes arises because teachers do not understand what the publication is getting at, and think that this is their problem. In fact, the problem is nearly always that of the authors. Published schemes of work need to be appraised confidently and critically by teachers—no matter how seemingly authoritative and definitive their source.

Bandwagons

Rudolf Radocy writes:

Most American music educators do not follow learning theories and other developments in psychology closely, yet they often may follow educational fads or 'bandwagons', where an idea or school of thought becomes popular rapidly, as many people endorse it, often without careful consideration of what the idea really represents or implies. (Radocy 2001: 125)

He gives the example of the so-called Mozart effect. Careful research (e.g. Rauscher et al. 1993; 1997) has suggested that music training, in particular listening to the music of Mozart, may improve young children's ability to reason abstractly in some specific contexts. These findings were over-generalized, not only in America, by members of the media, and some organizations with a commercial interest in the presence of music in education, and it was not long before special Mozart materials for use with children were being published, parents and teachers were deluging children with Mozart, and all sorts of people were claiming all sorts of educational benefits for music that may, indeed, be true (Mills 1998*b*), but which were certainly not proven. Some might ask whether this matters. If the end result of some—in effect—hysteria is that there is more music in education, then isn't that a good thing? Not necessarily. In addition to the intellectual dishonesty involved, which is at variance with the values that education generally attempts to instil in children, there is a danger that children's education may actually be harmed.

I recall a primary school where a very committed teacher, determined to do the best for her quite challenging class, was playing them Mozart during much of the time that she was teaching. Some of the students were visibly distracted by the music, and at times it was difficult for the students to hear the teacher's questions and instructions, and for the teacher to hear the students' responses. Moreover, the students were confused by being expected to talk when music was played during science lessons, for example, but told off for doing so in music lessons, and so their behaviour had deteriorated.

It would be difficult to argue that any of this was enhancing students' education.

Dogma

When considering the main influences on curriculum development in music over the last century or so, it is sometimes possible to spot the following pattern:

1. Someone has a very good idea: the Kodály concept, an approach to music education of the very highest integrity, and which originated in Hungary, would be a case in point.

2. Disciples grow up around that person, and the very good idea spreads.

3. The disciples attract their own disciples. These second-generation disciples may never meet the originator of the very good idea, or read anything that the originator has written: they copy what the first generation disciples do, without necessarily understanding why they do it.

4. The very good idea recedes behind the dogma that is developing. Teachers put particular ingredients into their lessons because these are part of the dogma, rather than because they relate to the very good idea. As the content of the curriculum becomes disconnected from the very good idea, practices develop that would be anathema to the originator, but which

are still credited to the very good idea. An example would be the dogma, frequently credited to the Kodály method (note the change of title from 'concept' to 'method' as the approach has become more dogmatic) that the songs first taught to children in England should use only the musical interval soh–me (descending minor third).[1] In fact, Kodály believed that children's first songs should be drawn from their culture. Hungarian folk songs are, I understand, frequently based on soh–me: English folk songs, and the music that English children hear as they grow up, are not.

5. The dogma becomes the focus. The disciples are replaced by gurus who train teachers to carry out procedures, without explaining what the procedures are *for*. Teachers feel that it is their fault that they do not understand what the procedures are for, and their confidence as teachers diminishes. They teach lessons that just consist of procedures, and that have not been planned to enable students to learn. The music education of many students suffers.

6. In due course, the dogma falls into disuse.

7. Some time later, someone has a very good idea . . .

In one respect, the cyclic nature of curriculum development is a strength: it ensures that the curriculum is re-created. However, the lack of awareness that this is happening is a weakness: we do not always benefit from the lessons of the past. Many teachers in England believe that composing in schools began with the introduction of GCSE in the mid-1980s, and so think of it as an activity that does not begin seriously until the age of around 14, and that must be carried out in a way that makes it readily examinable. The lessons learnt long ago by those teachers who encouraged younger students to compose and improvise more freely, before their creative response to music has been drilled out of them by more restricted—and in some cases repressive—approaches to music education, have largely been forgotten. As have those doubtless learnt by Walford Davies when he included children's melodies in his radio broadcasts from 1926.

Other examples of dogma include the use of pentatonic[2] scales when

---

[1] Often said by followers to be the call of a cuckoo. But cuckoos, in particular the ones that I hear from my home in Oxford, typically have a call that is closer to a major third.

[2] A pentatonic scale consists of only five notes, e.g. C D E G A or the 'black notes': F♯ G♯ A♯ C♯ D♯. Strictly speaking, any scale consisting of five notes is pentatonic, but pentatonic scales that use intervals of less than a tone, for example C D E F G (which has a semitone between E and F) are relatively rare. Pentatonic scales are found in many cultures that do not use the western scale. For example, the slendro scale used in Balinese and Javanese gamelan music is pentatonic. Slendro divides the octave into five roughly equal parts, but there is no standard tuning. Because pentatonic scales generally consist of intervals of at

students are composing, on the grounds that 'everything will sound all right'. If everything sounds all right, why bother?

Sometimes teachers create their own dogma. An inspector recently told me of a lesson that she observed in a secondary school, one of the very few secondary schools in England that still teaches the descant recorder to all students. (Most secondary schools never did this, or gave up a long time ago, having observed that the descant recorder is not popular with many young people.) The inspector looked up from her writing and saw that the student next to her was playing not a recorder, but her ruler. She held the ruler like a recorder, resting it on her lip, and placing her left hand above her right hand, and with her fingers nicely curled and their tips resting on particular centimetre marks. She sat upright 'so that she could breathe properly' and fingered the 'notes' of the melody that the class was playing from the board.

INSPECTOR: Why are you playing a ruler?

STUDENT: Because I have forgotten my recorder.

[Inspector pauses to consider, and notices other students playing rulers, and one student playing a biro.]

INSPECTOR: Why is that student over there playing a biro?

STUDENT: That's what we do when we forget our rulers.

What is the point of all that?

Not daring to be different

Some of the most musically exciting music teaching that takes place in schools is idiosyncratic, and borne of the specific enthusiasms, expertise, and interests of a particular teacher.

The recorder work at Corbridge Middle[3] School in Northumberland was a case in point. I have suggested above that teaching the descant recorder to all the students in a school is rarely successful. However, at Corbridge this worked a treat. The music teacher was thoroughly committed to everyone learning the recorder so that they had an instrument to use in their composing and playing, and for getting to know music, and this had become a distinctive but

---

least a tone, there are no dissonant semitone intervals when notes are combined: hence the view of some music educators that 'everything sounds all right'.

[3] Although students in England generally transfer from primary school to secondary school at the age of 11, there remain a few middle schools in some parts of the country. Corbridge Middle School is for students aged 9–13.

unquestioned part of the culture of the school. Students were composing on the recorder within a few weeks of their arrival at Corbridge, and worked progressively on their recorder skills throughout their four years there.

The music teacher was a keen jazz pianist, and one of the highlights of the Corbridge curriculum was a project in which all the students in their final year used their recorders to play jazz. The teacher sent me a tape of a jazz performance in which every single member of a class of 12-year-olds took it in turns to solo over the first eight bars of *Autumn Leaves* to a piano accompaniment provided by the teacher. This was an ordinary mixed-ability class of almost 30 students, including some with learning difficulties or other special educational needs. The music facilities in the school were not plush: the recording was made on a ghettoblaster. A simple tutti, that the whole class could play, was used as a foil while the student who was about to solo walked out to the ghettoblaster, and the one who had just finished walked back. All the solos were substantially different from each other, and one could tell from their structure that students had assembled them using a variety of approaches. The solos were all creditable, and a few were stunning by almost any standard.

There are many other schools with idiosyncratic approaches to creating, interpreting, and responding to music that are very good ideas that have been planned equally carefully and work very well. Some secondary schools base their curriculum around high-tech digital film and surround sound. At Exmouth Community College—which has few connections with Russia—large numbers of students are enthusiastically, productively, and creatively learning balalaika, and I have already mentioned the project in Portsmouth where whole classes of primary students learn to play jazz on the harmonica, before transferring to woodwind instruments. If you have got a really good idea that you think will bring music alive at your school, and you can persuade your headteacher to resource it so that you can try it out and evaluate it, then go for it!

And if your idea works, tell other schools about it, but do not necessarily expect them to copy you, or you may accidentally become the originator of the next dogma. There are some ideas in music—indeed in any subject—that work really well only because of the particular skills and passionate commitment of the teacher, and the chemistry of the teacher, students, and school. At an arts education conference where the Corbridge recorder jazz had been on display, I saw the head of music at a secondary school where recorder was taught to everyone—but much less successfully—strike up a conversation with the teacher from Corbridge. Good on him! Did the second school become a second centre of excellence in recorder jazz? No it did not. I guess that the head of music knew that recorder jazz was not him, and was not his school. But the Corbridge experience had led him to realize how dull and pointless the compulsory recorder work was at his own school. He phased it out within the next few years.

The difficulty of analysing one's own teaching

It is not always easy to 'stand outside' one's own teaching and analyse it. But I am not talking rocket science. Here is an example of a lesson that I once saw taught to a class of 12 boys aged 11 in an independent (i.e. fee-paying) school. The lesson lasted 35 minutes:

The teacher had said that the lesson would consist of a published listening exercise based on *Theodoric* from *Piae Cantiones*. In practice, the teacher first spent 25 minutes dictating verbal notes headed 'Important Information'. Some information was misleading (e.g. a crotchet equals one beat) and other information was poorly explained (e.g. a crotchet, said to have a black middle, was drawn on the board with a green pen). The teacher used terms including 'hook' without explanation, but dismissed a question about the meaning of 'treble clef' by saying that the class would not be able to understand this yet. Perhaps the 'important information' had been prepared for an earlier generation: it referred to a pop song and an advertising jingle from the 1960s, i.e. when the boys' parents were young children.

Finally, the class opened a book at an exercise based on *Theodoric*. They listened to the piece once, found a sequence in the first four bars (there isn't one) and ran out of time before starting the published questions.

It was easy to spot the boys who already knew about crotchets and so forth. It is difficult to believe that the others came closer to knowing about them as a consequence of this lesson. And why did the teacher spend the majority of the lesson imparting information about music, instead of having the boys do music? And if information is to be imparted, surely it should be accurate?

Some of the problems with this lesson are glaringly obvious. Had the teacher thought about this lesson from the point of view of the boys who he was teaching, I believe that he would have had little difficulty appreciating some of its more problematic features. Not everyone finds it easy to stand outside their own teaching, and 'observe' it from the point of view of someone else. Talking to students about what they feel that they have learnt can help. So can observing the lessons of other teachers, and inviting another teacher to observe your lesson, to help you evaluate it. It can be easier to work out what to look for when you have not got to simultaneously teach the lesson.

I said that the lesson described above took place in an independent school. I wonder how this lesson might have appeared from the point of view of the boys' parents, who were paying fees for their offspring to be educated outside the state education system. But that is another story . . .

The difficulty of analysing one's own musical development

Thinking about, and trying to analyse, your own musical development—the skills, knowledge, and understanding you developed and in what order—can help with working out what students need to learn so as to become a musician like you. But it does not follow that students' needs can be served best by giving them a musical education that is as similar to yours as possible—only perhaps on 'fast forward', as they may be starting parts of it rather later than you did.

When planning teaching, teachers can try to distance themselves from their own musical development—to consider it with the same degree of objectivity that I have suggested they use when evaluating their own teaching.

Teachers often learnt to read staff notation at such a young age that they cannot imagine functioning without it. Consequently, they may want to teach it to children before they need it. In *Music in the Primary School* I wrote:

Staff notation is simply a means of recording some types of western music. It is not a code that must be understood before any purposeful musical activity can take place. Some jazz musicians, and children learning the violin according to the Suzuki method, for instance, cannot read music. Some 20th century composers, including Luciano Berio, have occasionally found other forms of notation more appropriate to their purposes. And many musical traditions, such as Indian music and gamelan music, make little or no use of any written notation, let alone staff notation. Thus the study of written notation is not relevant to all forms of music making, and much worthwhile musical activity in any musical tradition can take place without recourse to it. Some music is not staff-notatable: other music is not notated.

Consequently, children need not be taught to read music until they are ready to use it. And once they have learnt it, it need not become the only way of recording or accessing music. Children who have learnt to read music in conjunction with piano lessons, for instance, still benefit from opportunities to compose by ear at the piano, and on other instruments. There is a parallel here with spoken language. Children do not learn to read and write until they have been speaking for some time. And once they have learnt to read and write, they do not stop talking to each other. (Mills 1991e: 70)

Since I drafted that text, I have observed music being taught in many primary schools, and other schools, and now have even stronger reservations about the use of staff notation. Thousands of students every year are confused by teachers' well-intentioned, but misplaced, attempts to teach them to read rhythms and pitches. It really is like teaching students to read before they have learnt to speak.

As recently as 2004 I observed a lesson where 11-year-olds were being 'taught' to read music by completing (in silence) a worksheet that required them to add up the 'values' (using the unspoken but misleading assumption that a crotchet is 'one') of various series of rhythmic symbols (such as a minim + a crotchet +

a quaver rest + a semibreve) and then use the numerical answers to crack an alphabetic code and 'find a mystery word before your friends'. Why? What were they supposed to be learning from this? And what was this activity saying to the students about music, musical activity, and music in schools? The mystery word was 'symphony', but who cares? An extra complication was that the worksheet used an unexplained mixture of US and English time names, so that some of the students thought, understandably, that a minim had a value of '8' as you count 2 for a minim, and so it must contain 8 quarter-notes (i.e. crotchets). But even setting aside this extra dimension, the lesson was very problematic.

Teachers sometimes forget that they learnt to read music using an instrument, for example the recorder or piano, which can make a sustained sound, and try to teach children partial truths such as that 'a crotchet is twice as long as a quaver' using clapping. A crotchet clap sounds exactly the same as a quaver clap—it is only the silence after it that changes in length.

Some years ago, I worked with 40 children aged 8–10, and five adults who do not read staff notation, to learn more about the information that they pick up from rhythms that are clapped or played to them (Mills 1991*a*; 1991*b*). As someone who learnt staff notation so young that I cannot remember life without it, I am unable to work this out for myself through introspection. I have known, seemingly forever, the convention that one uses claps to mark the onset of a sound that lasts until the next clap, and not just literally to denote the onset and duration of extremely short sounds with a lot of silence in between. I wanted to know what people who do not know this convention are picking up from clapped rhythms, so that I could work out how to teach them more effectively. I based my experiment on a simple rhythm: ♩ ♩ ♫ ♩ |♩ ♩ ♫ ♩ | that had been used in earlier research by a US researcher, Jeanne Bamberger (1982; 1988).[4] As in the US research, I clapped the rhythm, and then asked students to draw something that would remind them of it.

The response of Lucy, aged 8, was typical of many of the children who had taken part in the US research. Lucy had recently started learning the violin. After listening to the clapped rhythm, she drew her hand and showed, through labelling her fingers from 'beat 1' to 'beat 5' that she had spotted that the rhythm repeated, and also that the repeating cell consisted of five 'claps' (Fig. 5(a)). She also showed that 'beats 3–5' were a group of some sort. I asked Lucy if she could think of another way of drawing the rhythm. She drew five teddy bears that she numbered 1–5, labelling claps 3–5 'fast'. Lucy's response seemed reasonable enough to me: there is a sense in which 'beats 3–5' sound like a group. However,

---

4 A crotchet in one piece can be shorter than a quaver in another piece that is played at a slower tempo. Students sometimes find this confusing.

Fig. 5 (a)–(f)   Drawings illustrating the notation and perception of rhythm by a student aged 8

the US research had judged responses like Lucy's to be immature, and to suggest that she had not heard the rhythm properly.

I decided to try to find out more about Lucy's thinking. In particular, I wanted to know how she would approach the notation of some rhythms that really did sustain. A few weeks later I returned to her school, armed with a very simple electronic keyboard, in order to work with her individually. Instead of clapping rhythms, I taught her to play them on a single note of an electronic keyboard, using a tone which could be sustained for several seconds, but that ceased when the key was lifted. Once she had learnt a rhythm, I asked her to draw something which would remind her of what she had been playing.

On learning to play Fig. 5(b) on the keyboard, Lucy drew ten pigs, which she numbered from one to ten. She labelled pigs 2, 3, 7, and 8 'fast'. Next, without prompting from me, she clapped the rhythm and labelled pigs 4 and 9 'fast' too. It was as though the rhythm that she was hearing had changed into one that could be written more accurately using the notation shown below the pigs.

Thereafter, Lucy gave up drawing until she had first clapped a rhythm that she had learnt to play on the keyboard. It seemed that she thought of clapping as being something that you always did when a teacher asked you something about rhythm. For Fig. 5(c) Lucy drew eight butterflies, and labelled butterflies 2, 3, 4, 6, 7, and 8 fast—which suggests a rhythm more like that written below the butterflies. For Fig. 5(d), she drew nine tennis balls. She was in doubt about whether some of them were 'fast' or not, but the rhythm that they described is less like the original than the one written below the tennis balls. For Fig. 5(e), she drew 14 triangles. She started by marking the first few 'short' or 'fast' (she did not say), but realized that this was going to take a long time and changed her strategy, instead marking triangle 11 'long'. This drawing is more like the rhythm shown below the triangles.

Finally, I returned to the original rhythm (Fig. 5(f)). Lucy economized on her drawing by producing squares instead of teddies, and wrote out the repetition of the first 'bar', but otherwise her response was the same as it had been several weeks previously, when she had not had access to the keyboard.

Lucy's final notation could be viewed in several ways:

- ◆ inaccurate, duration-based notation of the rhythms I had taught her
- ◆ notation based on something other than duration
- ◆ accurate, duration-based, notation of rhythms reconstructed from the clapped rhythms.

Given that, in Fig. 5(b), I saw Lucy change 'accurate' notation of durations following clapping, I think my third suggestion is the most sensible. A long clap is no longer than a short clap: only the silences between vary in length. So Lucy is entitled to reconstruct the clapped rhythms like this if she wishes.

Clapping seems to alter Lucy's perception of rhythms. So why does she clap? The answer is that her violin teacher has trained her to clap rhythms before playing them. When Lucy plays a rhythm, her teacher cannot tell whether any mistakes result from inaccurate rhythmic perception or technical difficulties such as plucking a string, or changing bow, at the moment intended. Asking Lucy to sing the rhythm on a single note does not work either, because Lucy learns in a group, and the teacher cannot tell whether an individual is, for example, sustaining a crotchet for the duration of a minim. Asking Lucy to clap makes things easier for the teacher, who can see if Lucy is not clapping in the right place, even when she is clapping in a group.

The problem is that Lucy's teacher has not noticed that clapping changes Lucy's rhythmic perception. There is nothing intuitive about an assumption that a clap represents a note which lasts until the next clap is heard. When the teacher claps a rhythm she may, as I do, 'hear' a tone which sustains until the onset of the next clap. But Lucy seems not to do this. She may learn to. But I doubt that clapping rhythms before playing them will help with this. Clapping rhythms after playing them, or whilst other children play them, might prove more helpful, and would still enable the teacher to check individual responses . . .

I decided to probe further by investigating the responses of some adults who have never tried to learn to read music. Using just one note, I sang them the rhythms shown in Fig. 6(a), (b), and (c)—and gave them counters in two sizes and two colours to represent what they had heard. A woman used both colours of the small counters, and one colour of the larger counters, to represent the rhythm shown in Fig. 6(a), although it only contains two note values: crotchets and quavers. She used the second colour of small counters to show which of the quavers were strong, and so invented a system of notation for herself that is more precise than staff notation. She requested a third, intermediate, size of counter to use for the third beats in Fig. 6(b). I had not anticipated this response, and did not have a counter of intermediate size. She requested a third, intermediate, size of counter also for the final beats in both bars of the rhythm shown in Fig. 6(c). She was right, of course. When singing Fig. 6(b) and Fig. 6(c) I had phrased them by clipping the final crotchet of each bar. A child might not have challenged me.

The relationship between clapped and sustained rhythms can be different for performers and listeners, even among those who do not read music. I recall a group of students aged 9 who composed a piece for drums and claves consisting, they said, of 'longs' (the word their teacher used to distinguish crotchets from quavers or 'shorts'). The silences were much longer than the sounds. But the performers stuck to their claim that the sounds were 'long' (as

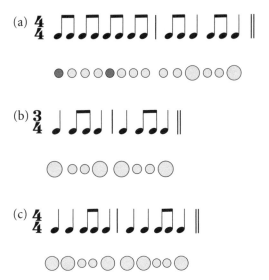

Fig. 6 (a)–(c) An adult who has not learnt to read music uses counters in two sizes and up to two colours to represent rhythms

did their teacher) even when other members of the class said that they could not hear what was 'long'.

Sue, aged 9, was a friend of Lucy. She has played cornet in a band for two years. I wrote down the rhythms shown in Fig. 7(a) and (b) and she clapped them. But whenever she came to a pair of quavers, the second one was a bit early. I clapped the rhythm shown in Fig. 7(b) for her, and she copied me accurately.

I asked Sue how she knew what to clap, and she said that she tried to count (here there was a wry smile). She showed me how she counted Figs 7(a) and 7(b) and explained her strategy as follows:

It's usually 4. It's 4 in this one [Fig. 7(a)] because it looks like it's going to end on this one [the crotchet labelled '4']. In this one [Fig. 7(b)] it's 3 because the fourth one [the quaver labelled '1'] doesn't look like it's going to end.

Sue has tried to make sense of what her teachers have told her. It is, however, not the sense intended. Sue's teachers tell her to count, so she counts. But she counts the wrong thing: incidents, not a pulse. Her teachers have taught her, during music theory classes, to work out the time signature of unbarred rhythms by looking for 'endings'. Here, she applied this skill in an inappropriate situation: the performance of barred rhythms. If Sue understood what she was doing in the 'spot the time signature' exercises, she would see that the performance of a barred rhythm was a different exercise. But as she has not understood the concept of pulse, there is little chance of that happening.

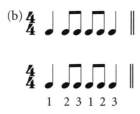

Fig. 7 (a) and (b)   A 9-year-old student 'counts' a clapped rhythm

John Holt, in his classic book *How Children Fail* (Holt 1984), first published as long ago as 1964, wrote of a child: 'What she needs is a broom to sweep out her mind . . . If she could only forget nine tenths of the facts and rules she has all mixed up in her head, she might begin to learn something.'

I think that Sue needs a broom too. But her problems may remain unrecognized. When Sue gets a rhythm wrong in the band, someone tells her to count, and demonstrates the finished product. She copies the finished product accurately, while trying to count the notes. The tune comes out all right, so Sue and her teachers assume the counting was all right. Sadly, the time will come when the music is too difficult to copy. By then it may be too late for the broom, and Sue will join the school leavers who have failed as music readers.

To teach music reading effectively, we must understand how the framework for music defined by staff notation looks from the outside. Those of us who have read music for a long time may not be able to apply Holt's broom to ourselves. But we can find out about this viewpoint from those who are on the outside: those who have not yet learnt to read music.

I wonder what Lucy and Sue are doing now. They will be in their twenties. Are they still playing violin and cornet? Perhaps they went to university. Perhaps they have trained as teachers. Perhaps they will be teaching some children to read music. If so, I hope that they have devised a way of doing this which avoids the confusion that they went through.

Did Lucy and Sue need to learn to read music at all? Perhaps they did, because they wanted to play music that is written in staff notation: they had just been taught badly. Peter Roadknight writes of teaching students notational systems in such a way that they believe that it is 'their' system: 'If it's their system, it will work' (Roadknight 2000: 6). Lucy and Sue needed an approach more like this, one that smacked less of the revelation of knowledge held by adults. However, I am quite sure that Sue did not need music theory lessons at this stage: she could have operated effectively in her band for several years without what was, for her, this additional source of confusion. Lucy and Sue remind us what can go wrong even when well-motivated bright children are taught to read music in a small group. The scope for getting it wrong when whole classes are taught music reading despite having no immediate musical need to read music, and possibly not wanting to read it at that stage of their development, is vast.

Teachers sometimes argue that whole classes need to learn staff notation so that they can use it to notate their own compositions. In fact, using staff notation to do this can be a constraint. Working in South Korea, Myung-Sook Auh and Robert Walker (1999) found that 12-year-olds produced compositions that assessors judged to be more creative when they used graphic notation that they had devised themselves, rather than staff notation. It was as though staff notation got in the way of the compositional process, even though staff notation has been an established part of the music curriculum in South Korea for many decades: students expect to learn it, and teachers have plenty of experience of teaching it. Moreover, the researchers observed that some of the staff notation that students handed to assessors bore little resemblance to their compositions, which they performed from memory. They observe that 'traditional notational ability and creative ability in music are likely to be unrelated' (Auh & Walker 2001: 108–9).

Any system of notation is, at best, an incomplete record of the music that it represents. While there are characteristics of music—namely what note to play and when to start playing it—that staff notation records quite precisely, there are others, such as timbre, dynamics, variations in tempo, and when to stop playing notes, which are notated somewhat crudely, if at all. And yet these characteristics may be among the defining features of a particular piece of music. Buy the sheet music for a well-known popular song, play exactly what the notation says, and your attempts may be met by gales of laughter. This is not because the notation is wrong, but because staff notation cannot neatly represent the particular sorts of syncopation, inflection, use of timbre, and other nuance, that make many popular songs what they are. The particular form of simplicity that staff notation imposes on music does not restrict only popular music. Kathy Primos writes of a

South African university student who 'did not recognise a well-known song from his own Tswana culture when it was taught to him [from staff notation], saying that the "feeling was all wrong" '. She continues:

Anticipating that my students would need to develop transcription skills to collect songs of their African culture, I used a taped example from a book of South African songs as a dictation exercise and gave them copies of the transcriptions from the book to compare with their own. This was met with a storm of protest: 'This is not correct. It's stupid. It should not be in 4/4 time.' (Primos 2001: 10)

Any form of notation, including staff notation, is perhaps best thought of as an *aide memoire*. Whether it records a prelude of J. S. Bach, a *Gymnopédie* of Erik Satie, a musical of Andrew Lloyd Webber, a Robbie Williams song, or the music of Andean panpipes, performers have to apply their imagination and knowledge of style if they are to bring it to life.

Underexpectation of students' musical development

Underexpectation of what students can achieve is another obstacle to teaching music musically. Expect students to achieve the moon, and they will often achieve the stars. Expect them not to be able to do even the most basic of musical tasks, and they probably won't be able to do them, particularly if a teacher has communicated this sense of their hopelessness effectively. Underexpectation can arise for many reasons, including the use of published schemes of work that expect too little, or dogmatic approaches to teaching. It can arise also through weak diagnosis of students' achievement. Here is a particularly gross example of this:

In preparation for introducing the vertical representation of pitch on the stave, a teacher checked that her class of [7-year-olds] understood the concept of pitch (high/low). She played two adjacent strings on her guitar consecutively, and asked the children which was the higher. Nobody answered. The teacher repeated the notes and told the children to choose one way or the other. The result was about 50:50. The teacher concluded that the children were guessing because the notes were too close together for them to tell apart. (Mills 1991c: 11)

This teacher had not successfully distanced herself from her own musical understanding in three ways. First, she did not notice that the string with the higher pitch was spatially lower, and so her question was unclear. She reminds me of a cello teacher who told her students that the sound was going up while sliding her left hand down a string, a trombonist who inadvertently gave some very strange messages about pitch by sometimes moving his slide down, and sometimes up, while telling students that the sound had gone down, and a TV schools programme in which pitch was demonstrated on the white notes of a piano ('That's not up, those notes are level,' said Darren). Second, the guitarist assumed that students listening to her two notes would focus on their pitch rather than their timbre or duration, for example. Why should they? Third, the guitarist allowed herself to come to a conclusion that conflicts with common sense. If the students really could not perceive a difference in pitch of at least a major third, they would not be able to sing even reasonably well in tune, and they would probably not have been able to tell, from the inflection of the teacher's voice, that she had asked them a question.

And here is a second gross example:

The teacher took a large suspended cymbal, and a soft beater. First, she hit the cymbal softly at the rim. Second, she hit the cymbal as hard as she dared. She asked the [11-year-old] pupils if they could tell her in what way the second sound differed from the first one. One pupil volunteered that the second sound was longer than the first sound. No, that was wrong. Another pupil ventured that the second sound was more metallic, and the first more wooden. No, that was wrong too. A third pupil suggested that the pitch of the second sound wavered, whereas that of the first sound was higher, and more constant in pitch. No, that was still not right. Eventually, a pupil pointed out that the second sound was louder than the first one. When she evaluated this lesson at the end of the day, the teacher wrote that most of the class had not grasped the concept loud-soft, and were consequently still working towards the achievement expected of [7-year-olds in the national curriculum]. (Mills 1996*b*: 10)

This teacher's expectations were way below the capabilities of her students. Like the guitarist, she had allowed herself to reach a conclusion that is not sensible: young babies frequently respond to differences in loudness that are much subtler than the ones she was offering, many toddlers apply the vocabulary *loud* and *louder* accurately, and it is not unusual for a 6-year-old to be able to produce a series of four sounds, each slightly louder than the one before it, on an instrument such as a wood block. Why did the teacher suspend her common sense? This may have been because, like the guitarist, she was trying to assess the students using a sort of 'test' rather than in a musical context. She was not in real life any more. And, although she may not have spotted this at the time, she was receiving some of the potentially confusing information that can result from trying to test students' musical understanding by giving them tests about very specific aspects of music. There is no such thing as 'context-free' music. You cannot give students a test of their pitch discrimination, for example, without presenting them with tones that have duration, loudness, and timbre, and it is difficult to be certain that students have homed in on pitch, rather than the other features of the music that are inevitably present. Pitch, duration, loudness, and so forth, are sometimes referred to as the 'elements' of music, but I believe that this is misleading, as they cannot be separated from each other in the way of the scientific elements.

It would be nice to think that the examples given above were just one-off examples of teachers getting it wrong. Most of us do, from time to time. But where there is a pattern of underexpectation, students lose their motivation, and with it their will to show the teacher how much they can do. Eventually, they may only be able to do the very elementary things that the teacher thinks that they can do. A teacher gave me a copy of the targets that he had set for each of his 15-year-old students to achieve in a lesson that I was observing. Two of the most advanced were:

Performing an arrangement of *Fur Elsie* [*sic*] on the keyboard. He is having difficulty fitting the chords to the melody. He is aiming to complete the first four phrases.

Working on her second composition creating her own accompaniment for her own melody (rather than using a preset auto-accompaniment on a keyboard).

The setting of these targets could, in principle, lead to some tolerably exciting work. At the other extreme of expectation lay two less appetizing prospects:

Poor attendance recently, will be beginning a performance of *Ode to Joy* on the keyboard focusing on the first eight bars of the melody if present.

Very poor attendance, if present he will be working on a keyboard performance of *Little bird.*

These students had followed the national curriculum in music since the age of 5, and opted to continue music beyond the age of 14! Could you be inspired to break the habit of staying away from school by the prospect of playing the first eight bars of *Ode to Joy* or, worse still, *Little bird* (Fig. 8)?[5]

Only a few miles away, in the same city, another comprehensive school working in equally challenging circumstances was deliberately using music to raise students' rate of attendance at school. The music classrooms, and the corridors outside them, were a hive of activity as individuals and small groups of 15-year-olds worked on individualized performing and composing projects, frequently exploiting digital or analogue recording equipment, that challenged them to achieve musical standards rarely found at school in their age group. The teacher's expectations were sky-high, and his support to them was of top quality. He always listened to a student's work properly before commenting on

---

[5] *Little bird* was a melody popular with writers of descant recorder tutors in the 1950s: when played in G major, it requires only notes that are played with one hand, and uses only crotchets, quaver pairs, and minims. It was also a song that many young children of the time knew, and this helped them with their music reading. While *Little bird* can also be played using only one hand on a keyboard, its lyrics are less obviously suited to contemporary 16-year-olds. They begin: 'Little bird, I have heard, what a merry song you sing . . .'.

Fig. 8 *Little bird*

it. The students were working on a school-certificated course that the teacher had written especially to meet their needs. *Little bird* and even *Elsie* were not in evidence, senior managers had noticed that students attended school more frequently on days when they had music, and the music teacher had been commissioned to observe teaching in other subjects, in order to advise his colleagues on how to liven up their lessons so that the students would flock in to them too . . .

Chapter 8

The musical student

My school teacher told me I wasn't musical but now I know she was wrong. [Participant in a community music project]
Youth Music Action Zones (Youth Music 2003: 49)

Given that you are reading this book, the chances are that you were once thought to be 'a musical child': a child with the potential to do well in some field of music.

Why was that in your case? Was it because you, like me, grew up in a home where there were musical materials that you could use to show that you liked doing music?

My mother sang to me: I sang back. She practised her horn as I played: I smiled, looked interested, and made an attempt at blowing it myself. She played the piano for hours whenever she got the chance, mainly Chopin and Brahms: I sang along with the pieces that she played most frequently. She let me plink-plonk freely on her piano, an activity that progressed to making up, and trying to pick out, melodies. She bought me a piano tutor book, showed me how to sing, read, finger, and play the first melody, and helped when I later met seemingly insuperable problems such as playing with both hands at once. In due course, Father Christmas brought me a descant recorder and an orange recorder book. I devoured it: a green book appeared and I joined the school recorder group and started playing with them in local non-competitive festivals. Later a tenor recorder arrived, and then a violin and a violin teacher. I went to a concert, and saw my mother playing horn in a symphony orchestra, and Martin Milner playing a Mozart violin concerto. I was fêted by elderly ladies in the audience who shared their cough sweets with me at a tricky moment. Every Christmas, Uncle Johnny got out his accordion, and played *White Christmas* on the piano, pub-style, by ear—and my mother and I, and later my brother and sisters, joined in. When the great-aunts came to stay I had an appreciative audience for any performance that I might wish to offer them, at more or less any moment of the night or day. You've got the picture. It was quite easy to be 'musical' in my home. There were lots of musical materials, the time and space that allowed me to use them in the ways that I wanted, and adults who noticed what I was doing and approved of it. There was a resident expert and musical role model, my mother, who could be depended upon to provide factual information or technical advice when I wanted it, and who doubtless steered my musical development a little in ways that I do not recall. But there were none of the constraints that are frequently associated with so-called 'hot-housing'. For example, no one told me to stop playing by ear, forbade me to try to play music that they thought was too difficult for me, or bought me a theory workbook.

As it was, I was delivered to my secondary school, as a product of my genes and my upbringing, ready to benefit from the first-rate music teaching available throughout my time there. Or at least it was first-rate for me, because I was ready for it. Some of my peers caught up quickly; others never succeeded in filling the gaps in their music education. I recall a friend who was still occasionally missing out beats as she prepared the first movement of the Mozart flute concerto in G major for her Grade 8 examination. With hindsight, I find her problem less surprising than I did then. I had been immersed in metric music for years before I met my first crotchet. She had probably met crotchets *and* quavers *and* minims *and* crotchet rests cold through an encounter with a blackboard, or during the same half hour that she learnt how to assemble her shiny new flute, and how to blow a note from the head joint. No wonder that she failed to simultaneously develop the 'internal clock' on which musicians depend: the one that goes 1 2 3 4 1 2 3 . . . repeatedly during any piece in 4/4.

People tended to view my friend as clever and keen but 'not musical'. What nonsense. I firmly believe now that all she needed was some focused individual teaching that was designed to help her resolve her problem. There is nothing innate about the ability to count 1 2 3 4 1 2 3 . . . *ad infinitum* while placing dotted crotchets or semiquavers on top: we learn how to do it. We may learn this skill with different degrees of ease, or in different ways. But we still have to learn it: and a student who has not been taught it may be no less 'musical' than one who has.

All this is by way of pointing out the difficulty, perhaps impossibility, of predicting that a child has unusually high potential in music. We may search for musical potential by observing children's musical behaviour. But children can only demonstrate musical behaviour if they have been given the necessary materials, and have learnt or been taught to use them. Perhaps we can spot that children *have* musical potential from their musical behaviour. What we cannot do is spot they do not have musical potential either from the nature of their musical behaviour, or from their lack of it. And the chances are that everyone has musical potential that substantially exceeds their actual musical attainment.

Teachers of every subject are involved in the business of spotting which of their students have particular abilities that should be nurtured and developed. But for music teachers there is an extra problem: that of selecting which students shall receive what is nearly always a limited supply of instrumental teaching from visiting specialists. There is a commonly held, but I think debatable, view that the instrumental teaching should go to the students with most musical potential. But even in schools that are more egalitarian, or where parents meet the full costs of instrumental tuition, teachers still need to decide whether there are some children who should receive some particular encouragement to start lessons. And once a child has expressed an interest in taking lessons, is there a particular instrument that they should be encouraged to learn?

How can a teacher working in a school, and who only ever sees students new to the school in teaching groups of 30 or more, identify any students who have unusually high musical potential? This is a real and intractable problem, to which some bizarre and obviously unsatisfactory 'solutions' have been offered over the years. For example, I recall a secondary teacher who had decided that what marked out 'musical' children was their 'stickability'. He summoned the students who had expressed an interest in learning an instrument to a series of meetings at which he did nothing other than set the time of the next meeting. Once the numbers attending a meeting had dwindled to the number of places that he had available, his selection procedure was complete. One can only speculate how many promising musicians were lost to society through this clearly unacceptable educational behaviour.

Some of the more plausible solutions to the problem of spotting musical potential relate to children's physical characteristics, aural abilities, and personality. The custom of trying to assess these characteristics prior to offering children instrumental tuition has a long history, and continues today. But that does not make it right or fair, as we shall see below.

Physical ability

Seventy years ago, Charles Lamp and Noel Keys, researchers working in San Francisco, became concerned that instrumental teachers were selecting children for instrumental lessons using ad hoc tests of physical characteristics that had not been validated: 'In the absence of scientifically validated conclusions, music instructors have been forced to resort to *a priori* reasoning and uncontrolled observation' (Lamp & Keys 1935: 587).

The theories that Lamp and Keys found being used by teachers included that stringed instruments require slender fingers, that the type of brass instrument selected by a student should be based on the relation of lip thickness to the size of the mouthpiece involved, and that regular teeth are a prerequisite of success on a woodwind or brass instrument. Lamp and Keys carried out an investigation of the validity of these theories. They screened over 150 students who were about to start their first ever instrumental lessons for teeth evenness, lip thickness, and finger shape, gave them a controlled programme of teaching and practice, and then assessed their standard of instrumental playing after a year. This was careful research. The evenness of students' teeth was gauged by means of a scale that was devised with a professor in orthodontics, and which used measurements taken from three photographs of each of the students involved. The slenderness of students' fingers was measured using micrometer callipers, and taken to be the ratio of the length of the middle finger to its width at the first joint. Thickness of lips, similarly, was determined with micrometer callipers of the type then used by dentists for mouth measurements.

None of the physical measurements behaved as expected. The student with the thinnest lips and the student with the thickest lips both became French horn players of marked ability. The evenness of students' teeth made no measurable difference to their success on woodwind or brass instruments. The slenderness of students' fingers proved very ineffective in predicting their success on the violin. Indeed, one could predict a violinist's success just as readily by considering the evenness of their teeth!

The research of Lamp and Keys had at least a brief impact on instrumental teaching in San Francisco. The high schools there started to offer students tuition on the instruments that they wanted to play, instead of the instruments that adults thought that they should play, and assessed their aptitude on the basis of the progress that they made. But although this research was published in a reputable international academic education journal, the *Journal of Educational Psychology*, and given extra credibility by its appearance also in the *Journal of the American Dental Association*, it seems to have had very little impact more generally. Instrumental teachers on both sides of the Atlantic continued to select and deselect students for instrumental tuition on the strength of assessments of their teeth, fingers, and lips. Moreover, they did not make these assessments with the precision or rigour of Lamp and Keys: their micrometer callipers were replaced by what one might refer to, with apologies for the pun, as rules of thumb.

Fifty instrumental teachers in England who I interviewed 50 years later (Mills 1985) had a lot of theories concerning the physical characteristics that promote success on various instruments, and some of them used the theories

This ties in with my present-day experiences at the Royal College of Music in London, where my work includes a course on 'how to teach your instrument' for undergraduates who are talented performers. A group of 60 students to whom I recently explained that some instrumental teachers select students by size and shape just looked at each other and laughed. One student spoke for others when she suggested that 'there are students of all shapes and sizes playing most instruments here, but it does not make any difference to how good we are'. A student who plays double bass, and who has already started to give bass lessons to children, admitted that she had spent some time explaining to parents that children do not need to be a particular size before starting to learn to play bass: 'If they are small, they can begin on an instrument that is not much bigger than a violin.' A very short woman and a very tall man, both cellists, offered the view that most physical characteristics bring both advantages and disadvantages. The woman envies the man's ability to stretch larger intervals with his left hand; the man wishes that he did not need to 'overlap' his fingers when playing a long way down the fingerboard, close to the bridge.

Observant teachers notice the individual physical differences of their students, and draw their students into the conversation about how to develop technical ways of achieving musical ends that are consonant with the shape, size, flexibility, and so forth of their bodies. This is what the teaching of technique is all about. Whatever instrument a student plays, their body is part of it. This is obvious in the case of singing, but also true of every other instrument. An oboe is more than the pieces of hardware that one puts back in the case at the end of a rehearsal. A piano cannot function without a pianist. In the past, teachers have sometimes not been adept at noticing physical differences between themselves and their students, and have tried to teach young people to play exactly like them, regardless of their shape. Students' physical differences need to be worked with, and on occasion worked around, just like temperamental oboes, wolf notes on cellos, and the idiosyncrasies of pipe organs and the buildings that they play in. I went through years of violin practice, trying to get an equal vibrato on all the fingers of my left hand, assuming—like my teachers—that the 'problem' was lack of application on my part. One day, in my late twenties, I noticed that, in comparison with my teachers, I had a relatively long index finger that 'got in the way' when I tried to vibrate it like my other fingers. I experimented with changing my left hand position, moving my thumb a little further up the neck of the violin so that it was closer to my middle finger, and the 'surplus length' of my index finger became 'absorbed' through the need to stretch slightly backwards. Within weeks, I had a much better vibrato, and was also making a much better fist of other left-hand challenges such as playing in octaves and thirds. What a shame that one of my teachers and I had not spotted the 'problem' at least ten years earlier.

During my 'how to teach your instrument' course at the Royal College of Music, I observe every student giving one of their peers, or receiving from one of their peers, a first lesson on an instrument that has not been played before. Gifted violinists receive their first ever lesson on trombone or cello, gifted clarinettists receive their first ever lesson on oboe or in singing, and so forth. It is the differences between lessons that different students give on the same instrument that I, and sometimes the students, find most fascinating. This year I sat through several conscientious initial violin and viola lessons that began with the 'teacher' showing the 'pupil' how to hold their instrument. Out of the blue, the next violin 'teacher' passed his 'pupil' a violin and said: 'Over the years, you have seen other people playing violin. Let's see how you naturally hold a violin yourself, and I will work with you to make this hold as comfortable and as useful as possible.' And that was what he did, explaining as he went that his 'pupil' was more likely to remember 'what to do' if this was related to what they did naturally. Ten out of ten, I would suggest.

Personality

A mythology similar to that relating to physical characteristics may be found also in relation to personality. Anecdotal views of the personality types suited to particular instruments abound. A professional orchestral clarinettist once summarized the symphony orchestra as follows: 'the brass are the drinkers, the wind are the thinkers, and the strings are the stinkers' (Davies 1978: 203). The observation that several string players play the same music in many orchestral pieces, that the horns tend to sit separately from the rest of the brass, and that trumpets sometimes make a lot of noise, has led to suggestions that the violin is suitable for 'quietly behaved children' with 'no outlet for boisterousness or exuberance'; the horn is the best instrument for children who 'prefer to relate to small groups and usually have just one or two close friends'; and the trumpet is suited to the 'individualist' with 'prima donna temperament' (Ben-Tovim & Boyd 1985). Beliefs such as these have, over the years, denied countless children and older learners the opportunity to take up an instrument of which they might have made a great success.

So close is the academic relationship between students and their instrumental teachers, perhaps particularly at conservatoires, that students sometimes end up looking and sounding rather like their teachers, personally as well as musically. A musician who had just started teaching at a conservatoire commented recently to me of his surprise—and to some extent alarm—that

But where teachers do give a reason for setting aural tests for students, they often speak of wanting to know what is going on 'in students' heads'. Probe further, and teachers may explain that they want to know whether students can hear that notes have differing pitch, even though they cannot play them yet, and so forth. But we do not know whether students who have the 'right' things going on in their heads will necessarily make 'better' instrumentalists, or if they will receive more social, educational, or musical benefit from receiving instrumental lessons. And it is, of course, possible that 'what goes on in students' heads' might be improved through experience of learning to play an instrument.

But setting these points aside, it is not even clear that such aural tests could help ascertain what is going on 'in students' heads'. Unless they have already had some musical training, students simply may not know what to do in the tests. Why should a student know automatically what we mean when we say that one note is 'higher' than another, when 'higher' is being used in a way that does not relate to the more usual, spatial, sense of the word? Students may not know what they are expected to copy about notes on a piano or clapping unless this is explained, or they have seen it done before. Counting the number of notes in a chord will not make sense to a student who has not been told what a 'chord' is.

In addition, three of the tests are easier for students who have experience of playing, or playing around on, a piano, for example because they have one at home. Because the timbres of a piano and a singing voice are so different, it can be difficult to match the pitch of a piano note with your voice—even if you can hear the note in your head, and remember the sound of it being played. A student who has learnt how to apply the concept of high/low to the timbre of instruments they play, for example their own singing voice and a descant recorder, may not, yet, be able to apply this to the less familiar timbre of the piano. And a student who has experimented on a piano, building up notes into 'chords' (whether or not they were called chords) will find it easier to reverse the process, and say how many notes are being played at once. But, actually, the 'face validity' of the chord dismantling test seems very low. Why, for example, might it help a beginning trumpeter to be able to work out how many notes there are in a piano chord?

In fact, children's ability to tell the differences (i.e. discriminate) between pitches is typically much finer than is often supposed. Everyone's ability in pitch discrimination depends on the frequency range used, and is often finest within their vocal range for singing. Working within this range, as long ago as 1893, J. A. Gilbert (Shuter-Dyson & Gabriel 1981) found that children aged 7 could, on average, assess the direction of some intervals as small as two-thirds of a semitone. In the early 1960s, Arnold Bentley (1966) found that they could assess one-third of a semitone. In the early 1980s, I found that:

- the average 7-year-old could assess the direction of an interval as small as one-sixth of a semitone, i.e. a 1% difference in frequency
- the average 11-year-old could assess the direction of an interval of about a 0.85% difference in frequency
- some children as young as 9 could judge the direction of an interval as small as one-tenth of a semitone; that is about a 0.6% difference in frequency (Mills 1988a).

The discrepancies between the three sets of findings are probably due to the differing quality of the recording and replay equipment available at the time. There is no reason to suppose that the children of the 1980s necessarily had pitch discrimination any finer than those of the 1890s. Researchers of pitch discrimination have often reported the results of work with children aged at least 6, because younger children may have difficulty coping with a test that requires them to write their responses. But there is no evidence that younger children do not perceive fine differences in pitch. Bridger (1961) observed that some babies under five days notice pitch differences of about four semitones, and they may be able to perceive much smaller intervals. Indeed it is difficult to understand how children could acquire language, and particularly accent, without pitch discrimination.

It is likely that an investigation of children's pitch discrimination using contemporary digital technology would lead to the finding that their discrimination is even finer than it appeared using the technology of the early 1980s. All this suggests that, if a student is not able to assess the direction of intervals as large as the smallest intervals to be found on a piano, there is something wrong with the test, or the way that it has been explained, rather than the student.

Students' ability to sing in tune is a highly dubious predictor of any sort of musical ability. The assessor may be interested in whether the student can 'hear in tune', yet a student who can hear fine differences in pitch may still lack the vocal control needed to sing a simple song, or isolated notes, in tune. Or they may just have been asked to sing in a pitch range that is too high or too low for them. In other words, a student who sings well in tune probably has fine pitch discrimination, but the converse is not true.

Students who do not sing well in tune at some point in time frequently learn to do so subsequently. Some even teach themselves. Back in the 1980s, I met Andrew, a 6-year-old who had been rejected from a neighbourhood choir because of his poor pitching. According to my tests his pitch discrimination was better than that of any of the other 250 children up to the age of 9 that I

those who would most like them, or who most need them. I recall a secondary school where the first musical activity that students completed, in their very first secondary music lesson, was a published musical ability test. As soon as the test was over, the teacher read out the answers, the students marked ticks and crosses against their own answers, and then added up the ticks and wrote down which of Bands A–E their total placed them in. So, for the next couple of years or so until they had filled their book, and been given a new one, the students in Band D (below average) and Band E (well below average) were reminded of this fact on every occasion that they opened their music books.

But the prize for being most discouraging to students who have just arrived at secondary school eager to make the most of the new musical opportunities there should go to the following establishment. Like all the other schools that I describe in this book, it is 100% real:

During their first lesson at a boys' comprehensive school, all pupils are auditioned for the lower school boys choir by singing *Happy Birthday to You* solo and unaccompanied to the teacher in front of their class. Those who pass the audition go to choir once a week for two years during timetabled time. The others go instead to something called *non-choir*. None of the teachers is accountable for what happens in *non-choir*. Supervision is provided, but not a curriculum, and it appears that the boys simply fill their time doing homework in any subject. These boys get half as many music lessons as their peers, because they did not sing *Happy Birthday to You* well in their first music lesson. (Mills 1996*b*: 7)

Some students do, miraculously, recover from this sort of diminishing experience. An organ student at the Royal College of Music told me how the piano teacher that he had at the age of 6 persuaded his parents to discontinue his lessons on the grounds that he was not musical. He has retained a clear memory of the piece—called 'Soldiers'—that involved playing with both hands at once, and which was his downfall. He had an experience similar to that of Anthony Kemp when he was 13, his parents gave him another chance, and he is now doing very well, thank you.

Others are less fortunate. Society is full of adults who think that they are not musical because a teacher told them so, they were asked not to make a sound when singing, they were told to stand behind a pillar when singing, or they were given a triangle to play instead. All children—and all adults—are musical.

Chapter 9

The musical school

'We class schools, you see, into four grades: Leading School, First-rate School, Good School, and School. Frankly,' said Mr Levy, 'School is pretty bad.'

Evelyn Waugh, *Decline and Fall*

What is a musical school?

When people speak of a 'musical' school, what do they mean?

I have written in earlier chapters of some of the many schools in the UK that live and breathe music: where the positive impact of music in the curriculum for all students spills over into other parts of the school. Schools that work to provide a wide range and depth of individualized musical opportunities for all their students, and where music has become part of their ethos. Many more such schools come to mind:

◆ An inner city secondary school with many fundamental educational challenges that made a point—for several years until it was no longer necessary—of using its main foyer as a space where a group of students could compose, so that visiting parents could see and hear for themselves the value of creative work in music.

◆ Another secondary school where more than half the students choose to continue music when it becomes optional at the age of 14.[1]

◆ A special school for students with emotional and behavioural difficulties where experience of African drumming and 'turntabling' gives them a 'can do' feeling that teachers skilfully build on also in other subjects.

◆ Another special school, this one for students with multiple learning difficulties, where whole mixed-age classes clearly enjoy composing, and then performing, their own pieces—with individuals placing their sounds exactly

---

[1] The average for England and Wales in 2002, for example, was around 8%.

had badges presented in assembly. We were told that the word *choir* was written in silver as a mark of the light, silvery, quality of our singing voices.

During each daily assembly, the choir sat smugly on benches at the front, facing the children with non-silver voices who were seated cross-legged on the floor. We marched out of the hall ahead of them. I enjoyed my time in the choir. Doubtless I learnt a lot from it. But what good came from leaving out other children? Would they develop silvery voices by being given less opportunity to sing? Did the odd brassy voice matter, particularly given that we were not even competing for anything? And were the *fails* all left unscarred by the daily reminder of their musical inferiority?

I left primary school in 1965, a time when the failure of individual children was publicized more blatantly than is usual now. Set in the context of unavoidable 11-plus examinations, streaming into separate classes (which were labelled 'A', 'B', and 'X') from the age of 7, classroom seating based on termly form placings (oh the ignominy of having to publicly clear out your desk and move to a new one because you had slipped in these placings), the regular reading out of everyone's reading ages to the entire class, and the dreaded annual sports days in which incompetents like myself had no option but to make public fools of themselves (while 'letting down' the blue team . . .), there was perhaps nothing particularly evil about the way in which the choir at my primary school was organized.

However, traces of the practices that I have described remain. There are still some schools that are thought to be 'musical', but which provide scant musical opportunities for most of their students. Some state secondary schools select some of their students for admission using criteria that they think relate to musical potential, and then provide an impoverished music curriculum for other students. The English government's well-intended initiative to identify, and then enrich the provision for, students whom they describe as 'gifted and talented' (G+T) in music has sometimes led to the almost arbitrary choice of students for enhanced provision, and has lowered expectations of and worsened the provision for other students. And while the *Happy birthday to you* approach of providing extra singing for students who can do it well already, and no help for those who cannot, that I described on p. 126, actually slightly pre-dates the government's G+T initiative, one can see how a myopic school might argue that this is aligned with it.

Some primary and secondary schools with fine orchestras, choirs, or steel bands for some students cut corners when it comes to providing class music for everyone, with class lessons that are too short, that are under-resourced with musical instruments, or that take place in accommodation so cramped that it is not possible for students working in groups to hear their work properly. And I recall a secondary school that organized students into one of three ability groups—sets—according to their perception of students' musical attainment, from the age of 11. The top set all had instrumental lessons: their class lessons were organized as a formal band rehearsal, and took place in the school's best music room. They did not compose, they did not sing, they played only their specialist instrument, and they listened to hardly any recorded music. The middle set was taught in the next best room, and they undertook a markedly wider range of activities, including some creative work. The bottom set was taught in a history room that contained no musical instruments, and no equipment for playing recorded music. They did very little, to be honest. Of the three sets, only the middle set was receiving their entitlement to the national curriculum.

But 'medium' is not always 'good'. Earlier I referred (p. 28) to a study in which a consultant visited ten primary schools, and her judgements about the quality of the music provision (including teaching, students' standards, and curriculum) were used to divide the schools into three groups: high, medium, or low (Mills & O'Neill 2002).

When Susan O'Neill and I analysed the information received from the consultant, children, and teachers about each of the schools, we noticed that it was the *medium* schools that were most similar to what I have suggested is the traditional notion of the musical school. To put it another way, the medium schools had features in common with the junior school that I attended, although they had fortunately avoided some of its more extreme practices. At the medium schools, the music teaching was less interesting, the curriculum was more specialized and focused on recorder playing, and the standards achieved by the students—even in recorder playing—were lower. The boys were particularly critical of the provision: they did not enjoy music lessons, and they thought that teachers had favourite pupils. The teachers tended to think that students' standards were higher than they appeared to the consultant, and running extracurricular lessons for relatively small numbers of students interested the teachers more than running class music for everyone. The music at the *high* schools had a broader curriculum, and their provision centred on that for all children. The students were happier, felt that their teacher treated them fairly, and sang, played, composed, and listened more effectively.

As with students, I would prefer not to describe schools as 'musical'. But my reason is different. The issue is not that schools other than those described as musical may come to think of themselves as 'unmusical'. It is that many of the schools which think of themselves as musical, or that others describe as musical, simply are not.

Sometimes headteachers, governors, and parents have to be persuaded that becoming a *high* school is the right way forward. A lot of the pressure to focus on

unhelpfully presented in ways that overlook or dismiss the musical skills of music teachers, so that teachers are less likely to enter into them openly and benefit from the professional development that, when well run, they can provide.

A curricular issue: music 'and' or 'in' the arts?

Schools that are 'musical' often also have many other strengths, and they may be strong in the arts more generally. But what do we mean by 'the arts'? However we personally define them, it seems clear to me that music is part of them. Yet in recent years, some writers and other commentators have taken to writing about music *and* the arts, rather than music *in* the arts, or just 'the arts'. I think that this is just confusing . . . or confused.

Up to about 25 years ago, if someone in education referred to 'the arts', one could assume that they were talking about all the subjects of the curriculum that were not 'the sciences'. We then went through an awkward phase—that unfortunately lasted many years—when subjects including music, art, dance, and drama tended to be labelled as 'expressive arts', 'creative arts', or even 'creative and expressive arts'. I found this phase uncomfortable for four main reasons.

First, it gave the impression that creativity and expression or expressivity (whatever these words mean) were vested only in these subjects, when of course they are part of all subjects taught well, not least the sciences.

Second, it portrayed these subjects as self-indulgent—a description that is inaccurate and tends to lead to their intellectual and academic aspects being overlooked, and their disciplines being devalued.

Third, it introduced disjunction between the world of education and the world of work. 'Artist' is a well-established generic term for someone who works professionally in one or more arts disciplines: some musicians and dancers, for example, describe themselves as 'artists'. On the other hand, someone who described themself as a 'creative artist' or 'expressive artist' would probably be thought to be working only in some area of the visual arts. Consistency with the labelling used in the world of work helps students to realize that the arts offer a range of employment opportunities for those who wish to explore these. It also facilitates greater understanding of the artistic roles of arts teachers including music teachers.

Fourth, it led to some muddled thinking, whereby some teachers who were enthusiastic about expression and creativity, but who possibly had only a modest personal experience of any of the subjects, started to assemble courses in which the subjects were viewed as interchangeable rather than interdependent.

This confused thinking contrasted sharply with very clear thinking by some music teachers of the time who, while taking pains to avoid suggesting that music *should* be taught alongside other areas of creative work, showed through their teaching that it *could* be.

But while some of the younger readers of this book may find this hard to believe, some course developers in schools, colleges, and university education departments sometimes argued that it mattered not whether children or teachers were given opportunities to work in one, or all, of the disciplines—or developed any skills that might lead them towards operating autonomously in future—provided that they 'had the opportunity to express themselves' in some field or other. This muddled thinking had many problems, not least that it overlooked the possibility that someone who became an enthusiastic and accomplished singer, for example, might not have become an equally accomplished painter, say, had painting been the only 'opportunity for expression' on offer at their school.

In secondary schools, some of the more disingenuous or opportunist headteachers responded to the muddled approach by cutting the resources including time for the 'expressive arts', and delivering them on a 'carousel' timetable—a vehicle which virtually ensured that students were not given the opportunity to develop skills progressively, and that particularly disadvantaged the students with relatively slender experience of the arts in their life outside the school timetable. Students were sometimes taught music for only one term of each year, and music teachers often found that they had to use much of that term building students' skills and motivation up to where they had been a year earlier.

In primary schools, the muddled approach sometimes led to music just featuring within 'topic work' as listening to Handel's *Music for the Royal Fireworks*[2] in a topic entitled *Fire*, or singing a song with lyrics loosely linked to the topic in hand: regardless of the musical demand or interest of the songs. This overlooked some much more exciting opportunities that topic work provides, for example:

Occasional planned links with other subjects can . . . provide pupils with opportunities to compose in response to a stimulus that they have reflected upon in depth . . . In addition there is the opportunity for pupils to listen to, and develop their understanding of, music from different times and places through work linked to the history curriculum. Some schools are approaching this effectively through music lessons that are linked rigorously to history topics, and capitalise upon pupils' immersion in a historical period. Pupils' historical understanding of Victorian or Tudor times, for example, gives them the background they need to try to analyse the ways that music hall

---

[2] Note that this piece is not even about fire!

the ability of their parents to pay. But by the 1990s, Sture Brändström (2000) found that the places at a music school that he was researching were taken up mainly by girls with well-educated parents.

Research into **gender inclusion** issues in music has focused on students' confidence, and their gender-stereotyped choices of instruments. In the UK, music among school-age students is a predominantly female activity. Girls do better than boys in the national curriculum assessments that teachers in England are required to make of all 14-year-olds, more girls continue to study music at school when it becomes optional beyond the age of 14, and girls gain better grades at GCSE music. Girls often also dominate the extracurricular musical life of schools. More girls than boys start to learn instruments, persist with learning an instrument, take graded performance examinations, and participate in ensembles such as choirs and orchestras that are based in their schools and in their regions.

Youth Music, a national charity that was set up in 1999 to provide music-making activities for children and young people from the age of 0 to 18, and which targets young people who would otherwise not have musical opportunities, has already had an improving impact on the range of extracurricular music activities available in some schools. Youth Music works primarily in the community, rather than in schools, but the higher profile that it has given to activities including DJing and turntablism—which have initially proved particularly popular with males—has led to some schools offering them too. I hope that, in the medium term, this will lead to a more consistently equal gender balance in all the musical activities that schools provide. I do not like to see girls failing to involve themselves in DJing, because of a limiting view that this is not a female activity, any more than I am pleased to see boys failing to take up opportunities to learn orchestral instruments, or to sing in a choir, because they or their families think that this is not a male activity. But perhaps some schools may need to go through a phase of gender-differentiated provision before an effect similar to that at Ernesford Grange occurs, and students start to realize for themselves that they have much to gain from developing their musical skills from as broad a cultural range as possible. Music teachers will doubtless wish to ensure that their schools pass through this phase as rapidly as possible!

The limited quantity of research that has so far taken place into girls' and boys' confidence in music shows how complex this area is, as girls have emerged as less confident than boys in two studies despite generally, as has been mentioned above, taking up musical opportunities in school more readily than boys. The first study took place in Australia, and related to graded performance examinations. Gary McPherson (2003) found that girls gave lower ratings than boys of their confidence that they would achieve their potential in forthcoming examinations. Of course, we cannot tell whether the same would apply also in other countries, and whether the Australian girls' low confidence relates only to the examination results that they anticipate, or is more general within music—or even beyond music. The second, earlier, study was in the UK and related to the use of music technology in different types of schools. The researchers found that girls in mixed schools thought that they had weaker music technology skills than did girls in single-sex schools, and boys in mixed or single-sex schools. The researchers suggested that this might be because boys had greater experience of using computers outside music lessons: this may, or may not, still be the case (Colley *et al.* 1997).

There is a long history of research into children's gender-stereotyped choice of instruments, and this shows that children develop their stereotyped views young, and that their views are similar to, or possibly derived from, those of their parents. While there is no evidence that children of either gender are predisposed towards success on any instrument, girls tend to choose small, high-pitched, relatively quiet, instruments, and boys tend to choose instruments that are large, low, and loud (see, for example, Abeles & Porter 1978; Griswold & Chroback 1981).

Gender stereotyping is regrettable because it decreases the choice of instruments available to boys and girls. In recent years, researchers have attempted to find ways of encouraging children to be more open-minded. When children aged 7–8 attended 'counter gender-stereotypic' performances on the 'male' instruments of trumpet, drums, and guitar, and the 'female' instruments of piano, violin, and flute, this immediately decreased their preference for the perceived 'own-sex appropriate' instruments. In particular, girls expressed less preference for the piano, and boys expressed less preference for the guitar. The experiment was carried out with 357 children in three clusters of schools. One cluster received concerts with gender-consistent role models, the second cluster received concerts with gender-inconsistent role models, and the third cluster were the control group, and did not have concerts (Harrison & O'Neill 2000). It is encouraging that it was possible to change children's perceptions of instruments in this way. But we do not, of course, know whether or not the children's new views were sustained, and if any of them took up 'non-gender-stereotypic' instruments and persisted with them.

Research involving 600 Australian schoolchildren found that gender-based preferences were more fixed among boys than girls. Drawing a parallel with Lisa Simpson, the intellectual daughter of the cartoon Simpson family, who plays baritone saxophone, the researcher, Betty Repacholi, commented:

they were judged by school inspectors to be failing to provide an acceptable quality of education overall. The lack of a continuing good reputation for music in some schools does not detract from the significance of what they were achieving when I visited. People do not have to be immortal or perfect in order to be worth writing about, and neither do schools. These schools all gave wonderful musical opportunities to the students who were on their roll at the time, and some of this may stay with the students as they choose their careers, make other important choices about how they will proceed through life, bring up their own children, influence the upbringing of their grandchildren, and so forth.

The first of the two schools was situated on one of those tower-block inner-city estates that are eerily quiet and seemingly empty during the day, and have a reputation for being very dangerous after sunset. The school was closing through default as students' parents chose to move them to more popular schools elsewhere, and as the teachers left for new jobs. There was a *Death in Venice* feeling to the school when I visited, with its long empty corridors, some still bearing the signs of former vandalism, and its typically empty classrooms. Through a quirk of fate the school still had a music teacher, and the caring, careworn, and realistic headteacher who had been brought in to manage what was, in effect, the terminal illness of the school, was rightly proud of the music teacher's work, and took me through the maze of empty spaces to the music room. To enter the music room was to go into Aladdin's Cave, or through the Looking Glass—or onto platform 9¾ at Kings Cross station if you prefer. Outside was emptiness. Inside, groups of students worked on performances and compositions as they would in a school with an infinite future. But it was the environment in which the students worked that was particularly striking. There were displays on the walls of almost every kind of music that you could imagine, put together by the music teacher and by students. The shelves were stacked with musical instruments of different types, all in good repair, that students could collect and use in their work as needed. There were no tatty published posters, or aged song books, and there was no other detritus in view. This was very clearly a music room—a room that existed so that people could make music in it—and it reflected a view of music that respected the interests of students, and also looked outward from these. Music in this generally decaying and dwindling school offered something very special to the students who remained: something of which any other school could rightly have felt proud.

The second school is set in another large city. It has a more secure future, although it continues to work in challenging circumstances. For many years the school has had an admissions policy that allows it to accept a limited number of students because of their ability in and enthusiasm for the performing arts. It offers them extra provision in the arts, and the opportunity to work with like-minded students during and after the school day. Some other schools offer provision like this. The reason why I am writing about one school in particular here is that the arts students have had an effect on standards in the school more generally. Their enthusiasm, high expectations, and high rate of attendance have spawned good attitudes and high achievement in the arts among the other students, and the self-esteem and confidence that this has brought has raised achievement in the school. This school is deliberately using students' enthusiasm for the arts to raise standards in all subjects.

In some schools in challenging circumstances, as in schools more generally, it may take only a little effort, advice, or encouragement from a manager in order to help a teacher rejuvenate practice that has become jaded. Finally, a secondary school where I was assigned to observe in the single-teacher music department for a full four days, from Monday to Thursday, and where the music teacher was so ground down by the incessant criticisms of the headteacher that he had resigned his post before I even arrived. When I first saw one of his lessons, at 09:00 on Monday, there were signs that both the teacher and I had a dispiriting week ahead of us. The lesson required the students to try to play some dreary staff-notated melodies on keyboards. The material was dull, few of the students were trying, and the behaviour of some students was poor. There were signs, for example through the way that the teacher played the keyboard himself, and spoke to the students who were misbehaving, that he loved music, liked young people, and wanted to share his love of music with them. But these signs were buried beneath the surface of a very dull lesson, and invisible to the students. At the end of Monday, as was my custom, I asked the teacher if he would like daily feedback on the strengths and any weaknesses of his teaching and—a little to my surprise—he said that he would. The advice that I offered him at the end of Monday, Tuesday, and Wednesday, typically in the form of questions, was hardly rocket science. Most of it was little more than suggesting that he give students a wider range of real musical activities to carry out during lessons, draw on their memories of music that they already knew through watching TV or listening, and encourage them to use their imagination and to compose. But the teacher went away at the end of each day, thought about what we had discussed, and came back a slightly better teacher than he had been the day before. By Wednesday, he had ideas that he wanted to discuss with me as well as the other way round. By Thursday, the discussion was so rich that I was sorry to be leaving . . .

I would be lying if I said that the teacher became sorry that he was leaving the school, or had started to reconsider his decision to retire very early from music teaching. And it would be stretching things to suggest that the students

this. This means that students in all schools need to be offered a curriculum that comprises more than western classical music and contemporary popular music. Here, I address the role of so-called 'world music' within all this. First, what does the term 'world music' actually mean?

What is world music?

The term 'world music' is sometimes used to describe music that is 'other' in some way. In particular, it is sometimes used by enthusiasts of western classical music to describe music that obviously has some historical origins outside western society.

This section is not just about music that is 'other' in some respect, perhaps because it feels to be 'other people's music' or 'music that falls outside my personal musical world'. By 'world music', I mean all the music of the world: past, present, and future. Thus world music includes western classical music, music that is being composed now for symphony orchestras and opera companies, fusion, music that is being played now on Indian instruments in England, music that is being played now on Indian instruments in India, and the music that the Ancient Greeks played, if only we could work out what it was. In other words, all music that is, or could be.

I doubt that anyone reading this book needs to be persuaded of the vast musical, educational, and social benefits to be derived by drawing from the full world of music—and not just a strand such as western classical music—when teaching music in schools. The broad educational and social benefits flow, for example, from the opportunity for students to make links between their lives and those of others, increase their understanding and valuing of culture, and acquire knowledge that counters the development of prejudice. The specifically musical benefits include those of acquiring new musical interests, improving one's understanding of (and having new insights about) the context of the music that one knows and perhaps loves best, and finding new ways of learning in music.

These musical benefits can affect teachers as much as their students. As a small example of this, I recall the enormous, instantaneous, and unanticipated improvements brought to my chamber music playing by my elementary experiences of playing gamelan. I had always enjoyed playing string quartets, but knew that I was too preoccupied with my own performance, in particular my perceptions of its note-by-note deficiencies. When playing gamelan, my focus was the overall sound, the requirement to work from memory enabled me to think of my part as patterns within structures rather than notes, I was more conscious of being part of a group, and I was able to evaluate my playing from a greater distance, i.e. more objectively. The next time that I sat down with my string quartet, I found that I had subconsciously brought all this with me. I focused naturally on our overall sound (rather than my individual notes), and I looked at my written music much less, because I had realized that I did not need it. I am not claiming that such insights can be gained only by playing gamelan, or that all classical musicians would experience the same benefits from playing gamelan. But this experience proved very useful to me, and illustrates the potential musical benefits of working in a wide range of music.

Accomplished performers also experience the musical benefits of working broadly in music. When I have interviewed distinguished western classical performers about their careers, almost all have spoken of continually looking for new opportunities to learn musically, in order to keep their performance alive and still an act of re-creation. Experienced performers almost invariably choose to learn a repertoire that is broader than the one that they perform at concerts, and speak of how playing the broadened repertoire has helped them with the repertoire that they perform professionally. For example, a pianist known for his performance of heavy romantic piano concertos—such as those of Brahms and Tchaikovsky—might speak of playing baroque music to help with relaxing his touch, or jazz to help him find new tone colours. And a classical guitarist spoke of how playing sax collegially in a dance band helped break his isolation on stage during solo guitar recitals (Mills 2004a). Opportunities to engage with a broad range of musical opportunities are valuable at all levels, and within all aspects, of learning in music. There is no need for classical musicians, in particular, to specialize to the extent that is sometimes supposed. Of course they must develop the skills that they need for the music that they want to perform. But doing so to the exclusion of developing other skills in other music is likely to be counter-productive.

Trevor Wiggins wrote of what he learnt about practice, music cognition, and learning from taking drumming lessons during field research in Ghana in the mid-1990s:

During most lessons there will be one or two teenage boys who help by playing some of the other parts of the piece I am learning. They have heard this music since (before?) they were born and know how it goes. A typical scenario would find me learning a particular pattern one day. The next, while waiting for a master drummer to arrive, I will be practising quietly and, inevitably, making some mistakes. I will try to correct my mistakes by playing more slowly, or by taking a particular passage and repeating it. The boys who also arrive early will be frustrated by my efforts and will try to show me how it should be. This will always be at full speed and will probably be a variant of what I am trying to do. It may also start from a different point but to them it is 'the same'; i.e. it is a manifestation of an unheard central paradigm for this section of the piece. They are most surprised when I am not able to copy their actions immediately—don't I know this piece? (Wiggins 1996: 23)

example, a girl motioned to me to join her, and then read to me in Arabic from the Qur'an, her eyes ablaze with what looked like love for what she was reading. She explained the passage to me in English. However, the teacher then organized the children in a way that disrupted their engagement. First, she showed lack of awareness of the children's knowledge of their faith by testing them on the names of the five pillars of wisdom: *shahada, salah, zakat, hajj,* and *saum.* (The children looked at her with contempt, and started to speak to her rudely.) Second, she showed lack of understanding of the children's cultural practice by asking them to divide into groups, and make up plays, supported by figural drawings and songs, to explain an aspect of Islam to the other children present. (The children did not do what the teacher had asked, and became boisterous.)

The third example involved a class of 13-year-olds working through a module on Indian music that was drawn from a published scheme of work. The teacher used the published materials rigorously and literally, reading out information given in the scheme, playing recorded extracts of Indian music at the points indicated in the scheme, asking students the questions suggested in the scheme, and setting some practical work (devising a raga on a glockenspiel) as recommended. He interpreted the published materials thoroughly, but there was nothing of himself in the lesson. For example, he did not demonstrate, introduce recordings that he had chosen, or refer to any instances of listening to Indian music other than in his classroom. The published scheme did not explain that playing a raga on a glockenspiel was something of an auditory compromise, because the scales available on a glockenspiel are not Indian, and so the teacher did not explain this either. It appeared that the teacher's knowledge and experience of Indian music might both begin and end with the contents of the published scheme.

There are now many resources that teachers wanting to increase their knowledge of Indian music can use. For example, the *Mapping South Asian Music in Britain* project provided valuable insights into the nature and role of South Asian music in formal and informal music education in the UK (Farrell *et al.* 2000).

But actually the teacher had a potentially valuable unused resource in the classroom. There was someone there who could have helped. The predominantly white class included an Asian boy. Like his peers, he had followed the teacher's instructions without question. When I spoke to him after the lesson, he told me that he played tabla. Indeed he had been playing tabla for several years. No, he did not think that his teacher knew this. Of course, one cannot assume that the boy would have wanted to help out his teacher during this particular lesson. But perhaps the teacher could have asked him?

World music in school—getting better

Andrew Alden (1998) interviewed students in a mixed-race inner-city London primary school about the music that they enjoyed listening to. First, he spoke to students in large mixed-race groups: they reported that they rarely listened to anything except charts music. Second, he interviewed Asian children in single-ethnicity groups: they told him that they preferred Hindi film music to charts music, and spent much more time at home listening to it. Third, he carried out some more interviews of large mixed-race groups, and was told, as before, that they were interested only in charts music. Finally, he spoke to some of the Asian students individually, and asked why they had not spoken up for Hindi film music when they were interviewed in mixed-race groups. They explained that they were embarrassed about expressing an interest in Hindi film music in front of their white peers. This study provides a further indication (see also p. 57) that it might be helpful to organize listening as an individual activity, at least from time to time.

Some schools create a culture in which students can state their musical interests, have them respected, and share them. I recall a primary school that, for some reason, was more successful in this respect than the school that is described above. This second school had roughly even numbers of black, Asian, and white students. There was a well-developed class curriculum that had been honed over many years, and which placed distinctive emphasis on internalizing music—hearing it in your head—whether a student was composing, performing, or listening. In addition to this, students could learn instruments including steel pans, keyboard, and recorder, and take part in Asian dance. Some students were doing all of these. The concerts and other performances that the school held for parents included a wide range of music too, and class teachers tried to build on students' varied instrumental experiences when teaching them class music.

Secondary schools can also achieve comparable results. Here is an extract from the inspection report written in 2003 on Hamstead Hall School, a comprehensive school in Birmingham. A majority of the students at Hamstead Hall are Asian or Asian British, one-fifth are black or black British, and one-tenth are white British. The extract is drawn from an account of the school's annual Awards Evening, which was attended by the winners of academic or pastoral awards and their families:

The music that was performed during the evening illustrates the racial harmony in the school and the confidence of students. It included Indian, Caribbean and western popular forms. Bryan Adams—*Everything I Do*—sung solo by a Chinese girl, was delivered with polish and commitment. The gospel choir included white boys and Asian girls.

The older dhol drummers noticeably guided the younger ones as they performed. The Bhangra dancers whom they accompanied included white girls. The dancers and drummers have already taken part in the Birmingham LEA *Sound City* project and community events. The drummers receive tuition from the local education authority music service and the dancers are taught by a deputy headteacher . . . (Hamstead Hall School: Birmingham 2003)

Where students and teachers engage with different types of music in the classroom or the community—play with it, rather than look at it as though through binoculars—the creation of a new type of music through fusion is a normal musical outcome. As samba, for example, has been introduced on a large scale throughout Britain in recent years, often through the work of community musicians, it has sometimes fused with, and been influenced by, the musical interests of the community musicians and the young people with whom they work. Samba in Cumbria may not be the same as samba in Leicestershire, for example. Fusion was not evident in the public performances at the primary and secondary schools that are described above, but perhaps it was beginning in the minds of some of the young musicians involved. In a sense, almost any act of musical composition or adaptation, individually or in groups, is an act of fusion, because a composer brings a new influence to the music that has gone before. Debussy was influenced by a Javanese gamelan that he heard at the Paris World Exhibition of 1889. George Harrison was influenced by Indian music:

[George] took up the sitar, became a student of the instrument's greatest living maestro, Ravi Shankar, and brought a twangly Indian feel to Beatles tracks such as Within You Without You and Norwegian Wood . . . it gave him an authority in the studio that he'd never had before. (Philip Norman in *Sunday Times*, 2 December 2001)

Teachers—perhaps particularly primary teachers—sometimes feel reluctant to include music that they find 'difficult' to listen to in their lessons, because they think that students will find it even more difficult. In fact, the opposite may be true, as young people, particularly primary students, can be more open and malleable as listeners.

Although the rewards can repay the effort, care is needed when music practice from one country is transferred to another. As I have already suggested, the hazards can be seen in many of the attempts made to transfer the Kodály concept from its native Hungary to the UK. Kodály enthusiasts have frequently approached transfer by resetting the songs used in Hungary to English words. The Kodály concept grew up around the pentatonic scales that form the basis of Hungarian folk song, but these pentatonic scales are found less frequently in English folk song, and hardly ever in the popular music that forms the basic listening diet of many students. Consequently, the Kodály songs that are sung in England sound alien to many students, and indeed are alien to them. Children may be introduced to songs that consist of *soh-me* and then *soh-me-lah* followed by *soh-me-lah-doh* and *soh-me-lah-doh-re*. Thus children are not introduced to singing semitones for a very long time. Were the approach to singing followed strictly, children could find themselves not being 'allowed' to sing *Happy birthday to you* for several consecutive birthdays!

What range of music should teachers include in their curriculum? There is no single answer to this question. Musicians including Robert Kwami (1998) have suggested the creation of a level playing field for different cultures through focusing interculturally on the use of musical devices such as drone (e.g. Scottish, African, and Indian music) and ostinato (e.g. African and Indonesian music). However, he was at pains not to recommend inter-culturality as the exclusive approach, and argued that the study of particular traditions was also an important part of the music curriculum.

Traditions related to western classical music influence the music education of much of the world. During the period when the music curriculum in England, in particular, has been importing traditional music from outside Europe, it has been exporting western classical music to these same countries. In some contexts this has led to what would be regarded, in the UK, as undue emphasis on classical music theory, i.e. *symbol before sound*. For example, Kathy Primos reported that in South Africa only 5% of the many black candidates for Trinity College theory examinations in the Johannesburg region also entered practical examinations. African music is sometimes introduced into South African classrooms through the inclusion of African melodies in recorder tutors that are otherwise western in all respects: 'This "tacking on" of African materials on to the dominant culture of music learning may be well-meaning, but smacks of tokenism' (Primos 2001: 11).

The heavy westernization of the music curriculum in Japan is shown, for example, through the emphasis on melodies such as Bayly's *Long, long ago* in the piano curriculum, but this is now being tackled through requirements including that all Japanese lower secondary pupils learn a traditional Japanese instrument (Imada 2000; Mito 2000; Murao & Wilkins 2001).

An emphasis on western classical music can lead to the neglect of popular music, and not only traditional music. Chrispo Caleb Okumo has made some strong arguments for including Kenyan popular music in the curriculum in Kenya. His arguments include that this music has origins which can be traced and elements that relate to other music in Africa, can be analysed musicologically and textually, and provides insights into social and cultural context: 'music educators have no excuse whatsoever to not include popular music in their study programmes' (Okumo 2000: 148).

Some countries place higher emphasis on their national music than is common in England. For example in Australia, Gary McPherson and Peter Dunbar-Hall (2001) explain that study of Australian music is mandatory in some states, and that study of Aboriginal and Torres Strait Islander music is required in some states, and recommended in others. This emphasis on what might be called 'first person music' is reflected also in Australia's approach to musicology, which has a role in the curriculum throughout the age range. Students are discouraged from using secondary sources: they are expected to carry out musical analysis by themselves, and emphasis is placed on interviewing musicians, rather than reading about their views.

I recently had the good fortune to attend a concert given by Sydney Symphony Orchestra in Sydney Opera House. The programme—of Mussorgsky, Prokofiev, and Sibelius—was stunning, as was the fabulous setting in Sydney harbour. However, it is usual for the SSO to include Australian music in their programmes and my hosts were genuinely disappointed that this had not happened on this occasion. It is difficult to imagine the same pride in contemporary English music being shown in England, and this is regrettable.

Some countries make efforts, through the way that they label the curriculum, to show that they value music as part of life. In South Korea, a subject with a title that means *Joyful Life* combines music with visual arts, mathematics, social studies, and literature in the early years of school (Auh & Walker 2001).

This chapter has taken an approach to world music that centres on students, teachers, and schools. I have assumed that it is acceptable for music to be brought from communities throughout the world into schools, and for it to be listened to, performed, and adapted. I have assumed that this is acceptable, because I believe this to be the case. However, there are issues of authenticity and respect that teachers should bear in mind.

Music that was grown in a community cannot be performed authentically— whatever that means—in any school. But, of course, the impossibility of authentic performance would be an excuse neither for failing to consider the roots of a piece of music that is to be introduced into school, nor for washing one's hand of its origins. Teachers find out as much as possible about the music that they introduce into school, and share as much as possible of this with students. If they have observed, or taken part in, a performance elsewhere, this is a great help. But the books and other resource materials from which songs and other music are drawn are often much more informative than was once the case. Thankfully, the days have gone when one gets to the back of a school song book and finds something—with no accompanying notes—entitled 'Ghanaian folk song', with a rhythm reminiscent of *Hymns Ancient and Modern*, harmony to match, and lyrics that are either in twee English, or in an undisclosed and untranslated language that is presented without a pronunciation guide. But while authenticity is important, it needs to be kept in perspective. No music stands still in time, even without the involvement of schools. It would be unauthentic to view any music as a museum piece, and to try to perform it only as it is thought to have been performed 'originally'. (When? And by whom?) Music is dynamic, it changes as it passes between musicians, and is part of a cultural context that does not stand still. We could not 'preserve' it, even if we wanted to. Music historians and ethnomusicologists do important work in tracking music back in time, and relating it to its social context. Period performers give us valuable insights into how Mozart or Haydn, for example, might have heard their compositions performed. But this does not mean that their music always needs to be performed like that today—even if, as seems unlikely, Mozart and Haydn would have wished this. The knowledge gained from listening to music historians, ethnomusicologists, and period performers helps us when we decide how to perform music today.

How we perform music today will, of course, be guided by respect for the music, and respect for students. Within its own cultural context, some music is performed only in certain seasons, only on certain types of occasions, or only at particular times of day. Or it may be associated with codes of conduct, such as the removal of one's shoes when playing Javanese or Balinese gamelan.

Respect for students includes respect for their religious beliefs, and those of their families. I recall a professional development course for primary teachers that a gifted and charismatic animateur opened by singing a song in a language other than English, and requesting us to join in. One teacher did not join in, and took an early opportunity to ask the animateur what the song meant, and then to explain that she did not wish to sing it as it conflicted with her religious beliefs. Students do not all share the confidence of this woman, and there are classrooms in which it would not be socially acceptable for students to ask for an explanation before following an instruction. Teachers can take some very simple steps, such as avoiding music that may give offence because of its erotic content, or an overtly Christian message, for example. Where parents and carers do not trust teachers to respect their religious beliefs when choosing music for the curriculum, it is easy to understand why they may seek instead to exempt their children from the subject.

Chapter 11

Making progress in music

The Better Music Measures The Government has declared that nobody in the 21st century should have to put up with CDs which suddenly go all peculiar and give out a wobbly sound without explanation. It has undertaken to cure this fault by 2007.

Extract from a satirical article on the UK Government's five-year plans;
Oliver Pritchett in *Daily Telegraph*, 21 July 2004

Progress in music

Progress in music, clearly, is about rather more than the quality of CDs. It is a subject that could occupy several chapters—or even several books. The present chapter, perhaps best thought of as an introduction to this vast subject, considers progress from some different, but related, angles: the structure of progress that is implied through the organization of the national curriculum for music in England; the development of musical concepts; the progress shown by two young children making music in their home; the planning of progress in music; ways in which progress may be facilitated (or inhibited) in the classroom; the assessment of progress in music; the issue of whether participation in music at school may also help students to achieve more generally.

What is progress in music?

At first sight, the national curriculum for music in England appears to have progress wrapped up. A ladder of nine 'level descriptions' is intended to help teachers make judgements about students' performance in the subject. These levels cover the full range of musical activity: composing, performing, and listening. The levels are loosely related to students' age—the average 7-, 11-, and 14-year-old is expected to achieve level 2, 4, and 5/6 respectively—but individual differences may be accommodated. Teachers choose the level that best fits a student, and make their decision about which this is by considering students against the descriptions for adjacent levels.

The notion that students move through levels or stages as they make progress is familiar to teachers in England and Wales because of the use of levels for other national curriculum subjects, and also because many of the most experienced teachers were trained in Piagetian stage theory when they were students. In music, it is frequently accepted that achievement in aspects of instrumental performance may be measured through a sequence of eight graded performance examinations, such as those set by the Associated Board of the Royal Schools of Music or by Trinity Guildhall. Turning to other countries and continents, Kathy Primos (2001) has observed that wherever English is spoken, such graded musical performance examinations are to be found. So what could be wrong with the national curriculum level descriptions?

There may be nothing wrong with having levels for music per se. While Piagetian notions of staged development have had their day, the issue here is the progress that students make through being taught, rather than the progress that they make naturally through developmental interaction with their environment. Perhaps it would be possible to organize programmes of teaching to deliver particular packets of learning that could be described in a 'level', were that what one wished to do? However, the organization and structure of the national curriculum in England presents several obstacles to this. Here are three of them:

First, teachers—of any subject—are not encouraged to use the national curriculum levels as the fundamental basis for planning their teaching. Such practice is sometimes referred to pejoratively as 'teaching to the test'. In the hard-copy version of the national curriculum, the levels are not presented to teachers as its heart: they are at the back of the document, rather like an appendix. The heart of the national curriculum for a subject is its 'programme of study', which is not linked explicitly to the levels, and is more general. When planning programmes of teaching, teachers are supposed to read, absorb, and cover the 'programme of study'—probably with the levels in mind—and then apply the levels to measure students' attainment. Thus the levels are presented to teachers as though they were developmental levels, rather than teaching levels.

Second, the national curriculum levels are not organized in an unambiguous developmental sequence. There are stories of teachers being trained in the national curriculum by being given the statements that comprise the levels on individual cards, being asked to sequence the cards, and all coming up with different answers (none of which was the same as in the national curriculum)— and these stories are not all apocryphal. Consider, for example, the statement:

- they improvise and compose in different genres and styles, using harmonic and non-harmonic devices where relevant, sustaining and developing musical ideas and achieving different intended effects (part of level 6) which leads to:

- they create coherent compositions drawing on internalised sounds and adapt, improvise, develop, extend and discard musical ideas within given and chosen musical structures, genres, styles and traditions (the parallel part of level 7).

It is less than clear why a student whose achievement matches the description for level 7 more closely than that for level 6 is necessarily more advanced than a student whose achievement only matches level 6. The gain of level 7 over level 6 seems to be mainly related to having compositions that are coherent, doing some composition in one's head (internalized), developing musical ideas in more sorts of ways (for example by discarding some of them), and working within structures and traditions in addition to genres and styles. Yet students are specifically expected to work within 'structures' at level 2, 'coherence' is implicit at level 5, 'rejection of ideas' is implicit at level 2, and 'styles' are frequently related to, or situated within, 'traditions'.

Third, the levels that have been written for music are at a high level of abstraction. Whereas the levels for mathematics include points such as:

- students know the angle sum of a triangle and that of angles at a point (part of level 5) and
- they add and subtract fractions by writing them with a common denominator (part of level 6)

the music levels open with statements including:

- students recognise and explore the ways sounds can be combined and used expressively (level 3)
- students identify and explore the relationship between sounds and how music reflects different intentions (level 4)
- students identify and explore musical devices and how music reflects time and place (level 5)
- students identify and explore the different processes and contexts of selected musical genres and styles (level 6).

Each of these statements has a wide range of meaning. For example, a PhD student specializing in composing might be working on the expressive use of sounds (level 3), while most 5-year-olds would have little problem telling you which of two musical excerpts might be heard at a disco, or coming from an ice cream van (level 5). It is easy to see why, when given these statements on separate sheets of paper, teachers and musicians may order them in ways other than the 'right' one. Indeed, one could possibly argue an educational case for ordering these statements in any of the 24 ways that are possible (3, 4, 5, 6; 3, 4, 6, 5; 3, 5, 4, 6; 3, 5, 6, 4 . . . 6, 5, 4, 3).

For reasons such as the above, I think that there is more to be said about progress in music than that it is a matter of deciding which national curriculum level is the best fit for a particular student.

Progress in music is not linear. Composers, for example, do not get better only by using more instruments or writing pieces that have more movements or even—dare I say it—by working within particular 'traditions' as well as 'styles'. Performers do not make progress only by playing pieces that are more difficult technically, or faster, or longer. They show that they are getting better also by playing relatively easy pieces better than they did previously, or even just by revisiting pieces that they learnt previously, in order to consolidate them. In fact, progress is sometimes not linear even in subjects that are reputedly easier to organize linearly. Take mathematics, for example. Brenda Denvir and Margaret Brown (1986) showed, when working with low-attaining children aged 7–9, that learning mathematics is not a linear process, and that being immersed in one aspect of mathematics can frequently lead to unexpected learning in another aspect.

Keith Swanwick and June Tillman (1986) tried to take account of the non-linear nature of progress in music by proposing a helical model of musical development. Students move up the four turns of the helix with age, and as teaching or interaction with a learning environment enables them to do something better. But when something new comes along—a new instrument to play, or some computer software to use for composing, or they engage as listener with a whole new type of music that they have not encountered previously—students may drop down by a couple of turns or so as they absorb this new experience.

The notion of students dropping down the helix to absorb new musical experiences makes common sense. But it limits the extent to which the helix can be used for assessment. We could not label the completion of turns 1, 2, 3, and 4 as national curriculum levels 2, 4, 6, and 8, for example, and leave it at that, as we would not know whether a student who was at level 3 (say) was there because it was the highest that they had ever reached, or because they had temporarily dropped from level 8 as a holiday in Java had led to them engage with gamelan music that they were still getting to grips with.

Margaret Barrett's (2002b) work helps to illustrate how complex progression can be. She works regularly as a researcher in a kindergarten in Tasmania, setting up a 'music corner'—including classroom percussion instruments, paper, and texts—that children can join as part of the daily programme of activities. Children may be asked to sing songs, or to make up their own music, and to 'find a way of putting their music down on paper' so that they could recall it, or so that someone else could perform it. Margaret Barrett uses the children's invented notations as an insight into their musical thinking processes, and has found that children 'revert' to forms of notation that are seemingly less sophisticated, according to the nature of the task that they are set, or that of the response which they may wish to make to it. Thus a child who has seemingly 'moved on' from notating their music by drawing a picture of the instrument on which they play it, to showing the patterning of rhythm within their piece, for example, may subsequently decide to notate a new piece through a picture of an instrument. This may be because the piece is 'about' an instrument that a child has not had an opportunity to play before, or 'about' a particular use of instrumental timbre that the child wishes to emphasize over any rhythmic patterning, or just because this is what the child felt like doing. If we accept Swanwick and Tillman's thesis that musical development may be represented through a helix, students may appear to drop down it by a turn or more for reasons less tangible than the need to absorb a new musical experience.

Esther Mang's work in Canada, already cited, illustrates how young children have competence that greatly exceeds that which the national curriculum for music in England expects of them. The national curriculum in England for children aged 5–7 includes that children should be 'taught how to use their voices expressively by singing songs and speaking chants and rhythms'. Amber (see p. 18) does not need to be taught how to do this! Bertil Sundin, working in Sweden, collected songs that were 'made up' or 'found' by children aged 3–6. Some of the songs were reminiscent of Swedish folk songs:

such as this 'dancing' song by Irene, age 6 years. The words are about a girl who is sick. Her father has died and her mother tells the girl that she has been buried. The girl starts weeping and then (the song shifts here from minor to major) 'everybody comes with fruit and candies for her'. (Sundin 1998: 46)

The high standards of this untaught work serve as chastening reminders of how teaching with low expectations, or that treats students as empty buckets to be filled, can result in students ceasing to show us what they can—or in due course could—do. In South Korea it is usual to believe that a child's cognitive, emotional, and physical development begins from conception (Auh & Walker 2001). A dose of this approach in the national curriculum for music in England would be no bad thing.

Conceptual development[1]

Conceptual development is an aspect of musical development. The concepts, or abstract ideas, that musicians apply when making music include those of fast/slow and high/low. Children are not born with mastery of musical concepts: it develops as they learn.

Establishing what students understand in music, and working out how to move them forward in ways that make sense to them as musicians and learners, is not always easy. Teachers are typically among the successes of music education. Many of us mastered our musical concepts at so young an age that we cannot remember how they were explained to us, or what, if anything, was tricky about them at the time. And those of us who play instruments have often been applying the musical concepts we understand to the instruments we play for so long that we have forgotten about the scope for confusion. Consider high/low for example. On the guitar the highest string is at the bottom, and on the cello the sound goes up as you slide your hand down a string, or rock your bow onto a string to your left. When did anyone who calls themselves a guitarist or cellist last find that confusing? Other instruments also have other potential confusions. What does it really mean to play a crescendo on an instrument that has a sound that does not sustain much, such as a piano? Particularly in the early stages of learning to play the piano, before one has graduated to the pedals, and while notes are often played one at a time and quite slowly, the sound does not get progressively louder at all—it just reaches a louder peak as we depress a note more firmly, before dying away very quickly. And students who have mastered the crescendo on an instrument that has relatively little safe dynamic range, such as a descant recorder, may be thought by a teacher to have failed to grasp what a crescendo is, should they try to do something on a similarly small scale on a trumpet, for example.

Concepts such as high/low, fast/slow, and loud/soft (or loud/quiet should one wish to use the special vocabulary of the national curriculum for music in England) are not difficult for students to understand, once they have been explained in a way that relates to what students know already. Where students appear not to understand, teachers try to put themselves in students' situation, and work out what is not, for whatever reason, making sense. Teachers who are so embedded in music that they cannot remember learning whatever it is that a student does not understand, sometimes find it helpful to draw on another teacher who learnt the matter in hand more recently. Or to ask another student to do the teaching, or to explain to the teacher what the problem might be. But

[1] Parts of this section are based on an earlier publication: Mills 1994*b*.

it is almost always a mistake to assume that students do not understand anything in music through perceptual incapacity.

The ability of even very young children to perceive and respond to musical sounds and structures, and changes in musical sounds and structures, is often considerable. Parents sometimes report that their children are calmed by some specific pieces of music, excited by others, and respond to a third group with what appears to be total attention. Bridger's work which showed that babies aged under five days can discriminate pitch changes of as little as a major third was mentioned earlier (p. 123). It is, of course, possible that the babies could detect changes of pitch even smaller than this: they just did not show researchers that they could do this by making a response such as a movement. Chang and Trehub (1977*a*) found that babies aged five months noticed simple rhythmic changes, for example: • •　• • • • rather than • • • •　• •. They also found that the babies appeared to have grasped the concept of melodic shape. The babies were played a six-note melody until they became used to it, and their heart rate returned to normal. When the melody was changed to another key, their heart rate remained constant: when the order of the six notes was changed, their heart rate decreased (Chang & Trehub 1977*b*). Related experiments showed that babies could also detect changes in tempo and dynamics.

The results of such research show us that babies with normal hearing are not limited by their perception from developing the concepts of loud/soft, fast/slow, and high/low, for example. They have the 'perceptual apparatus' needed. And the chances are that they notice differences in pitch, for example, much finer than those for which researchers such as Bridger, Chang, and Trehub were able to show results. The problem is finding a way of spotting that young children notice the difference. Once children become able to talk and write, such matters become much easier, and the sophistication of children's perception can then sometimes be surprising. I have already said that in research using written responses (Mills 1988*a*) I found that most 7-year-olds recognized that notes one-sixth of a semitone apart were different, and that some 7-year-olds spotted differences of one-tenth of a semitone. But remarkable as this is, it is clearly not the same as grasping the concept high/low, for example, or—more advanced still—being able to talk about concepts using 'official' vocabulary. That young children perceive so well is important for teachers. It means that a child who cannot tell you which of two notes a tone apart is *higher* is not likely to be able to tell you the direction of two notes a perfect fifth apart either, and needs help with what 'higher' means, rather than help with perceiving that the pitch of notes differs. Conceptual development lags behind perceptual development.

It is sometimes said that children who are described as gifted in music have abilities that are 'innate' or even, to wind the clock back another nine months to conception, 'genetically determined'. Clearly, the knowledge that a note which sounds what we call 'higher' should be labelled thus cannot possibly be innate, just as skills that require engagement with a culture other than via amniotic fluid (such as fluent use of western harmonies) or interpersonal relationships other than that between foetus and mother (such as ensemble skills of the ilk required when playing nineteenth-century string quartets) cannot possibly be innate either. To suggest otherwise would be rather like claiming that newly born babies have the complete works of Shakespeare, and a developed understanding of how to stage them, inside just waiting to come out as they personally progress from 'infant, mewling and puking in the nurse's arms' to competent adult. It may, or may not, be the case that some individuals have greater genetic potential than others to develop very fine pitch discrimination, for example. I am not sure that we will ever know, or that this is educationally or musically important. What the research that I have described tells us is that children—probably all children—have perceptual abilities that remain underdeveloped musically by the opportunities that they receive, inside and outside school, as they grow up. Music education in school is about helping all young people to achieve more of their potential as musicians.

Teachers often attempt to assess students' musical understanding through the quality of their performance of music. A violinist who plays with consistently good intonation may be supposed to have grasped the concept high/low. A singer who changes the colour of her voice to convey the changing mood of the lyrics of a song may appear to be applying concepts associated with timbre including, for example, dull/bright. Much of the time, this type of assessment works well. But it can let teachers down. Students who have mastered a concept may be unable to communicate this through their performance because of physical difficulties. A student who does not sing in tune, for example, may have a secure grasp of the concept high/low, but insufficient physical command of his voice to communicate this, particularly if he is trying to sing a song that lies partly outside his comfortable vocal range. String players—indeed players of all the instruments where players have even a little control of the pitch of notes—are familiar with the frustration of being told that a note was flat or sharp, when they knew full well that it was, and the problem was doing something about it at the same time as attending to all the other challenges of the piece they were playing.

The examples given above are of students who did not do full credit to their understanding in their performance of music. It is also possible for students to give the impression through their music-making that their understanding is deeper than it really is. I recall a lesson when a teacher laid out a selection of triangles, wooden blocks, drums, cymbals, and tambourines and so forth, and asked a group of children aged 7 and 8 to choose an instrument each, go as a group into an adjacent workspace and 'compose a rhythm on percussion instruments'. After a suitable interval, the children returned to the classroom and played a rhythm the teacher did not recognize on the instruments they had chosen, and the teacher wrote down that the children understood what 'compose', 'rhythm', and 'percussion instrument' meant. Actually, I learnt through further work with the children that this was not the case. When I laid out a wider selection of instruments from the classroom 'music table', and asked the children to say which were percussion instruments, they picked out a recorder as a percussion instrument, and insisted that a cymbal was not a percussion instrument. When, after a game in which we had taken it in turns to make up a rhythm for everyone else to echo (but I had not used the words 'rhythm' or 'compose'), I said 'whose turn is it now to compose a rhythm?' they looked as me as though I had just arrived from a distant planet. The children had 'succeeded' earlier because 'percussion instruments' were the only instruments available, 'rhythm' was all that one could do with the instruments as they were untuned, and 'compose' was what one did when asked by the teacher to go into a group and do something with instruments.

And the labelling of musical concepts can also be confusing. Musicians speak of high/low and loud/soft, but a request to turn down the radio is a request to reduce the volume. And the labelling of different pitches with the spatial terms of 'high' and 'low', though shared by many cultures, can appear arbitrary. There are few instruments on which notes of higher pitch are, in any unambiguous spatial sense, 'up'. They are to the right on the piano, towards you on the harp, to the right and/or towards you on the violin, and often in much the same place on woodwind and brass instruments. The scope for misunderstanding students' understanding is considerable.

Making progress: Amy and Tom

I have suggested that progress depends on provision, and that young children are often more capable than we might expect. Here is an example:

Amy is ten days old. Her father lays her across his lap as he improvises at the piano. The harmonies are rich; the timbres are full; the mood is reflective—but the music is neither gentle nor spare. Amy turns her head towards the piano, remaining motionless until her father stops playing more than five minutes later. We do not know the shape of Amy's thoughts. But her attention to the music—its sounds, vibrations and the movement of her father's hands—which she is perhaps sensing through her ears, eyes and throughout the 'piano-side' of her body, remains rapt.

What is happening here? Is Amy displaying signs of musical precocity? Is she going to become a great musician? Perhaps she is, perhaps she isn't. Another way of looking at the above is simply that Amy is:

- receiving some music provision

- responding to it

- lucky enough to have at least one adult observer who notices her response, values it, and who is in a position to give her some further musical provision.

It is possible that any child would respond as fully as Amy to the opportunities that she receives. If Amy is lucky, then the music provision that she receives subsequently will build on her responses. However, the route by which she develops as a musician will depend on the nature of this provision. There may, or may not, be some sort of generalizable order to the musical development that children pass through simply by virtue of getting older. But the effects of this may well be very modest when compared with the musicianship that is developed through confident engagement with musical provision.

So what happened to Amy? How did she develop as a musician? Let's move the clock on almost three years from the example above, and focus on her relationship with the piano. Amy is now 32 months old:

Amy is not one to 'plink-plonk' on the piano, but loves to watch her father play. He shows her how to play E-D-C: she copies him and says 'That's *Three blind mice*'. She works out how to continue *Three blind mice*, playing E-D-C E-D-C G-F-E G-F-E. She then stops abruptly, and goes off to play with some toys.

What can we tell from this about Amy's musical development? Clearly, Amy knows the song *Three blind mice*, and furthermore recognizes it when just the beginning is played using the 'wrong' timbre—the piano instead of the voice—and without words. To put it another way, she has internalized the melody. The way that she continues it—repeating E-D-C without stumbling, and later G-F-E—suggests that she has spotted the pattern formed by the simple repetition of motifs. We do not know how she knew that the note after the second C was a G. It is possible that she was just lucky. We do not know if she has spotted that E-D-C and G-F-E is a sequence: she may just work out G-F-E note by note. The sudden breaking off of playing at the end of the extract may mean that she has anticipated the greater challenge of the next phrase, and decided not to attempt it—at least while she has an audience—or it may just mean that Amy fancies doing something else. Either way, it is clear that formal piano lessons of half an hour or more might not be the best way of meeting Amy's current needs as a learner. Indeed, a regular routine of lessons might constrain Amy's development by stopping her learning through play—like she does in the other aspects of her very exciting life. There is plenty of time for Amy to have piano lessons later. But this is not the end of the story . . .

Two days later, Amy's grandmother asks if Amy would play *Three blind mice* on the piano, and shows her the first note: E. Straight away, Amy plays E-D-C E-D-C G-F-F-E G-F-F-(D)-E. (The D was a slip that Amy instantly corrected.) Granny encourages Amy to play this again. 'No thanks', says Amy, and goes off to do something else.

Consciously or subconsciously, Amy has been doing some mental rehearsal of *Three blind mice* since she played it two days previously. The repetition of the Fs, which reflect the syllables of the lyrics, suggests that she has been thinking about playing piano while singing the song, either out loud, or in her head. Amy is learning rapidly, but not in a way that could be bottled in a piano lesson. She has access to expert musicians who set her challenges that the national curriculum would suggest are well beyond her, but which she meets with room to spare. And she adds to her own learning in between the times when adults are intervening to help her, just as she does with all the other aspects of moving on and growing up. She is also about to start contributing to someone else's musical development:

Amy, aged 34 months, has a brother, Tom, aged 5 days. When he cries, she tries to calm him through singing. She chooses songs from her repertoire that she feels will soothe him—such as a slowed down version of *Twinkle twinkle little star*, and sings to Tom in a special *sotto voce* voice.

In national curriculum terms, Amy is doing pretty well for a child under the age of 3. Through matching the mood of her music to an effect that she intends, and through showing the vocal command needed to do this consistently, she is well into the 'level 2' that is expected of children aged 7. That she has decided to do this for herself is interesting. Children can show their capabilities more clearly when they have the opportunity to act spontaneously, and for real. Had Amy been asked in a classroom situation to choose a song and sing it so as to make it suitable for a lullaby, she might have found this much harder. Amy might find it difficult, just yet, to explain in words what she is doing and why, but this does not diminish the fact that she knows what she is doing, because she does it.

What is the effect of Amy's intervention on Tom? In those early days, Tom tended to cry because he needed to, and so Amy's singing rarely had the intended effect of quietening him, much to her disappointment. However, within a few weeks, Tom is showing that he is developing sensitivity to singing:

Tom, aged 3 months, gave his mother his full attention as she sang their family song (Fig. 9):

Mum, Mum, Mum, Mum, Mum, Mum, Mummy
Dad, Dad, Dad, Dad, Dad, Dad, Daddy
Tom, Tom, Tom, Tom, Tom, Tom, Tommy
Amy, Amy, Amy, Amy, Amy.

Fig. 9 The family song

As she began to repeat the song, he started to join in with short phrases of gurgling. For two captivating 'Dads' he gurgled the same pitch as his mother sang. Half way through the third line all this effort became a bit much for him, and he fell silent. But he still gave his mother, and her singing, his full attention.

While it is impossible to check this out directly with Tom just yet, given his age, his parents, at least, think that he has got the idea about singing. And the sheer fact that he is responding makes it more likely that his parents will carry on singing to him in future. If Tom has not, contrary to impressions, got the hang of singing yet, it is difficult to see how he can avoid getting it in due course.

Amy's singing, on the other hand, is now going through a phase that one kindly might describe as 'interesting'. She is just 3:

On being invited by her father to record her singing on the computer, Amy decided on *Twinkle twinkle little star*. She chose her own starting note. Perhaps it was a bit high. But she stuck in there, exercising her voice more thoroughly than had she started on a note chosen for her, and perhaps learning through experience that a lower note next time might be easier. Amy finds the 'st' of 'star' difficult to say, and so she stops after 'little' to take a breath, and gives a good loud 'star' which disrupts the phrase. Amy chose a tempo that was too slow for her to sustain, and she speeded up a bit.

Play Amy's 'performance' to an examiner, and the chances are that it would not get a good mark. Put on a backing track in a key and at a tempo that she can manage comfortably, and she would probably get much better 'marks'. But wouldn't it be sad if Amy never had the chance to work things out for herself? Amy's rendition of *Twinkle twinkle* was 'work in progress'—'performing' rather than 'performance'. Amy is busy learning through play—with songs as well as almost everything else that comes her way—and an important part of learning is that of setting herself challenges which do not always quite come off.

There was time for another recording:

Supercalifragilisticexpialidocious, from *Mary Poppins*, which Amy sang after finishing *Twinkle twinkle*, was even more obviously full of play. The relish with which Amy worked her way round the difficult words of the first two and a half lines before collapsing into silence, and then a brief giggle, as the word 'precocious' eluded her was almost tangible. These were not the giggles of a child who was trying to please adults by being 'cute', but of a child who, mercifully, saw the funny side of having just made a bit of a mess of a recording. Being allowed to make mistakes is an important part of learning to be a great success. Amy is using singing to play with language, play with her voice, play with her memory. And when things go wrong it is still all fun. She is engaging with the raw materials of music, and learning continually.

These brief case studies of Amy and Tom illustrate:

- the enhancement of progress through the offer of opportunities for learning, i.e. teaching, that are packaged so that children may take them up, on their own terms, as they become ready

- teaching that enables young children to develop their musical talents, but which—through its child-centredness—differs from the formal instrumental lessons that are often offered to children who are thought to be musically talented

- the capacity of children—all children—to learn much more in music than is often supposed

- the importance of someone being around to notice what children have achieved, if this is to be acknowledged

- the hazards associated with taking snapshots of children's—or indeed anyone's—musical achievements. There are, of course, occasions when musical performances do need to be judged as 'stand or fall' occasions. Someone who gives a recital at a prestigious classical venue in London, such as the Wigmore Hall or the Purcell Room, will be judged according to how the show goes on the night, without consideration of how the show went that afternoon in rehearsal, or what the musician might be able to do in the future. And so it makes sense for some examinations of young musicians who aspire to turn professional to be conducted in much the same way. But anyone who assessed Amy's *Supercalifragilisticexpialidocious* or *Twinkle twinkle* in this way would have missed the point. Amy is, from the point of view of an examiner, going backwards so that she can go further forwards in future, or in Swanwick and Tillman's terms has temporarily dropped down the helix so that she can go further up it in future. Although I doubt that she would see either progress or her performances in quite that way. And the view of Amy, as the learner, is clearly very important.

Planning progress in music

The planning of progress in music takes place on many different scales. Amy and Tom's parents, in a sense, plan their children's progress whenever they reply to a child's musical response with some further provision. They may not have mapped out specifically where they want their children to be musically one year, or even five years, from now. In fact, they might reject any suggestion that they had thought of doing this, as they might associate this with 'pushing' or 'hot-housing' their children. But, deliberately or not, there is some planning going on, doubtless informed by both parents' experiences of learning to be musicians, and of being parented. Like teachers, Amy and Tom's parents have their personal philosophy of music education, although as parents they may not have articulated it formally.

Schools, on the other hand, are expected to be more explicit about their philosophy of music education, and the learning that they have planned for students. A school curriculum exists within its national curriculum, but the latter is more specific in some countries than others. During the decade—the 1990s—that England defined, and twice redefined, its national curriculum, Sweden outgrew its longer-established national curriculum, and replaced it with local guidelines that are intended to help schools and society work together more closely (Olsson 2001). That one country becomes more specific in its national curriculum, while another becomes less so, is not necessarily a problem: an indication that one country, or possibly both countries, have still not 'got it right'. The range of changes that could or should be made at any point in time, and in any place, in order to improve music in schools for the benefit of students, depends on the history—in the widest sense—of what has gone before, and the cultural environment in which students spend their life outside school. And should a national curriculum—any national curriculum anywhere—ever become the curricular equivalent of wallpaper, so that teachers cease to notice it, but simply carry it out mechanically without thinking about what they are trying to achieve, it would have exceeded its usefulness and be counter-productive. Skilful national curriculum planners anticipate this point in time by months or years, and preserve the essence of their national curriculum by giving teachers a reason to start thinking anew—as Sweden has done by relaxing the detail of a curriculum that teachers had started to find prescriptive—so that teachers can refocus on what that curriculum is intended to achieve. Perhaps a time will arrive when the planners of the national curriculum for England feel that they can do the same.

What might be this 'essence' of the music curriculum? Is there some irreducible core of any music curriculum that should always be preserved? I do not believe that there is detailed musical content that should always be taught, regardless of the context in which students are growing up and being educated. For example, I do not believe that there are particular songs that all children should learn, or particular skills—such as those associated with learning to use staff notation—that all students need to develop, in order to be musically educated, although there may be pragmatic reasons for building specific content into the curriculum set for a school, region, or country. However, I do believe that there is an 'essence' that lies at the heart of any music curriculum that deserves that name. Different curriculum writers will express that essence in different ways, and it is right that they should do so, as it is only so that they will own it, and be able to bring it to life. But it is to do with:

- acknowledging and welcoming the musical skills that each child brings to their first day at school
- doing this in such a way that students see and appreciate the complementarity of the music they do at school and the music that they do out of school
- having students finally emerge from this curriculum as competent and confident musicians—composers, performers, and listeners—with the skills and attitudes that they need to get as much as they want out of music as they move through life.

Having a national curriculum brings both advantages and disadvantages. In England the advantages include that schools cannot choose to make music optional for any student under the age of 14, and must provide a broad curriculum that includes singing, playing instruments, composing, and listening. The disadvantages anywhere can include that teachers lose their focused understanding of *what music in schools is for* because they have to argue the case for their subject less frequently. Even in countries where there is a national curriculum for music, teachers need to generate their personal philosophy of music education.

While the preparation of a national curriculum is doubtless always carried out with the best of intentions, as a means to giving more young people the benefit of a high-quality education, its very existence brings the disadvantage that teachers cease to be involved in planning their teaching from first principles. Where the curriculum is of the sort that tells teachers what to do, and in what order, without explaining adequately what it is all for, there is a danger of teachers finding their role reduced virtually to that of 'teaching by numbers'. One can find oneself doing what the curriculum says, without first working out what students need. It is rather like negotiating the way from A to B in a town using the sort of sequential directions that run 'first left, second right, carry on until you get to the fourth roundabout and then take the fifth exit'. These directions are fine until you find that the second right is closed for roadworks, or mistakenly count a mini-roundabout that the route planner assumed you would ignore, and find yourself hopelessly lost and unable even to work out what direction you are pointing in unless you can see the sun. Directions that are explicitly drawn from a map (which is also provided) offer better protection against getting totally lost. Should we find that a road has been turned into a one-way street that runs the other way, we stand a chance of negotiating our way round it, and still finishing up where we intended to be, or possibly somewhere even better, having enjoyed a more scenic route on the way.

So it is with the curriculum. If you understand what it is all for—the map—you can get back on track when something goes wrong (such as a class finding an activity more difficult than you thought they would) or you deviate from your plans to make the most of an unusual opportunity (perhaps the offer of some workshops with a visiting musician). And everyone may have enjoyed some richer learning along the way than had they stuck to the official route.

How to facilitate—or inhibit—progress in music in the classroom

Progress in music, like progress in all other subjects, takes place when students acquire new knowledge, understanding, or skills. That said, progress in music can occur on many different scales. Music teachers often try to promote progress for students:

- during each individual lesson. Students should leave a music lesson with more skills, knowledge, or understanding than they had on arrival. It is helpful if they also know that this is the case

- over time. Students consolidate the progress that they make in individual lessons, and leave each term or year of their course in school with more skills, knowledge, and understanding than they had when it began. (Again, it is helpful if they know that this is the case)

- across a range of music. While there would be no merit in trying to teach students about all music—in any case an impossible feat—students can be taught to make progress by moving beyond the forms of music where they feel most comfortable, at least from time to time

- across a range of musical contexts. As we all know, students do not just do music during music lessons, or when they are doing their music homework. Many of them are involved in music, at least as listeners, for much of their waking hours. Clearly, much of the music that students do between lessons does not lie within the control of their teachers. Nevertheless, music lessons need to be capable of moving students on, however much music they have done since their last music lesson. Students who sing extensively between music lessons, perhaps in a band or a choir, should nevertheless be able to make progress when they sing during class music lessons. Students who compose their own material for their band, or who play jazz clarinet, should still have something to learn from composing in class.

Progress in music, like progress in all other subjects, has a *before*, a *now*, and an *after*. Students enter a lesson or course with prior attainment. The teacher builds on this, and leaves students equipped to respond to more demanding lessons or courses in the future. Clearly, teachers cannot hope to know everything about every student's prior attainment when they start a lesson (although they could sometimes know rather more than is the case). But through planning activities that allow for the possibility of achievement far higher than that which the teacher expects, and through observing acutely students' response to their teaching, teachers can often take account of students' *before*, give them a constructive *now*, and leave them equipped and motivated for their next experience of learning music, in or out of school.

Questions that teachers can ask themselves about progress might include:

- Is the composing in Year 4 better than that in Year 2? Is it two years better?
- Is the singing in Year 6 better than that in Year 5, even though children in Years 5 and 6 are taught together for singing?

Earlier sections of this book have contained many examples of students being helped to make progress through the efforts of their teachers. Here are some more:

Students age 12 quickly learnt to play suspended fourth chords by copying the teacher playing them on keyboard, and applied them in their compositions.

This teacher used three of the students' senses to teach them suspended fourth chords effectively and efficiently: sound (of this family of chords), sight (of how the hand looks on a keyboard when fingering a suspended fourth chord, and touch (how the hand feels when fingering a suspended fourth chord). He avoided approaches based on staff notation, which would have been much slower.

The school had just taken delivery of a new state-of-the-art keyboard, and two 13-year-olds spent the lesson investigating its scope. One of them recalled the ground bass and opening theme of Pachelbel's *Canon*, which he had last been asked to play six months previously, and they used the keyboard facilities they had discovered in an arrangement.

Note how the students voluntarily drew on their previous learning, and that the teacher let, and encouraged them, to do this. He did not, for example, require the students to learn to play a facile melody while also getting to know the new keyboard—although he probably had a more structured task prepared, ready to pass on to the students, had their work become aimless. Thus a lesson that might have led students temporarily to drop down the Swanwick–Tillman helix, because they were learning how to use a new musical instrument, had instead led to upward progress.

A class of 16 years olds were being introduced to serialism. They found serialism difficult to understand, and serial works difficult to listen to. They were reluctant to do any practical work, for fear that it would be 'wrong'. The teacher handed out a well-structured worksheet that reinforced her exposition about tone rows, inversion, retrograde and retrograde inversion. She sent the students in groups to the practice rooms, and insisted that each group return in 20 minutes able to play an original tone row, and its statement in inversion, retrograde and retrograde inversion. She made it clear that she would not mind if some of the work that students returned with was 'wrong': this would provide her with a basis for helping them to get it 'right'.

The teacher had realized that students' negativity about serialism, and about their own ability to understand how serialism works, was getting in the way of their learning—and escalating. By insisting that they compose and then manipulate their own tone row, and perform their work to the class, she obliged students to start to work with tone rows, and to start to develop the aural skills needed to do this. She also provided herself with a basis for diagnosing, and remedying, any gaps in students' understanding. By the end of the one-hour lesson, some students were starting to spot aurally when their peers had inadvertently repeated a note in their tone row, or had made some glaring mistakes in the ways that they had manipulated their tone rows. A few students were starting to volunteer positive comments about the aesthetic qualities of their peers' work. The negativity had largely gone, and had been replaced by a spirit of enquiry and problem-solving.

Teachers sometimes allocate their best resources, for example instruments or rehearsal spaces, to the students who they feel have earned them, for example through good behaviour or through attending extracurricular activities. This can lead to a downward spiral, with the students who have to work without adequate resources behaving ever more challengingly, and becoming less and less interested in their work. This teacher broke that cycle:

During a class lesson, a group of 13-year-old boys found it difficult to meet their obligations because they were in the wrong environment. They were trying to compose in the same classroom as two other groups. They were frustrated, unable to function as a group, and beginning to interrupt the work of other students. The teacher intervened and found them a practice room. Their imminent disarray was transformed into motivation, and they rapidly produced the composition that was required of them.

And, finally, I have already written of the disruption of progress that can occur when students transfer to secondary school at the age of 11, and they are unlucky enough to have a secondary music teacher who assumes that they have done little, or nothing, in music previously. In some parts of England, all students change school at the age of 13, or even 14, and students can find themselves 'going back to zero' even later in their education. It is a bit like playing Snakes and Ladders, with the probability of landing on one of those very long snakes being particularly likely after a move to a new school. When students enter a secondary school from lots of contributory schools at the age of 14, just as they begin their GCSE course, it can be tempting for music teachers to begin with lessons of the most basic kind—for example on music theory—which almost everyone finds easy and dull, so that students stop working as hard, or with as much interest, as in their previous school. The next teacher actively used the widely ranging musical strengths of his contributory schools to raise students' expectations of themselves, and their understanding of the scope of music:

This was the second week of the school year, the GCSE group included students from over ten contributory schools with a wide range of musical strengths, and the teacher had asked all the students to prepare a performance that they would give to the rest of the class. The standards were high, because students were using their musical strengths and those of their previous school, and the diversity of the performances was greater than would usually be found within a single school. For example, a pianist played Beethoven from memory, a classical guitarist performed one of his Grade 8 pieces from notation, a group of six students played an arrangement of *Stand By Me* on steel pans, a tenor saxophonist improvised on *Summertime*, and an electric guitarist played blues. The students were intently interested in each other's performances, came to understand that the scope of music is broader than they had previously thought, and had the potentially inspiring experience of seeing other students doing something musical better than they could do—yet.

Sadly, teaching does not always enable students to make progress at quite this rate.

This is an approach that I have called *praise them regardless*:

The teacher pulled down the blackboard to reveal some short rhythms consisting of crotchets, quaver pairs and minims, and asked the class to clap them. The class [of 11-year-olds] started together, but thereafter the clapping verged on chaotic. It was impossible to tell if the students were even clapping the correct number of times. Perhaps some of them were reading the wrong rhythm. The teacher commented that the students were 'starting to get the right idea', and reminded them that crotchets are 'longer' than quavers. (Are they? A clapped breve sounds much the same as a clapped hemi-demi-semi-quaver: it is the silence after the clapped sound has decayed which changes in length). The students were praised, and the lesson bell rang. (Mills 1996*b*: 11)

Here is another example of lack of progress:

Students aged 15/16 studying for GCSE use just one mallet when they play the xylophone.

Why is this an example of lack of progress? Because this is neither exploiting the potential of the instrument nor teaching students to play it more effectively. Professional xylophone players use both their hands; indeed they sometimes play with as many as four mallets in each hand! The one-mallet problem has similarities with that of allowing students to routinely remove the unneeded bars of xylophones, glockenspiels, and metallophones when playing music based on a pentatonic scale: an approach that is sometimes argued for on the grounds that 'everything will sound all right'. (So is it worth doing, then?) I am not suggesting that students should never play with only one mallet, or never remove bars from their instruments. But doing either of these routinely means that technical problems that are impeding students' access to a wider repertoire are not grappled with and, in due course, overcome.

Here is a further example:

The class of 11-year-olds spent the first 20 minutes of the lesson clapping on the first beat of the bar of a march.

This was a march with a very clear downbeat that had been composed specially for use in school—it was not even 'real' music. The students got the idea of how to clap on the down beat in a lot less than 20 minutes. And what was the point of clapping on the downbeat anyway? Where, if anywhere, was this activity leading?

And then:

There was no music at all until minute 25 of this one-hour lesson for students aged 11—and then only the open strings of a cello, played pizzicato.

This was one of a series of lessons on instruments of the orchestra, and was about the cello. I use the preposition 'about' advisedly. The first 25 minutes of the lesson were spent talking about cellos, writing about cellos, and looking at a cello that the teacher had brought to the lesson. But none of this was related to the making of music by one or more cellos. When the teacher played the open strings of the cello, the increased engagement of the class was palpable. But they soon sank back into their seats on realizing that the teacher's performance of each of the open strings, only once and pizzicato, was both the beginning and the end of the music that they were going to hear—and that none of them would get the chance to even touch the cello.

I continue:

While one half of the class of 13-year-olds practised one-hand five-note melodies (C–G) on keyboards, the other half copied out a handout about the life of Liszt.

These students had been learning keyboard for over two years, and the school was accustomed to organizing keyboard lessons so that only half of the class played keyboard, and the other students did activities that merely filled their time. It is perhaps particularly ironic that the week's handout was about the great pianist Liszt . . . This approach to planning lessons does not show respect for students' time and so, I would argue, it is unacceptable. But actually the students' limited progress with keyboard was not just a result of them only having about half the opportunity that they should have had to get their hands on an instrument. It was also to do with the school's limited expectations of their keyboard playing. Had the students played keyboard for only an average of five minutes a week for two years, they should still have moved beyond one-hand five-note melodies on C, D, E, F, and G.

Some problems with progress develop over a long period of time, for example:

Both boys have been learning viola for four years, since they were 7. They still play only in first position, and still use 'fingerboard spots' to guide their intonation. The taller boy has not learnt to adjust his playing position as he has grown. He has a very low bowing arm, and rests his left elbow against his chest.

Here, it is as though the viola teacher does not know what to do with viola students who do not give up! Just think how well these students might be doing now, given their tenacity, if only they were being taught more systematically, and with greater ambition on the part of the teacher.

Progress is fragile. Once gained, it can still be lost:

Many of the 12-year-olds at this school can play the ground bass of Pachelbel's *Canon* with their left hand, while adding the opening theme in their right hand. But the 15-year-olds struggle with the opening theme of *Jingle bells* in C major, and have the note names written underneath the staff notation.

This is not because the older students are particularly lacking in keyboard ability, or because the music provision at the school has recently been improved—for example through the appointment of a more demanding teacher for the younger students. The older students included some who attain very highly in other subjects, and the teachers of each of the classes have both been at the school several years. The issue was that the teacher of the older class was not aware of the curriculum lower down the school, and taught the keyboard to 15-year-olds as though they had never studied it before—with the result that they became bored and their performance deteriorated.

Just occasionally, progress does not seem to have been planned at all:

The 9-year-olds were on a 'taster' course in learning to play a musical instrument given by the local education authority music service. The idea was for the students to all have a chance to see whether they wanted to learn an instrument and, if so, which instrument they would most like to play, without initially needing to commit themselves to playing for a term or more. In groups, students had four lessons on each of four instruments: flute, trumpet, violin, and clarinet. This was just long enough for many students to come to the conclusion that they were no good at playing any instrument. For example, students who were just starting to make progress in getting a note consistently from a flute during their fourth lesson were not allowed to have a fifth lesson, but had to try a trumpet instead. And students who had been particularly successful on one of the instruments they tried earliest sometimes had this happy experience erased from their minds by a less successful experience on another instrument. And finally, when the 'taster' course ended, no further provision was available for several months, so that the students who had wanted to carry on playing lost interest—and no one continued to play an instrument.

So at the end of this, doubtless well-intended, taster course, some of the students had come to the (almost certainly incorrect) conclusion that they were no good at playing any instrument, while the remainder were left without an opportunity to make further progress.

Issues in assessing progress in music

Much has been written on assessment in music. For example, the US publication *Assessing the Developing Child Musician* by Tim Brophy (2000), runs to almost 500 pages. I do not intend to duplicate all that effort here, but to make some observations about what it might mean to assess progress in music musically.

The system for assessing music in the national curriculum for music in England is 'holistic' rather than 'segmented'. Instead of giving students marks (perhaps out of ten) for many different aspects of music, and adding them all up to give a total mark that tells you how good a student is (segmented assessment), teachers are expected to consider a student 'in the round' (what I would call holistically), and to consider which of the published 'level descriptions' they match most closely. While I have already questioned some of the content of the published level descriptions (p. 156), I think that this is a musical approach to assessment.

Let us take the example of performance in music. As I leave a concert, I have a clear notion of the quality of the performance that I have just heard. If someone asks me to justify my view, I may start to talk about rhythmic drive, or interpretation, or sense of ensemble, for example. But I move from the whole performance to its components. I do not move from the components to the whole. In particular, I do not think: the notes were right, the rhythm was right, the phrasing was coherent, and so on—therefore I must have enjoyed this performance. And I certainly do not think something such as:

SKILLS + INTERPRETATION = PERFORMANCE

I recall performances that have overwhelmed me, despite there being a hand-ful of wrong notes. I remember others in which the notes have been accurate, and the interpretation has been legitimate, and yet the overall effect has been sterile. A performance is much more than a sum of skills and interpretation.

Segmented marking systems are used routinely in some other subjects, and may be appropriate in some fields of music. For example, teachers assessing students' recall of factual information about music, or success in solving a mathematical problem, typically use such schemes. The point is that the assess-ment needs to fit the behaviour being assessed. A musical performance is not a mathematical problem.

Mathematical problems are sometimes set to provide a context for the assessment of qualities such as aspects of mathematical thought. Here, it makes sense to use a segmented marking scheme that will tease out the aspects to be assessed, and to ask students to present their solutions so that they can be given a mark for each of the aspects that they have grasped. Otherwise, a student who has been through the intended thought processes, but has produced no evidence of this, and who perhaps gives an incorrect answer because of some trivial computational error at the end, for example, will not receive appropri-ate credit.

Musical performances are not like this. There is no need for musical performance to be set in a context: it provides its own. The musical perform-ance assessor is fortunate in being presented with the actual behaviour that he or she is to assess. It makes no sense to dissect the performance, give a mark for each of the bits, and then reassemble them by adding up the marks.

One sometimes hears teachers arguing for segmented assessment on the grounds that holistic assessment is 'subjective'. Of course, all assessment is subjective, in the sense that human beings determine how it is done. Even the most detailed mark scheme for a mathematics problem—perhaps one that justifies exactly what a student has to write in order to gain each mark—is subjective because it was designed by a human being. Other human beings might have set a different problem, or structured the mark scheme in some other way. That assessment is subjective, in the sense that human beings are involved in it, is surely something to be celebrated rather than bewailed. The material being assessed is, after all, human endeavour.

Subjectivity, then, I would argue is not necessarily a problem. But what of reliability? Are students who are assessed holistically more likely to be given differing marks by different assessors than students who are assessed using a segmented scheme? Not necessarily. Holistic assessment is not totally reliable, in the sense that all assessors will always come to complete agreement. On the other hand, neither is segmented assessment totally reliable. It is not clear why marks for components of performance, such as rhythm, should be any more reliable than marks for performance itself, and a segmented marking scheme simply combines a series of marks for such components. In fact, Harold Fiske (1977), working in Canada, reported an experiment in which holistic assessment was found to be more reliable than segmented assessment. Fiske collected cassette recordings of a series of trumpet performances, and asked music students to assess them on five scales used in local music festivals: overall, intonation, rhythm, technique, and interpretation. He found greater inter-judge reliability for the overall grade than for any of the segmented grades. In other words, there was much less agreement about ratings for intonation, rhythm, technique, and interpretation than there was for overall ratings. Why should this be? I would suggest two reasons:

1. Overall performance is real. In other words, all the judges hear the same performance. If we are to assess a component of the performance, such as rhythm, on the other hand, we must filter out much of the other material. Our ability to do this, or our technique of doing this, will vary. Thus our perceptions of the rhythmic element of a performance may differ. Abstracting rhythm from melody is not a conceptually simple matter like filtering out impurities from a sample of rain water, or absorbing light rays within some defined frequency range: melody consists of a dynamic relationship between rhythm, pitch, and a host of other variables. Indeed, it is not clear what the expression 'the rhythm of a performance' really means.
2. We are practised in the assessment of overall performance. Every time we listen to a TV theme tune, a pop song, a Mahler symphony, or the ringing of a mobile phone, we have the opportunity to make judgements about what we hear. On the other hand, we are less frequently presented with examples of pure rhythm or intonation, whatever either of these mean, to assess.

It might be possible to train assessors to become more reliable in segmented assessment. But why should one bother to do this? If holistic assessment is already more reliable, surely it makes sense to use training in an attempt to strengthen it further?

Holistic assessment is sometimes criticized on the grounds that assessment is credible only if it is possible for an assessor to verbalize exactly what they are doing. Musical performance is an essentially nonverbal activity, and its reduction to a verbal common denominator seems of uncertain value. Yet there are elements of holistic assessment that can be verbalized, as an experiment that I carried out some years ago illustrates (Mills 1991*d*).

I started by arguing that, as holistic assessment has some inter-judge reliability, it is reasonable to suppose that there are common aspects to individuals' holistic assessments. However, we do not know what these common aspects are: the experiment was intended to find them.

The theoretical background to the experiment was drawn from *personal construct theory* (PCT) (Kelly 1955). George Kelly, a psychotherapist, believed that a person sees other people through a personal system of constructs. A psychotherapist who knows a client's construct system has a basis for planning, and then starting, therapy. But clients typically cannot explain their construct system to the psychotherapist: it has to be elicited. Consequently, Kelly developed a technique that he called triangulation: a client is presented with the names of three people he or she knows, and asked to state a way in which two are the same and the other is different. The extent to which the factor suggested is one of the client's constructs is then explored.

In my experiment, I looked for the constructs that might be being used as a framework for holistic assessment of performance in music. Again, they were hidden. But a substantial difference from Kelly's situation was that I hoped to find a universal, not personal, system. However, triangulation again proved a useful technique.

Initially, I made a videotape of five solo musical performances, each on a different instrument. All the performers were judged by their teachers to be of at least Grade 8 standard, and were of similar age (15–19). Eleven student teachers with widely differing musical experience watched and ranked the five video performances, and then I interviewed each of them individually. I chose three performances, and asked students to describe a characteristic that two performances had, but the other lacked. I then asked students to tell me whether the remaining two performances had, or lacked, this characteristic. By repeating the exercise with different groups of three performances, I established what was, I hoped, some of the individual's constructs. I then pooled the supposed constructs of the eleven individuals, obtaining the following list:

C1   The performer was CONFIDENT/NERVOUS

C2   The performer DID ENJOY/DID NOT ENJOY playing

C3   The performer WAS FAMILIAR WITH/HARDLY KNEW the piece

C4   The performer MADE SENSE/DID NOT MAKE SENSE of the piece as a whole

C5   The performer's use of dynamics was APPROPRIATE/INAPPROPRIATE

C6   The performer's use of tempi was APPROPRIATE/INAPPROPRIATE

C7   The performer's use of phrasing was APPROPRIATE/INAPPROPRIATE

C8   The performer's technical problems were HARDLY NOTICEABLE/ DISTRACTING

C9   The performance was FLUENT/HESITANT

C10   The performance was SENSITIVE/INSENSITIVE

C11   The performance was CLEAN/MUDDY

C12   I found this performance INTERESTING/DULL.

The next stage was to see what happened when another 29 assessors were asked to use C1–C12 to judge performances. This time, the video recording consisted of a series of ten solo performances, each on a different instrument. There were two groups of assessors:

Group 1:   12 music teachers and student teachers specializing in music

Group 2:   17 student teachers specializing in subjects other than music. Some members of this group had shown interest in music through, for example, joining their college choir. But none had studied music at school beyond the age of 16, or taken instrumental lessons since leaving school.

The assessors were asked to imagine that each performance was part of a Grade 8 examination, and to assess the performance as seen and heard without making any allowances, for example for performers who looked younger. For each performance there was a double-sided sheet to be completed. On the first side, the assessor gave a single mark of up to 30 using the Associated Board of the Royal Schools of Music's criterion-referenced classification system (distinction, merit, pass, and fail) as a guide. On the second side, the assessor rated the performance on each of the 12 bipolar constructs using a four-point scale.

The marks given by individuals for performances were converted into ranks, with the performance given the highest mark being assigned a rank of one. The constructs were scored from one to four according to their placing on the four-point scale. There was a positive correlation between each of the constructs and the overall rank ranging from $r = 0.4$ (C6) to $r = 0.7$ (C10 and C11) ($n = 290$).[2] I followed this up with another statistical technique: multiple regression

---

[2] Correlation coefficients (denoted r) can range from 1 (perfect positive correlation) to 0 (no correlation) to –1 (perfect negative correlation). So the marks that assessors gave the performance were influenced most by whether the performance was clean or sensitive, and least by whether they thought that the tempo was appropriate.

analysis.[3] This showed that the constructs accounted for more than two-thirds of the variance in the ranking of the performances, for both Group 1 and Group 2. This indicates that the holistic assessment could be accounted for in terms of common constructs to a substantial extent.

It is interesting that there is so little difference in the results for Groups 1 and 2, i.e. that there is little apparent difference in the holistic assessment according to the extent of formal musical expertise. This offers tentative support to the theory that the reliability of holistic assessment stems, at least partly, from practice in everyday situations.

We have seen that holistic assessment has advantages over segmented assessment. It is more musically credible, in the sense that it is more like assessment made of musical performance in the real world. In addition, it can be more reliable, and no more subjective.

This discussion has been possible only because there is some general understanding of what is meant by 'performer' and 'performance'. We have some idea of what assessment systems in this field are trying to predict. We can tell if the marks produced are nonsense.

This is an unusual situation. Much educational assessment with an outcome of a single mark or grade takes place in a less certain context. We may know what a performer is, but do we know what a musician is? Yet we routinely combine marks obtained for listening, composing, and performing to give a music GCSE, or A level grade. Is there an understanding of what a mathematician or a scientist is? Yet we combine marks to give single grades also in these subjects.

It is sometimes argued that there is something particularly difficult about assessment in the arts. Might it not be that some areas of the arts offer opportunities for particularly rigorous assessment? If we understand what behaviour we are trying to measure, then we can tell if the marks we obtain are sensible. Perhaps those who devise summative assessment systems for non-arts subjects could learn something from looking at aspects of the arts.

---

[3] The multiple regression analysis searched for values a_1 to a_{12} such that a 'regression' equation of the form:

$$\text{Rank} = a_1 C1 + a_2 C2 + a_3 C3 + \ldots + a_{12} C12$$

accounts for as much as possible of the variance in ranks, when calculated across the $29 \times 10 = 290$ performances heard.

The regression equation that was calculated here accounts for 71% ($n = 290$) of the variance in the ranks. The separate figures for Groups 1 and 2 are 73% ($n = 120$) and 69% ($n = 170$) respectively.

Indeed, for many years there has been evidence that holistic assessment can be of value beyond arts subjects. In the early 1980s, Cliff Denton and Keith Postlethwaite experimented with the use of tests and teachers' own assessments (sometimes supplemented with checklists) in the identification of students who would achieve well in mathematics or physics GCE O level examinations (see p. 36). They found that teachers' assessments were just as reliable as tests (Denton & Postlethwaite 1985).

Clearly, a single mark or grade can only ever provide severely limited information about achievement in any sphere of activity. Recent moves to provide a wider range of information about achievement through the use of profiles and reports are welcome. However, there will always be circumstances in which achievement must be summarized in the form of a single number or grade. Assessment is always high on the educational agenda. Further thought about how grades and marks are derived will probably always be timely.

I have suggested that it may be easier to establish the credibility of holistic assessment in performance than in other aspects of music. This is because performance is a holistic task. The setting of holistic tasks in other fields of music can assist in understanding what we are assessing. An example of a holistic task that I particularly like is *Musical Ideas*, one of the non-statutory tasks that accompanied the 1995 version of the national curriculum for music in England (SCAA 1996). Teachers were encouraged, but not required, to use the task to assess the attainment of 14-year-olds, and some teachers still like to use it today. The task is intended mainly to help with the assessment of students' abilities as composers, including their ability to evaluate their compositions.

Students are given a page from a fictitious composer's notebook (Fig. 10) that his daughter has sent to a real contemporary composer, Lin Marsh. The page contains ideas for a composition, and the daughter asks Lin Marsh if she would compose a piece using them. The students try out the ideas for themselves, choose the ones that they will include in a piece of their own, compose it, log the ideas that they used and how they developed them, and listen to the compositions of others in their class, spotting how they used and developed the original composer's ideas. Finally, the students listen to Lin Marsh's composition, spot the ideas that she used and how she used them, and listen to comments that she noted down as she composed including:

I liked the two patterns of the Dorian mode and the raga—knew I wanted to use both . . . Looked to see if text came from a poem—couldn't find it! . . . I like the voice as an instrument and the 'voice awakening' as the earth seemed interesting. I could introduce other text later (?) . . . How to make the voice sleepy! Closed mouth/hum/yawn/sigh? . . . Have rejected the dotted rhythm—find it out of place with my melody

34, Minsted Road,
Derby
15 February, 1996

Dear Mrs Marsh,

I recently discovered these jottings in a notebook my father used to carry. A friend of mine suggested that I send them to you as he thinks that they will interest you.

I know that my father composed music for many different events and occasions, including music for films and television. I also know that it is most likely that these jottings were to be used for a new piece. Initially I thought that the ideas were for a number of pieces but having looked at them more closely I could see that perhaps they were intended for the same piece.

The words give me a problem because I cannot tell whether they were to be sung or spoken or just for inspiration!

There are only a few clues to help anyone but I did wonder if you might be able to make a coherent, completed piece from some, if not all, of the ideas. Obviously, I would be grateful if you would send me any tape recordi~~~ scores.

I look forward~~~

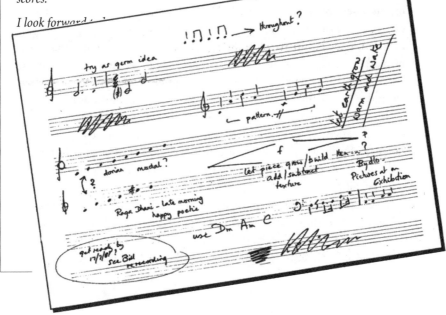

Fig. 10   Composing from a composer's notebook (reproduced by permission of QCA)

. . . Like the 5ths in the melody—think this comes from the [original composer's] idea but I'm not sure now—the original composer's ideas are mixed with mine too much . . .

Lin Marsh's composition for voice and piano is powerful, and students and teachers are often moved by it. It includes many of the ideas from the notebook, some very obviously, and others more subtly. It is fascinating to watch 14-year-olds listening to her comments in a way that that they might not, had they not already attempted the same composition task as her. It is an example of how students can be fired up by tasks similar to those undertaken by professional musicians, and can be assessed doing them.

There is scope to make much more of the music curriculum, and music assessment, like this.

Making progress not in music[4]

Does participation in music at school also help students to achieve more generally? Does doing music help children to become better at mathematics, at French, or, more generally, at working in groups or getting organized, or concentrating, for example? There are those who believe that it is unwise even to ask this question, as a conclusion that music serves some extra-musical end may lead to music being discarded when some more effective, or cheaper, means of serving that end is found. I think that this view is simplistic. It is obvious that the primary reasons for teaching music must be musical ones, just as the primary reasons for teaching art and design relate to art and design, and the primary reasons for teaching mathematics relate to mathematics. It is obvious also that the music curriculum should be assembled, and music taught, so that all students get as much musical benefit from learning music as possible.

But, that said, it makes sense also to consider whether, and if so how, music could be taught so as to also help learners learn more generally. This is not because I feel that it would be 'missing a trick' in marketing music if one did not do this, but because students go to school to learn many diverse things— not just subjects—and it is important that music plays a responsible part in this. Music must always be taught in school primarily for musical reasons. But if it is also the route to wider learning for at least some students, fine and good. And if doing music enables students to develop knowledge, understanding and skills that help them to learn more generally, this will help them to learn in music too.

So, can music improve the mind?

---

[4] Parts of this section are based on an earlier publication: Mills 1998*b*: 204–5.

As I explained in Chapter 2, I have little doubt that it *can*. This view has a long history in English education. For example:

> It is an acknowledged fact that, when properly carried out, class-work in music . . . has most certainly the effect of stimulating the mental faculties of those who take part in it, and, as a result, of improving the standard of work in other departments. (MacPherson 1922: 13)

Whether it *does* improve the mind, is another matter.

The 'can it?' question asks whether there are circumstances or conditions, perhaps a particular sort of music or a style of music teaching, under which music may improve the mind. The 'does it?' question asks whether any sort of experience that could sit under the general heading of 'music' always improves the mind.

The 'does it' question has recently attracted considerable interest in educational circles in the UK. Rightly or wrongly, some musicians and music educators have thought that the place of music in our national curriculum was under threat, and have sought to defend it by arguing that music offers psychological benefits that extend beyond the realms of the subject. Some of this defence has been responsible, careful, and thoughtful. However, there have been examples of carefully crafted research findings being taken out of their context and over-generalized to the point that music, any music, has been portrayed as a panacea. Researchers have been commissioned to investigate whether or not music is a panacea. In fact the 'does it' assertion is easy, and not costly, to refute. One just needs to find a single counter-example of music failing to improve the mind, an example of 'does not', and it has bitten the dust. I suspect that we can all think of an example of 'does not' from our own experience. Depending on our prejudices, we may need to look no further than the nearest rave, radio station, supermarket, or crush bar for our counter-example. The 'can it' question is much more interesting.

Working in Switzerland, Maria Spychiger and colleagues (1993) investigated the effect on some primary children's general attainment of giving them more music provision each week, at the expense of other subjects including mathematics and language. The children kept up with their peers in all areas of the school curriculum, and performed slightly better than them in language and reading skills. This is an appealing study if only because of the audacity, given the usual hierarchy of subjects, of the finding that children who did more music in school, at the expense of language and mathematics, became better at language and reading and no worse at mathematics. Educationally, I do not think that it matters much whether motivation played as great a part as music in securing these results, because the motivation was bound up with the music. Maria Spychiger showed that, in the particular circumstances of her investigation, the answer to the 'can it' question is 'yes'. However, common sense tells us that the 'can it' finding cannot be extended into a general 'does it' finding. Were we to require all the schools in England to give children more music at the expense of mathematics and English we would soon find rather more than one counter-example of a school where standards in mathematics and English plummeted, if only because the teachers would not have been persuaded that this experiment was likely to work. Spychiger's study is interesting, not because it is generalizable, but because it questions the educationally unquestionable. It provides plenty of food for thought. For example, do mathematics teachers sometimes waste some of the relatively large amounts of time that they have at their disposal? The *Times Educational Supplement* has reported (*TES* 2003) that 20 secondary schools in England are experimenting with compressing the three-year curriculum that students follow from the age of 11 into a two-year curriculum as, for example, there is often repetition in the science curriculum, and scope for the mathematics curriculum to be accelerated.

And there may be aspects of Spychiger's study that are generalizable, if only we could isolate them. For example, what was it that led to improvements in language and reading skills, despite less time being available?

To return to the 'can it' question, I have little doubt that music can, under particular circumstances, improve the mind. One need do no more than sit in the classroom of a really good music teacher who believes that music can improve the mind and observe the students growing intellectually in front of your eyes to be convinced of this. What I am sometimes less certain about is what, exactly, this teacher is doing that leads to this improvement, and whether other teachers could be trained to do it too. If we are to exploit the potential of music to improve the mind, we need researchers, and possibly also school inspectors, to help isolate the conditions under which this happens. Perhaps it helps if teachers have a particular sort of commitment. Perhaps it helps if the teaching is particularly carefully planned. Perhaps it helps if students are taught to perform from memory, or to sing at sight, or to try to refine their compositions through thought experiments, instead of always reaching for a keyboard. Doubtless there are a host of other possible factors. Perhaps we need just one of them to be in place. Perhaps we need them all. Once we know more we will need to establish whether these factors can be packaged in a music education that is excellent musically. If they cannot, then the investigation may have added to the sum of human knowledge, but will not be of educational value. Whatever the potential of music to improve the human mind, the main purpose of teaching music in schools is excellence in music.

Chapter 12

The other 18 hours

If I had to live my life again, I would have made a rule to read some poetry and to listen to some music at least once every week.

Charles Darwin, *Autobiography* (Everitt 1997)

This book is about music in schools. But students typically spend only about six hours of each school day at school. And, for most students, fewer than 200 of the 365 or 366 days in a year are school days. A student who never misses a day of school through illness, or for any other reason, will still spend less than one-seventh of each of his or her school years at school. The same student will spend only about one-fifth of his or her waking hours at school. Given the almost continuous immersion in music of many—even most—young people outside school, and also that school exists partly—even mainly—to prepare young people for the time when they leave school, it would be a naïve teacher who tried to teach a music curriculum that is hermetically sealed from life outside school. To try to do so would miss opportunities to build on achievements outside school, and also try to influence them. It would also risk alienation by those young people who value their existing music life outside school above the musical life that the teacher is attempting to build for them inside school.

In earlier chapters, we have acknowledged the centrality of students' musical life outside school, and the need to build constructively on this, when considering what is meant by a musical child, a musical school, or progress in music. This chapter presents some further examples of links between school and 'the other 18 hours' that are going well, and others that are not.

Building on music in the community: ways of working

The music-making that students undertake in their community can frequently be brought into school, and enrich a school's music life. Indeed, there is a sense in which children cannot but bring this music with them into school, and it is just a matter of whether or not teachers notice, build on it, and help children to share it with their peers. Keith Swanwick writes that 'most communities have rich seams of music-making ready to be mined' (Swanwick 1999: 100). Personally, I would prefer a metaphor that spoke more of collaboration, and of opportunities to learn from community musicians, and which did not risk an association of mining with exploitation, but the point is a sound one.

At St Saviour's and St Olave's School in Southwark, London, a comprehensive school for girls where gospel singing has grown into an important part of the curriculum and extracurricular activities, the idea to bring gospel into school from the local community came originally from a group of girls who sing gospel in their churches, wanted somewhere where they could rehearse at lunchtime, and asked Lynne Buckley, the school's head of music at the time, if they could use one of the school practice rooms for this purpose. Fortunately, she said 'yes'. In due course, the lunchtime rehearsals spawned school gospel groups and compositions that girls submitted for examination courses, and gospel became embedded into parts of the curriculum provided by the school. But, throughout this, Lynne Buckley spoke of herself as the facilitator, rather than driver, of the integration of gospel into the school's musical life. The many girls in the school who are proponents of gospel know it first hand in a way that she could not, because it is central to their whole life. She has developed much of her knowledge of gospel through working with them.

Lynne Buckley has had many opportunities to observe the girls as they develop gospel performances, and described their way of working as follows:

In all these songs by various singers a similar process has taken place over varying time scales—usually *many* hours:

1. Decide on a song (this can take 45 minutes of a one hour rehearsal or even longer!)

2. Sing it several times—words written down if not known by all, new verses made up if not enough in original, and everyone embellishes the melody with known or invented harmonies.

3. Try out instrumentation, allocate solos/free style/bridges etc to individuals, pairs or small groups and develop a structure.

4. Sing it many, many times with *frequent* break downs for discussion. Sometimes directors emerge.

5. Eventually settle on the final version but no guarantee that it will be the same on the day.

There are many differences between this process, and the highly organized and teacher-directed ways in which students are often expected to work in groups during lessons led by teachers. Here I focus on just four of these differences.

First, the girls take longer than is often allowed during school lessons when deciding on the song that they will develop, but this seems to work. In fact, as the 'deciding' stage involves singing and trying out ideas, one could view it as a valuable part of the warming up and rehearsal process. In addition, the deciding stage has included initial work on other songs that could be returned to for a later performance.

Second, the girls simply carry out, without being asked, the musical tasks that need to be completed in order to produce a performance, such as extending the lyrics, embellishing the melody, organizing the structure of the final performance, and discussing why a performance has broken down and how it can be repaired. In school, students are often spoon-fed through this, or a similar, sequence of activities.

Third, directors emerge where they are needed, instead of being chosen for every group by an organizer at the beginning, the girls do not argue about who the director will be, and the directors know what it is that they need to do. There is none of the teacherly organization sometimes seen through statements such as 'Each group needs a leader: Claire, you are the leader of your group', 'Claire, take your group into the second practice room on the right', 'Let's hear from Claire's group now'.

Finally, it is accepted, within the girls' understanding of the genre, that the agreed version of the song may be varied for the final performance. If someone introduces a new embellishment to the melody during a performance, this is viewed neither as a 'mistake' nor as a selfish act that carries the risk of 'putting others off'.

To put it another way, the relationship between rehearsal and performance is more dynamic and organic than is frequently the case when teachers and other adult musicians organize performances of western classical music. In addition, the girls show that they have skills of organizing themselves which work, but that are different from those frequently taught in school. In particular, the girls begin by collaborating, with a director emerging when one is needed for musical reasons. This is very different from having an organizer, one who behaves like the chair of a committee, in place from the very beginning of a long sequence of group work.

Perhaps teachers in primary and secondary schools may feel that they cannot incorporate some of this into their ways of working, from time to time. But it could be worth a try, and it is a reminder that students who do not respond well to a teacher's method of organizing them may, in fact, have ways of organizing themselves that are more effective. To draw a parallel with another subject, the teaching of numeracy in England has recently undergone a sea change, in that students are now encouraged to find, use, and explain calculation methods that work for them, with which they are comfortable. The emphasis on students always using calculation methods that work well for teachers has gone, or at least diminished. This change in approach has revealed students who can calculate when they are allowed to choose their methods, but who sometimes fail when they are obliged to calculate using the method preferred by a teacher or the writers of a textbook. It may be that students already have ways of working in groups on performances and compositions that we could tap more effectively. As I write, Lucy Green, of the Institute of Education at the University of London, is working with some secondary schools to try to introduce some of the modes of learning that she has observed adult popular musicians using in real life. The modes of learning that she has described include listening to and copying recordings, peer-direction and learning in groups, acquiring technique, practice, and acquiring knowledge of technicalities.

There is not just one way of approaching any of these. For example, extracts from interviews carried out by Lucy Green (2001) show that some popular musicians learn recordings by trying to sing the line that they want to play in 'real time', such as:

I'd listen to the line over and over again till I could sing it, the bass line. And then I'd work it out from singing it. (p. 61)

while other musicians use 'step time':

if I liked the record, yeah, I'd probably know it, know how it goes and like play it and just stop, yeah, play it and then, yeah: so if I wanted to work it out, hear one chord, stop the tape, work the chord out, next one, next one, until I got the song right. (p. 62)

and then sometimes develop 'chunking' techniques that enable them to work faster:

now it's more—I haven't got perfect pitch, it takes me a little while to work out what key it's in, but I recognise chord sequences, so I know most chord sequences are based round I IV V in the pop music of nowadays and I can hear patterns and recognise them and know that that's going A D G and put those in there and play them . . . (p. 62)

Similarly, while none of Green's interviewees felt that they had built up their technique by acquiring a teacher as soon as they gained access to an instrument, in the way that is common when learning western classical music, there was still some variety in approach. One musician deliberately acquired a teacher when he was in his early 20s:

I'd never thought too much about how I was doing things 'til I went to Bob. (p. 85)

Another musician had his need for technique pointed out by a friend who played classically:

I did it all by ear until at the age of, I'd just turned 19, it must have been around March or April when a guitar playing friend of mine said 'Your hand technique's dreadful,' and I said 'Well I'm fast, I can do this, that and the other', and he said 'No, no, no it's dreadful.' And he showed me correct classical guitar technique . . . and I turned professional in the September . . . By this time I'd become obsessed with technique and I used to watch every bass player that I regarded as being an icon at the time, and I noticed that the majority of them did use the technique that my friend had shown me . . . I had from March 'til September to really get my stuff together . . . most things with me, when I like them, are obsessions and so, you know, it would have been something I would have been doing *every* night. (p. 84)

But a third musician—an acclaimed drummer with an undoubtedly fine technique—had never made a conscious attempt to develop one and did 'just whatever came naturally, really'.

It will be interesting to see how Lucy Green's experimental work with schools works out.

How not to build on music in the community

Here are some examples of young people who are or who were as actively involved in music outside school as the gospel singers at St Saviour's and St Olave's—but whose music-making was not acknowledged by their schools.

Cheryl has no formal musical training, but her father plays in a folk band. She can play the accordion, guitar, whistle, harp and she sings. She is the most accomplished member of the band. Her music teacher is keen on brass bands and does not consider folk music worth listening to. He is not aware of Cheryl's accomplishments and gave her an average grade for effort and attainment on her Year 9 report. She will not be taking GCSE music.

Spider is a brilliant drummer who plays in a bhangra group. He has long hair, always wears a hat and can appear to be sullen. He asked about drum lessons at school but failed the audition given by the drum teacher. The audition was decided by the teacher talking to the students and deciding who he thought would have the best attitude. Spider had a neighbour with a drum kit and used to go round to 'have a go'. After school he had no qualifications and became unemployed. He has recently started community workshops and young people love his music. He asked about giving some lessons in his local school but when he appeared in 'ripped' jeans was asked not to return.

Ravi plays the sitar, tabla and sings. His family are all musicians and he regularly performs at weddings and concerts in the local community. He is bright and attends a local selective school which sets pupils in most subjects. Sets for music are decided according to the Bentley music test. Ravi is in the middle set. Music lessons consist of playing through some melodies on a keyboard. The pupils have to bring their own headphones and if they forget they are given written work to copy out. (NIAS 1997: 11–12)

Cheryl, Spider, and Ravi are all doing well musically without the support of their schools. But these examples are regrettable for three main reasons. First, the schools, and the schools' students and teachers, are not benefiting from

Cheryl, Spider, and Ravi's expertise. For example, the students are not being inspired to develop their musicianship through Cheryl's performance on accordion, guitar, whistle, and harp, and through singing. Second, the schools have not worked with Cheryl, Spider, and Ravi to enhance their musicianship. There is no prospect of an 'Ernesford Grange' effect (see p. 137) happening here, for example with Cheryl asking for classical singing lessons, or joining the school choir, in order to improve her folk singing. Third, Cheryl, Spider, and Ravi are likely to look back on their school days as irrelevant to their musicianship, and may even perpetuate this problem by expecting too little, in due course, of the schools that their own children attend.

Complementarity in the community

Of course, not all the music-making that takes place in the community can be acknowledged and built upon in school. Some young people may want their private life to remain just that. But where teachers show that they recognize, and take an interest in, the musical enthusiasms of their students, they are opening a door to effective links between music in the community and music in the school if that is what the students want. Making equipment and accommodation available, as at St Saviour's and St Olave's, can help here.

I recently visited a community music project, run on a financial shoestring, where a band—formed from sixth formers in one school—had travelled more than 20 miles from their home, at their own expense, to record a demo disc in a recording studio. The session was run well, the band learnt a great deal, the demo disc was completed—and perhaps it will, as the young people hope, be the passport to them gaining at least one gig in their home town in future. So in that respect it was successful. But I happen to know that the young people's school was just as well equipped for making recordings as the community recording studio. These were well-motivated, academically minded sixth formers with good attitudes to school and their teachers. Why had they not used the facilities at school, thereby saving themselves money and time and—although I did not mention this to the young people—freeing the community project to support the less advantaged young people with whom it is funded to work? The students' answer related to the availability of keys to rooms and cupboards at the school. Everything is kept locked up, rooms may be unlocked only when the teacher is present, and the teachers were not thought to be available for band recording sessions. I have a great deal of sympathy with the teachers at the school. I remember the anxiety that I felt, when a school teacher, through being the holder of door keys that gave access to equipment owned by the school that young people wanted to use, but that I was worried about them breaking, or leaving unlocked ready to be stolen, so that it would not be available for use in my lessons. But this is something that teachers need to work round and through. It is good when students want to use equipment that is owned by a school.

It is far better that young people want to use the resources of a school than that they should consider them in the following terms:

[Music in schools is] all *East Enders* theme tunes, glockenspiels, and things missing. What they call a drum kit is one snare drum and a pair of hand cymbals, everything's got the wrong speakers, and no-one's allowed to use it anyway! (Ings *et al.* 1998: 41)

The young musician who said that was working in a band that had been organized through a music project run by the youth service.

Some youth projects work consciously to avoid provision that appears to be like that in schools in order to draw in young people. Youth workers setting up a project in Glasgow came to the conclusion that:

The fact that keyboard lessons flopped early on was the discovery that young people associated them with school and formal education. (Ings *et al.* 1998: 53)

And young people sometimes get much more than music out of making music in the community. Here are just four examples. In the words of a youth worker:

Some of the kids I work with have very poor self-esteem. The band has transformed them and the school says their work's improved. The knock-on effect has been amazing. (Ings *et al.* 1998: 62)

In the words of a parent:

It's brought them together. They've stopped fighting and it's given them something constructive. They are singing when they go home, playing the rhythms with their sticks on the walls. (Youth Music 2003: 53)

And, finally, in the words of two young people:

I really don't wanna go back walking around the streets in the freezing cold 'cause I don't see the point anymore. I just wanna settle down and get to my work. I think it's showed me that if you really work at something you do actually come out better in a way. Yeah, I've achieved something. We've got a CD, we've all achieved something. (Youth Music 2003: 11)

To perform is my chance to get rid of all the anger and hurt inside of me, afterwards it's just like Ahhh, I'm clean again. (Youth Music 2003: 39)

Building on musical skills in the community

Above, we considered some examples of young people who enrich the music in school by bringing in music from outside school. If music in school is indeed to form a worthwhile part of music in lifelong learning, then it needs to help young people develop knowledge, understanding, and skills that they want to take away with them when they leave school at the end of each day, at the end of each term and year, and at the end of their school career.

In the past, teachers have sometimes justified the introduction of lessons on keyboards and guitars, for example, into the school curriculum on the grounds that these are skills that students may wish to use outside school. True, but provision on keyboards and guitars has frequently become institutionalized, so that students develop skills that they are not likely to wish to use outside school. Consider, for example, the simple five-finger C–G melodies, with flat rhythms that can be easily, if dully, notated using only crotchets, minims, and pairs of quavers—and perhaps the odd semibreve—that many young people spend years perfecting in secondary school.

And if we provide instrumental lessons (rather than music lessons involving the use of instruments) primarily so that young people will develop skills that they can use in the community, why is so much time spent in teaching boys and girls in primary schools to play the descant recorder—or indeed any recorder? The recorder is an instrument that had its musical heyday several centuries ago. It is studied in conservatoires, and played at contemporary concerts, primarily by musicians who are particularly interested in early music. Only a small proportion of contemporary composers write for recorder. Prior to the invention of the silicon chip, the introduction of mass-produced descant recorders into schools undoubtedly gave some children a route into instrumental playing that they would not otherwise have had. The continued large-scale teaching of recorder to children who might prefer to be learning another instrument is harder to justify.

Provision that is targeted towards what young people want is more likely to be helpful, and appreciated by them. At Ernesford Grange, students took classical singing lessons so that they could sing more effectively in their bands. Karaoke presents a challenge to schools that has some similarities. In Japan, the ubiquity of karaoke has significantly raised the profile of singing in society. Until a few years ago: 'the traditional style of folk singing meant that only good singers tended to sing at parties or festivals, and others participated by clapping hands or softly joining in (or lip syncing)' (Murao 1994: 5–6).

This has all changed with karaoke. While karaoke was popular initially mainly among adults of middle age, it is now integrated into the social interaction of all age groups. And the emphasis on being part of a group in Japan means that it is difficult to decline the opportunity to take one's turn at singing into a karaoke microphone. In karaoke, any blemishes in singing are amplified, and conveyed to a large listening audience. This has put pressure on students and adults in Japan who consider that they do not sing well in tune to do something about their problem. The situation is not unlike a nightmarishly magnified twenty-first-century version of that in which Philomathes, a self-styled non-singer, found himself in Thomas Morley's *Plaine and Easie Introduction to Practicalle Musicke* of 1597:

supper being ended, and Musicke books, according to the custome being brought to the table: the mistresse of the house presented me with a part, earnestly requesting me to sing. But when after manie excuses, I protested unfainedly that I could not: everie one began to wonder. Yes, some whispered to others, demanding how I was brought up. (Morley 1952)

In Japan, karaoke sets are now found in bars and pubs, hotels, sightseeing buses, restaurants, private houses, and 'karaoke boxes' (small singing rooms that provide snacks and drinks). There are stories of elderly people ceasing to go on sightseeing trips for fear that they will show themselves up if passed a karaoke microphone on the tour bus, and of business men considering that they were passed over for promotion because they were too embarrassed about their voices to take their turn singing karaoke during social evenings with colleagues. There is now a new interest in learning to sing well that schools could build upon.

While karaoke is not as popular in the UK as it is in Japan, and it is more acceptable socially in the UK simply to decline to take a turn at singing, some of the same pressures can still be found, albeit generally on a reduced scale.

Homework

Finally, a brief section on the topic to which, until a few years ago, a chapter with this title might have been confined: homework.

Working in Israel, Eva Brand (2000) capitalized on the enthusiasm of many Israeli children and their parents for homework by sending children home with cassette recordings of unfamiliar songs for them to learn, so that she could research their learning strategies. Working in the USA, Ruth Brittin (2000) found that children at school sometimes wanted a break from the more repetitive musical influences in their home life: when she asked children aged 8–10 to select accompaniments to suit particular melodies, many of them rejected accompaniments that reminded them of a particular TV melody: *Barney and Friends*. The links between home, school, and homework are complex. And what works well in one school will not necessarily work well elsewhere.

A teacher working in an English secondary school that has very poor facilities for music had set up some very effective links between learning at school and learning at home. This is a comprehensive school set in a locality where many families are economically advantaged. The students typically have their own bedroom and their own computer with broadband access to the Internet, and the students who have instrumental lessons typically own instruments of high quality. Many of the students who continue music beyond the age of 14 have access to professional composing software, and some of them have what is, in effect, a small recording studio in their home. The school, on the other hand, is very short of space and equipment. There is only one computer in the music 'suite'—a distant building that is not connected to the school intranet or the Internet—and which consists of one classroom, three practice rooms, a cupboard, and a corridor.

In many schools, GCSE students do most of their composing in the classroom. At this school, many of the students prefer to do their GCSE composing at home, where they have more equipment, peace and quiet, and the opportunity to work undisturbed for longer periods. The teacher works constructively with the situation in which she finds herself. The students who prefer to work at home use lesson time for strategic consultation with the teacher and each other about their developing work. During a lesson that I observed, a student who plays piano was trying out the piano part of an oboe sonata movement composed by one of his friends, an oboist, who had scored the accompaniment using software. Later in the lesson, the oboist got out his oboe, and played through the oboe part of a quartet that a clarinettist had written, explaining what would, or would not, work—and offering advice accordingly. Meanwhile, the students who prefer to compose at school were at work in the practice rooms.

Clearly, the teacher and the students are working in a school that is resourced unacceptably poorly for music. But aspects of the way in which the teacher was organizing her GCSE course could usefully have been retained, whatever the quality of the facilities, because they promoted effective links between learning at home, and learning at school.

The homework that students do of their own accord is sometimes overlooked. I wrote earlier (p. 75) of some young brass players—who had been learning cornet at primary school for a term or so—who were composing at home during their practice time, but not sharing their compositions with their instrumental or class teachers.

What a missed opportunity! These students—like instrumental students in many other settings—were all doing composition homework for free, voluntarily, because they wanted to, and nobody was acknowledging it, capitalizing upon it, and building musically upon it. Think how difficult it would be for the brass teacher or class teacher to MAKE the students do a composing homework, of a nature and at a time of the teacher's choice. Is the main point of homework that it is an imposition? Or is it that students do some work, which enhances their learning at school, at home?

Chapter 13
___

Why is music so boring?

I . . . wish I had been taught theory of music . . . in a more exciting and enlightening way, not in a brutal and boring way, which is what I got and which made me give it up as soon as I could.

David Lodge, novelist and critic, in *New Statesman*, 2 October 2000

I . . . wish I had been taught music properly. We got lessons in English folk songs only, and just sat round singing them.

Sir David Attenborough, writer and broadcaster, in *New Statesman*, 2 October 2000

Subjects are . . . likely to be found boring if pupils fail to see their relevance to their lives . . . Few could see any use in learning art and handicraft, and fewer still in music.

Schools Council 1968

Personaly it is not the noise i object to in music it is the words. i could not care less if i find the minstrel boy in the ranks of death the sooner the better he is uterly wet and unable to lift his fathers sword.

The fictional student Nigel Molesworth in Willans & Searle, *Down with Skool!*

Why is music so boring?

Why is music so boring? It isn't always, and it needn't be. Or at least not as boring as we are sometimes told that it is.

I am not going to pretend in this chapter that music at every school is always interesting and exciting. Even if I had suddenly started to believe this myself, which I have not, I have written far too much in the past about the dull lessons that I have observed, and read about, for me to expect anyone to take me seriously.

But I am clear that some of the research, and other writing, of the last 20 years or so that has been used to criticize music as dull has overstated the case. In both primary and secondary schools there has always been a substantial body of good, motivating, and thoroughly musical teaching—plenty of evidence, in other words, that music in school can be organized so that it is interesting, exciting, and thoroughly worthwhile. Even in the first three years of secondary school, the years that are arguably most difficult to teach, and where music has recently received particular flak from commentators, there is still plenty of good teaching around. For example, the findings of inspection by Ofsted during (almost) every year of the 1990s were that, while there was more unsatisfactory teaching in music than almost all subjects (clearly bad news!) there was nevertheless also more good teaching than in most other subjects. In comparison with other subjects, there was relatively little music teaching in the first three years of secondary school that was barely satisfactory: it was either worse, or more usually, better than this. Good teaching is good practice, just waiting to be disseminated. There is no evidence of which I am aware for the sometime expressed view that music should be removed from the curriculum as it is such a hopeless case. Music is simply not in the terminal condition that some commentators believe it to be.

There was a piece of research more than 35 years ago, alluded to at the start of this chapter, that undeniably showed that music in many schools was in dire straits, and there has been some more research since then which suggests that music in some schools still has a long way to go. But alongside this just criticism of music has been much that is poorly argued, under-researched, and logically untenable. And this criticism has often been carried out by those who could be advocates of music education, namely musicians who describe themselves as educators. While commentators in most other subjects make their reputations by developing, defining, or uncovering good practice and disseminating it, reputations in music education are sometimes made by attacking the subject, on the strength of evidence that is, at best, skimpy. While some of this may just be a matter of naivety, it is sometimes difficult to escape a more cynical explanation. Music, more than other subjects such as history, geography, or design and technology, would take place somewhere even if it never took place in school. Work in school is open to scrutiny, and sometimes also to inspection.

Music in 1968

The research of more than 35 years ago that I mentioned was *Enquiry 1* of the Schools Council, which was published in 1968. This only related to secondary schools: primary students are rarely asked what they think about anything (Pollard *et al.* 2000). *Enquiry 1* was a very thorough investigation that asked secondary students which subjects they thought were useful, and that produced results which were alarming in the case of music. But let us not forget that 1968 was a long time ago. Readers who are old enough to have memories of 1968 are likely to recall that their personal world, the world of music in schools, and the world more generally, have all changed substantially since then. In 1968, I was a spotty long-haired adolescent who had just graduated to a full-size violin, Arnold Bentley's well-known musical ability tests (*Measures of Musical Abilities*) were only two years old, the Beatles released *Yellow Submarine*, Cliff Richard came second in the Eurovision Song Contest with *Congratulations*, Bobby Charlton still had several years to run at Manchester United, mass-produced electronic keyboards had not been invented, those ghastly 'blue-box' glockenspiels that have mainly now been consigned to the scrap heap were still several years away from becoming ubiquitous, and a computer was a set of enormous machines that occupied several rooms and nevertheless did much less than one of today's laptops.

The year 1968 was also when the Russian army entered Prague, Robert Kennedy and Martin Luther King were assassinated, Enoch Powell was expelled from the shadow cabinet following a speech promoting the repatriation of African and West Indian immigrants, and the 1960s turned sour, with violent demonstrations by students about Vietnam and courses of study in cities including Paris, London, and Chicago. It was a long time ago, wasn't it? We should not still be dining out on the findings of *Enquiry 1*.

What was music teaching like in 1968? Doubtless, it varied. It is, however, more difficult than now to establish where the balance between boring, and less boring, practice lay. This was a decade before HM Inspectors began routinely publishing national surveys of education (see, for example, DES 1978) and we need to refer back to sources including textbooks, and the recollections of those who were being educated at the time, in order to establish a picture of this. On this basis, I am clear that the music education that I received at secondary school in 1968 was very enlightened for the time. This was my third year at secondary school, and the third year in post of an enlightened head of music, who had already modernized substantially the curricular organization that he had inherited. 'First year choral'—in which all 120 boys and girls age 11 gathered for a weekly lesson to sing songs including *Hearts of Oak* and *The British Grenadiers* with just one teacher and his piano at the front—had been disbanded, as had the practice of allowing students to give up music in favour of taking an additional modern language after only two years at secondary school. In that latter respect my school was 20 years ahead of the many secondary schools that were forced only by the Education Reform Act of 1988 to ensure that all students studied music for at least their first three years at secondary school.

By 1968, the music curriculum at my school in all years was strongly practical. Lessons for younger secondary students were frequently based round a 'class orchestra' that played specially written arrangements of repertoire including, occasionally, that also being addressed by the school orchestra. Everyone was in the class orchestra. If you were taking instrumental lessons, you sometimes played your specialist instrument in the class orchestra—but the school's full range of orchestral, classroom, and improvised percussion instruments was also available. We were not taught 'music theory' separately from practical music, we did not spend long periods listening to classical music on the crackly recordings of the time (a practice misleadingly called 'music appreciation'), and when new exciting music publications came along, such as *Daniel Jazz*, they were introduced experimentally into the curriculum straight away. Once music became optional, and we started working towards the public examinations of the time for 16-year-olds, the practical work did not stop. We learnt to write harmony by ear—in our heads—rather than by rules, and we arranged and played as much as possible of the works set for historical and analytical study, and other music by the composers of these set works. Our set works included Mendelssohn's incidental music to *A Midsummer Night's Dream*, and so I was sent home with the music for Mendelssohn's Violin Concerto, and had a lot of fun playing through the easier bits, with my mother at the piano.

Important, also, was the musical image of the head of music. Yes, he did all the things then expected of music teachers such as playing the piano and conducting. But he was also learning the bassoon from scratch—a practice that helped him to stay in touch with more elementary learning and also helped to establish bassoon playing at the school—and he was something of a pop star. His 'group' of teachers, the Master Singers, had a contract with Parlophone (the same record company as the Beatles!) and one of the Master Singers singles had made it to No. 2 in the charts. This was a plainchant setting of the common text then used for the weather forecast on BBC radio:

Good morning, here is the weather forecast, for the next 24 hours

First the general situation . . .

The Master Singers were occasionally to be seen singing on TV where their visual presence, possibly because they ranged greatly in height and all wore business suits, was of the same ilk as the infamous *I Look Down on Him* sketch of John Cleese and the Two Ronnies, which was first seen on a *Frost Report* of the same period. The adjective 'cool' had not then acquired its current meaning, but the Master Singers certainly were . . .

This broad and exciting approach to music in school continued when a new head of music—a composer—was appointed when I was in sixth form. As a member of the school's Motet Choir (which actually performed *a cappella* works from any period) I was invited to go to the already famous Strawberry Recording Studios in Stockport and sing in the backing group for Hotlegs (later 10cc), a group of young men that was then doing well in the charts. I accepted with some alacrity.

I knew, even then, that this was not the general situation of music in secondary schools. My school was certainly not the only one that taught music musically and relevantly at the time, but its approach was unusual. More generally music appreciation, *The New National Song Book*, and music theory (paper study that was not linked to making music) reigned supreme. New publications such as *Daniel Jazz* were tackled by few music teachers, perhaps partly because the piano accompaniment was quite demanding, the fewer than 3% of students who continued music beyond the age of 14 worked towards harmonizing square melodic phrases in the style of *Hymns Ancient and Modern* using rules rather than their ears, and the handful of students who continued music beyond the age of 16 aspired to harmonize whole hymn tunes in the style of J. S. Bach: an undisputedly great composer, but nevertheless one who had been dead for more than two centuries. The nearest that many secondary students got to learning an orchestral instrument was a descant recorder, and readers who were at school in 1968 are likely to have memories of the *School Recorder Book 1* (orange) and *Book 2* (green, for those who made it beyond top G) (Priestley & Fowler 1962).

The Schools Council responded to *Enquiry 1*, in due course, by setting up two music projects, including the *Music in the Secondary School Curriculum* project, led by John Paynter from 1973 to 1980, that 'introduce[d] schools, in some cases no doubt for the first time, to a possible approach to music which reaches all pupils, involves all pupils and enthuses all pupils (Harry Rée in Paynter 1982: vii). This project built on the pioneering work described in *Sound and Silence*. It was about creating, interpreting, and responding to music, and it was about the music of the time. While the immediate impact of the project on the music curriculum in many schools was less than the project deserved, it would be very difficult now to find a secondary school that has not been touched by it in some way, and which continues to teach music as it might have in 1968.

Music since 1968

As I have already said, there is now plenty of good practice around, just wait-ing to be disseminated. The music chapter of *The Arts Inspected* (Rose *et al.* 1998) is full of accounts of good practice in schools where music is manifestly not boring, because large numbers of students—occasionally more than half the students in a school—choose to continue the subject once it becomes optional. Times change, teachers move on, and none of these schools will be exactly as they were in 1998. Music has strengthened further in some of these schools, but it may well have declined in others. But there are plenty of indica-tions that good practice is growing overall, and of music educators working to spread and disseminate good practice. The more teacher-centred sections of the weekly *Times Educational Supplement* frequently describe examples of teachers working to generate new good practice by developing their school's music curriculum in imaginative ways, finding that their students are capable of much more musically than either adults or children had dreamed, building better curricular links between primary and secondary schools, building 'music gardens' that allow younger students to develop their classroom music-making as they work with high-quality so-called junk instruments outside at lunchtime and playtime . . . The time has at last almost passed when a journal-ist or education writer might publish an article suggesting that a lesson on design and technology construction techniques might be followed up by singing *This is the house that Jack built*—and that this would do fine for music in school that week.

Yet despite all this effort and progress, music in schools continues to get an unjustly critical press. Some of this results from popular or popularized report-ing of research projects that emphasizes their more negative findings, or that generalizes, without due caution, from a sample that is very small or which may not be representative.

A study in 1999 of young people's attitudes to cultural venues included the following depressing account of music in school: 'I was forced to sit for hours with my friends, as my music teacher just used to play us bits of music and make us write down about them and that's why everyone hated music lessons and that's why I gave it up' (Halsey & Kinder 1999: 90). However, this study involved only 20 young people, and we are not told what the other 19 thought.

A study in 2000 of the effects and effectiveness of arts education in secondary schools (Harland *et al.* 2000) was very critical of music in its oft-quoted sum-mary. For example, the summary stated that music had 'critical problems', 'student enjoyment was often absent' in music, and there was 'an urgent need to tackle the quality of teaching in this subject'. However, as one works one's way through the 602-page book that the summary was intended to summarize, the extent to which the critical judgements about music are justified by reported evidence becomes less clear. I give just two examples of this here.

First, there is the assertion that students do not enjoy their music lessons. The researchers judge such effects by counting the number of students who report them, which is fair enough. However, it appears that more students reported enjoyment of music than enjoyment of dance or drama, and so the basis for criticizing music, but not these other subjects, is unclear.

Second, there is the assertion that the quality with which music is taught has serious weaknesses. To judge from the annual reports of Ofsted, it may indeed be the case that, in general in England, music is taught less effectively than other subjects to students aged 11–14. However, the researchers do not refer to this evidence, or other relevant external evidence, anywhere in the lengthy book, and so the issue is the extent to which the researchers have supported their claims from their own evidence. In fact, the research appears not to have considered the quality of teaching, which is raised as a concern only in the summary. Two music lessons are indeed reported at considerable length (almost ten pages apiece), but without evaluation of the teaching. And, from what one can tell, given that the researchers did not report what the teachers intended that students should learn, or precisely what the students were doing, these lessons actually sound rather good—as one would expect given that they were drawn from schools that had been included in the study because of their good reputation in arts education.

The researchers miss some opportunities to present music in a more favourable light than other subjects. For example, music is undersold by the manner in which the researchers count students' reports of extracurricular involvement. Students' reports in music are divided into two categories, with the result that music slips behind drama, which has only one category.

If research is to have any point at all, it has to be reported objectively. This is a matter to which I will return in Chapter 14—when I turn to learning from research. However, research findings about music that are unduly gloomy tend to slip by without being challenged, because they resonate with so much of what we read about music education elsewhere. Music in schools has been the butt of professional humour for many years, with those who attempt to reform the dull and dusty image of the subject receiving as much flak as those who maintain what is perceived as the status quo. Consider, for example, the reflections on singing teachers of one Nigel Molesworth, a fictional schoolboy of the 1950s:

As singing masters stray into the job so to speak you get all sorts and there is no real telling. i mean we had one you kno the one with the super sports car *urum-urum-urum-uraaaaaa* who used to sa O.K. hep cats snap into the boogie. which was super but the trouble with singing is headmasters hear it they can't help it. That master was soon in his sports car headed for town *urum-urum-urum-uraaaa* which was hard cheddar really. (Willans & Searle, *Down with Skool!*)

Less amusing are the ostensibly serious pieces that deride music in schools for failing to do something that is unimportant, ambiguous, or verges on impossible. I have in mind those newspaper articles that complain every few months that 86% of 6–14-year-olds have not heard of Mozart or Beethoven (I am more interested in whether the children have heard, or preferably played, their music), 60% of children cannot play an instrument (it all depends what you mean by 'play'—and 'instrument') and 85% of children do not bark 'cello' when shown a picture of one (never mind whether they can, or cannot, recognize a cello from the sound that it makes).

In this context, it is unsurprising that the stereotypical image of the young person as classical music hating is reinforced through further writing:

Beethoven to beat vandals
Classical music is to be played at railway stations to stop vandalism after a trial showed that youths move on rather than hang around on platforms when they hear Beethoven, Mozart or other similar music.

After a successful experiment at Harold Wood station, First Great Eastern [train company] is now to install sound systems to play classical music at three other Essex stations – Hockley, Rochford and Burnham – and is looking at expanding the scheme to other areas. (*Daily Telegraph*, 12 January 2002)

This story fired the imagination of readers, including those who wrote to the paper as follows:

I was delighted to learn that vandals are being driven out of our railway stations by classical music . . . Could I exhort stations on Virgin Trains' routes to introduce Wagner? During an average journey, it should be possible for opera lovers to fit in the whole of *Das Rheingold* and perhaps the first act of *Die Walkure* as well. (14 January 2002)

As well as playing Wagner on train journeys, perhaps we could also give some of the Neibelung hordes a job with Railtrack, where thay could get their little hammers out and mend some of the cracked rails. (16 January 2002)

One publican I know found the ideal way to empty his pub of yobs and boozers was to play a little Mozart. But occasionally this had little effect. [Once] it took eight minutes 23 seconds of a very modern Scandinavian composer to shift the lot. (16 January 2002)

While this correspondence has its funny side, this use of music—of any sort— to repel people, much as one might formerly have used a scarecrow to try to keep birds away from one's vegetable plot, is clearly not conducive to improving the image of music in schools. The same is true of the use of background music to calm or mollify students, however tempting this may be at times.

I have argued above that while music in school is sometimes boring, it need not be. And that there is plenty of good practice, of an applicable kind, on which we can all build.

One answer to the question 'why is music so boring?' is that this is what people want it to be. They have thought of music in schools as boring for so long (sometimes even though their own music education was not boring!) that they find the idea that it might not be boring quite threatening.

I sometimes wonder if this is why there is still so much recorder teaching in primary schools. I loved playing recorder as a child, and for me the recorder led to many other interesting things, as I have previously explained, but for most children learning the recorder leads nowhere except to a feeling of failure. In 2002, a brief mention that many children are not motivated by playing recorder in the report of the *Young People and Music Participation Project* (O'Neill 2002) grabbed the attention of the media, and several newspapers developed the story with some very amusing results (Fig. 11).

Why did this story capture the imagination of so many journalists? Presumably because so many of us remember learning the recorder at school, and remember how many of us hated this . . . What does it say about our view of childhood, and our view of education, that we want to put today's children through experiences that we knew were unconstructive for most children a generation ago?

It need not be like that. This book has already given many examples of music going well in schools. And music education can actually be used to set students who are running into difficulty at school on a less troubled path. John Finney and Michael Tymoczko have described an experiment in which four 13-year-old students, viewed as potential negative leaders in their school, were given the challenge of teaching a class of 12-year-olds. Teachers described the more negative aspects of the student-leaders as follows:

Tyson, amiable and good on the surface, but very disruptive . . . has difficulty in accepting authority . . . others look up to him, some through fear rather than respect . . . loses concentration easily and gives up if he feels the work is difficult . . . enjoys being at the centre and the one to whom others defer . . . probably the strongest personality in the group, he is an intelligent boy.

Rachel, attentive but often seems to be at the centre of some issue with other students, with some much more high profile agitators within the group . . . prone to arguing with her peers . . . poor attitude . . . on occasion refuses to work with other students . . . the quiet one who works with Morgen to divert the lesson plan.

Morgen, no motivation, no ambition . . . distracts others . . . very talkative . . . sits at the front yet easily distracted . . . subtle negative leadership . . . gives up if she feels the work is too difficult . . . can be very negative as a way of maintaining authority over others.

Brian, underachieving . . . his tactics are very covert and he is adept at putting the responsibility for his behaviour on to someone else . . . can be malicious with words

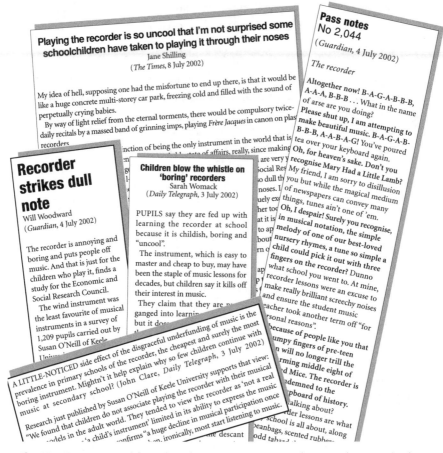

Fig. 11 Newspaper articles written in response to a research report that contained a brief reference to the recorder

. . . enjoys winding people up . . . always not on task . . . does not respect the right to teach and learn . . . full of his own importance . . . easily distracts others . . . stirs the others to misdeeds. (Finney & Tymoczko 2003: 40)

These students liked the way that they were taught in music:

They appreciated the active and participatory nature of their music lessons. In music their ideas were taken seriously . . . The teacher showed and told them what it was that they were learning and what they had to do and he did this by being a musician . . . They were taught that, like their music teacher, they were musicians too. (Finney & Tymoczko 2003: 41)

They were supported by music teachers as they planned, and then gave, a sequence of three music lessons. The sequence began with a routine to a track by Justin Timberlake, and culminated in a performance by the class. This was rigorous work. The students had to plan the objectives of the sequence of lessons, and how they would achieve these. They thought through the ways in which they would teach. They were determined that the experience of the three lessons would be a good one for the class. They thought about the class's prior learning, and how they would build on it. They observed the class being taught by someone else, so that they could learn about their behaviour and how it was managed.

This was a difficult project for the researchers to keep on track. Three of the student-leaders became excluded from lessons because of unsuitable behaviour elsewhere in their school life: 'Sustaining the project required a considerable degree of diplomacy and a supportive head teacher' (Finney & Tymoczko 2003: 42). However, the project was a huge success, whether judged by the videos of the lessons that were taught, the responses of the recipient class in question-naires or at a focus group, or the personal growth of the student-leaders. Time will tell whether the confidence that the student-leaders gained through doing something good for other people, and the empathy that they developed with their teachers, will be sustained, but the early signs are encouraging.

A music-related project at another school was also far from boring, and helped to transform the behaviour of students—particularly boys—during the lunch break. There was vandalism, there was bullying, and many students joined lessons after lunch in no fit state to learn anything. The school decided to try capitalizing on the students' enthusiasm for break dancing. An instruc-tor was hired to work every lunchtime and, supported by a PE teacher, he gave a break dance class in a ground-floor gym with a large window onto a playground. The break dance class became the centre of school life at lunchtime: the place to be. On some days, so many students arrived that a number had to be turned away. It was 'first come first served'. The students who had arrived too late to be admitted, along with large numbers of other students who preferred to be spectators, would watch the class from outside the gym, with their noses glued to the gym window. Vandalism and bullying were not on their minds.

Chapter 14

Learning from research

I take it that educational researchers are as committed as teachers, trainers and policy makers to the educational endeavour, to improving the efficiency and effectiveness of educational experiences. In my view, what earns research the adjective 'educational' is this moral commitment to putting learners in the way of a better lot in life through making some contribution to the effectiveness of educational processes. From this point of view, the purpose of educational research is to extend the knowledge base for teaching and learning using best social science practice. Clearly the purpose goes beyond the normal social science objective of deepening our understanding of the human condition. Educational research, if it is to be judged effective, must make a difference to the experience of participants in educational settings.

C. Desforges, *Familiar Challenges and New Approaches* (2000)

Unfortunately, there is a tendency, these days, to jump to conclusions when faced with research findings especially if they seem to suggest that there is some aspect of education which is in urgent need of reform.

C. Plummeridge, 'The Rights and Wrongs of School Music' (1997)

There is much that we, as teachers, can learn from the findings of research. I have applied some of what I have learnt from reading other people's research, over many years, in preceding chapters. Given the symbiotic relationship that I personally see between teaching and research, I would now find it hard—perhaps impossible—not to do this. It is not just the 'final findings' of research that interest me, for example statements that Z% of children do this or think that—but the whole process. What question or questions were the researchers seeking to answer through the research? Why were these questions of interest to them? What methods did they use to address them? What do they feel their 'final findings' mean and imply, in the context of the questions they asked, and the methods used to address them? What should they, or others, do next?

But I do not read research only in the third person. While my interest in research has to begin with consideration of it in its own terms, as above, that is not where it ends. I inevitably find myself evaluating the research too: admiring particularly nifty examples of research design or statistical analysis, and asking questions such as 'Is that research question quite as relevant to the classroom as researchers say it is?' or 'Have the researchers over-generalized their findings, given the size and structure of their sample?'

And reading research (as well as listening to it reported at conferences) continually sparks off the beginnings of thoughts and ideas for my practice as teacher and researcher—two parts of myself that I now see as virtually insepar-able. I say 'the beginnings' of thoughts and ideas because it is rare—if indeed if ever happens—for me to think simply 'the researchers have found X so I must do Y'. Reading research leads me to challenge my own views, including the views that sometimes worry me because I feel that I have held them for a long time, so that I wonder whether I am criticizing them enough. Or on reading the results of research carried out in a selective school, for example, I might hypothesize about what would be found were it carried out in a comprehensive school—or in a sample of schools that were chosen to be representative of their locality, or their country. Or the research might prompt me to think of a related educational problem that needs to be solved. For example, some research by Hiromichi Mito (2002) into the difficulties encountered by pianists in Japan with absolute pitch when asked to transpose has prompted me to think more deeply about how pianists are trained.

In any case, it was actually not Hiromichi Mito's 'results' that I found most interesting and relevant, so much as the educational issues raised by his experimental task, in which pianists with absolute pitch came into a room to sight-read Bach or Chopin, and were completely thrown because their digital piano had been mistuned by a diminished fifth. As a musician without absolute pitch, so that I found myself at a significant disadvantage when asked to write down seriously atonal melodies and harmony as an undergraduate, my initial reaction on being asked to view absolute pitch as a learning difficulty is not unreservedly sympathetic. But, moving beyond this, the research suggests that pianists with—and probably also without—absolute pitch, could benefit from learning a wider range of strategies for sight-reading. And given that digital pianos provide the potentially useful musical facility to adjust the key of an accompaniment to suit a singer, for example, it seems unfortunate if pianists are not trained to make use of it. And while it is highly unlikely that a concert pianist would ever arrive at a prestigious concert hall to find the piano mistuned by as much as a diminished fifth, it is conceivable that the piano in a less acclaimed venue, for example a village hall where a pianist had been asked to accompany a dance class or pre-school music class, might be mistuned by a semitone.

Where 'final findings' are applied hastily, over-literally, and without sufficient consideration, this is often because, as Charles Plummeridge has suggested above, they confirm a personal view that something needs to be reformed. But they may also be used hastily to confirm a lazy view that things should continue exactly as at present—without bothering to think whether or not this is really right. Research is used, either consciously or subconsciously, as the reason (or excuse?) for doing (or not doing) something that one would have liked to do (or not do) anyway, but without taking personal responsibility for the decision. For example, research is sometimes misapplied to support the popular claim that education in the UK is perpetually in decline. In some earlier writing, I have likened this to the Shepard scale (1982) in which listeners are tricked into believing, through judicious choice of the harmonic spectrum used when playing the tones of a descending major scale, that they are hearing perpetual downward movement (Mills 1996a).

Ted Wragg helpfully reinforces this thought annually, when the results for the UK GCSE and A level examinations are published nationally, and the popular press invariably reports that standards in schools are falling. If fewer students than the previous year have passed the examinations, this means the standard of the students has fallen. If more students have passed than previously, then the standard of the examination has fallen. In other words, neither students nor their teachers get praised, whatever happens! In 2003, Ted Wragg adapted the lyrics of the nursery song *The Grand Old Duke of York*[1] accordingly:

> And when they were up they were down
> And when they were down they were down
> And when they were only half way up
> They were definitely down.
>
> (Ted Wragg in the *Times Educational Supplement*, 12 September 2003)

---

[1] The original version of *The Grand Old Duke of York* goes as follows:

> The Grand Old Duke of York
> He had ten thousand men
> He marched them up to the top of the hill
> And he marched them down again
> And when they were up they were up
> And when they were down they were down
> And when they were only half way up
> They were neither up nor down.

What is the (music educational) research process?

The research process is often portrayed in print—through the layout of theses, dissertations, and research papers—as linear:

1. **Title**

   An area of research is chosen, and a title proposed.

2. **Literature review**

   The researcher establishes the background to the research through carrying out a literature search: reading, analysing, evaluating, and reflecting upon reports of the research that has already been carried out in the area, or related areas.

3. **Research questions and hypotheses**

   The researcher articulates the precise questions to be addressed through the research, and sets hypotheses that the research will test. In music education research, the questions are chosen because answering them has the capacity to improve the learner's lot in music.

4. **Research design**

   The researcher designs the research that will answer the questions and test the hypotheses. This stage includes determining which research methods to use; deciding how large a sample is needed, how the sample will be structured, and how the people that it comprises will be chosen; designing research instruments such as questionnaires and interview schedules; deciding what data will be collected and how they will be analysed.

5. **Research**

   The research that was designed is implemented; the data are collected, coded and analysed.

6. **Results and discussion**

   The results of the analysis are reported and discussed.

7. **Conclusions and implications**

   Conclusions are drawn, and implications for music education are proposed.

In practice, of course, the process can be more complex. The title of a research paper may be adjusted at a late stage of writing, in order to signal more clearly to readers what its focus is. Literature is frequently read at all stages of a research project. Researchers need to have some idea of their research questions before they carry out their literature review, or they would not know what to read. And so forth.

Moreover, the researchers' approaches are influenced both by the nature of the questions that they are seeking to answer, and the make-up of their own background in the social sciences. While much published music education research has traditionally been psychological in approach, some of it is essentially sociological, philosophical, or historical. Increasingly, music education researchers have a wider repertoire of research approaches, and draw their methods eclectically from across the social sciences.

But three aspects remain constant. First, there are research questions that the research seeks to answer. These might be exploratory 'blue skies' questions along the lines of 'what happens if . . .', which could have answers that are unimagined at the outset, or they might be focused on specific objectives, for example: 'if I do X, does Y improve?'

Second, the research questions are chosen because of their relevance to improving the learner's lot in music. There is no such thing as 'fundamental research' in education. Charles Desforges has argued (see above) that educational research is good social science with the capacity to improve the learner's lot. Thus, music education research is good social science with the capacity to improve the learner's lot in music. It follows that music education research questions have to be grounded in initial knowledge of what is already happening to learners, or particular groups of learners, in music. While research questions need to be set by researchers, rather than teachers, it makes sense for researchers to talk to teachers, and other parties in education, as they draft them. While the research questions that are asked will not necessarily be the questions that teachers think it most pressing to have answered, they need to be questions that teachers, properly briefed, agree have some relevance—and could not answer reliably themselves without the research. There is no space in music education research for questions that view the world as though from a distant satellite or planet—or even using the wrong pair of spectacles. There is no space in music education research for questions that are asked because a researcher thinks that the answers might be 'interesting' rather than 'potentially useful'. Such 'research' is a waste of time and money, and brings the work of researchers into disrepute.

Third, there has to be a 100% logical flow from the research questions through the design of the research, to the carrying out of the research, to the techniques used to analyse the findings of the research, and finally to the interpretation of these findings and listing of their implications. Without this 100% logic, we do not have research. There is no space for woolly thinking, fudging, sleight of hand, or spin in research.

Looking beyond the findings

In his book *1089 and All That* David Acheson (2002), mathematician, described attending a boys' independent preparatory school where the same test was set every week. Question 23 was 'what is the secret of all life', and the official answer was 'chlorophyll'. If this was the correct answer at all, then it was the correct answer only within a particular context, one that related to natural science rather than philosophy or religion, contained only the earthbound scientific knowledge that a boy of the 1950s could reasonably have learnt, and where a query along the lines of 'what came first, the chlorophyll or the sun?' might have been viewed as perverse.

Looking only at the findings of music educational research, without considering their context, can lead to 'interpretation' that is not valid, and 'application' that isn't.

Here is an extract from the New Statesman Arts Lecture given by Gerry Robinson, the Chairman of the Arts Council of England, in June 2000:

Research shows that, at age five, a child's potential for creativity is 98 per cent. By the age of ten, that potential has dropped to 30 per cent; at 15 it is just 12 per cent; and by the time we reach adulthood, our creativity potential is said to fall to a mere 2 per cent.

These are astonishing statistics and are profoundly important in making the case for placing the arts at the heart of education. (Robinson 2000)

Stirring stuff—and I am sure that we are all pleased that someone is arguing for the arts to be placed at the heart of education—but what does the first paragraph actually mean? How did the researchers define 'creativity potential' and how did they measure it? How many 5-year-olds, 10-year-olds, 15-year-olds, and adults were measured? One could get the results described above by measuring just one child at age 5, 10, and 15, and then speculating about what will happen to them over the 60 or so years that they are likely to enjoy as an adult! Was the research done last week, last year, or 30 years ago?—in which case we might get different results today, or no longer accept the researchers' definition of 'creativity potential' as relevant. Where was the research carried out? Gerry Robinson is talking about education in the UK—but was the research carried out in the UK, or at least in some context that the researchers argue is equivalent, in some way that they have explained and we agree is justified, to the UK? Who did the research? Because of the authoritative way in which it is reported, we may assume that it was carried out or supervised to an international standard by at least one undeniably distinguished researcher— but it could have been a new researcher's first attempt at research, or even a piece of coursework that a lone 17-year-old had submitted for their A level psychology examination. Where is the research written up? Is it published in a source that we feel we can trust, or was it posted on an unmoderated website? Where do we need to go to read more about this research, and check that we understand it? And so on.

Without the answers to questions such as these—and I do not know the answers to any of these questions—we cannot tell whether or not we agree that the statistics are 'astonishing', and whether or not they are 'profoundly important'. Gerry Robinson's argument for placing the arts at the heart of education would have been just as strong and compelling had he not mentioned the research. When research appears to confirm something that an audience wants to believe is true, they may not subject it to quite as much scrutiny as it deserves.

Lack of clarity with definitions can also lead to other problems:

Tests prove tone deafness
The strange case of a woman called Monica who really cannot name that tune, whether classical or popular music, is reported today by scientists.

Monica suffers from a musical disability that leaves her unable to recognise or enjoy any kind of music.

Her case is the first validated example of tone deafness that cannot be explained by a brain lesion such as a stroke, hearing loss, cognitive deficits, or lack of exposure to music. In the journal *Neuron*, Prof Isabelle Peretz of the University of Montreal reports that Monica was evaluated with a battery of musical and other auditory tests, revealing that she performed no better than random guessing when asked to discriminate or recognise melodies, rhythms, or generally familiar music.

Prof Peretz's team has found that the root of Monica's problem is a difficulty in discriminating pitches. While most people can distinguish sequential pitches one quarter-tone apart, Monica cannot distinguish pitches smaller than a whole-tone (the interval between C and D, for example).

There has been a debate about whether tone deafness exists, but the work shows it is real and may result from a specific impairment in the low-level process of pitch discrimination.

'Music is probably the only domain which requires fine-grained pitch discrimination to be appreciated,' said Prof Peretz. 'Therefore, a poor pitch perceptual system would mostly, if not exclusively, interfere with the development of musical competence.' (Roger Highfield, Science Editor, in *Daily Telegraph*, 17 January 2002)

Interesting stuff—although Arnold Bentley showed 40 years ago that people can distinguish sequential pitches that are much closer than one quarter-tone apart. But is Monica really what is usually meant by 'tone-deaf'? Rightly or wrongly, people tend to describe themselves as tone-deaf when they have difficulty pitching their singing voice accurately, i.e. singing in tune. And if the term is to be used literally here—in relation to hearing rather than singing—is it right to call someone who can distinguish sequential pitches that are a tone apart 'tone-deaf'? Surely, to qualify as literally 'tone-deaf', one has to be unable to distinguish sequential pitches however far they are apart.

Faced with this potentially confusing complexity, it is easy to see why many readers of the *Daily Telegraph* on 17 January 2002 just clung onto the headline, and interpreted it in a way that was consistent with what they had always thought 'tone-deaf' meant, i.e. having difficulty with singing in tune. The *Daily Telegraph* gets read hastily over one's breakfast cereal, or in snatches en route to work: it does not routinely get the same sustained critical attention that one might give to a research paper. Readers of the *Daily Telegraph* saw the headline, absorbed it, and possibly did not read the article at all, or gave up halfway through.

Many music educators have been trying for decades to dispel the notion that a difficulty with singing in tune necessarily means that one has something wrong with one's ears. The false argument that a difficulty with singing (which in any case could probably be solved through taking lessons!) implies that one cannot hear properly, which implies that one is 'unmusical', lies unconstructively at the root of many people's low self-esteem as musicians. I have lost count of the occasions, over many years, on which someone has told me sheepishly that they are tone-deaf and hence 'unmusical', I have asked them whether they can hear that some speaking voices are higher than others, or that some notes on a piano are higher than others, they have agreed that they can, and I have offered the thought that they are not tone-deaf and not unmusical, whatever either of these terms mean. But now—a few years on from the *Daily Telegraph* report—one still only has to suggest at a party or music education meeting that everyone has potential for music that remains unfulfilled, or that people do not divide into 'musical' and 'unmusical', in order for a bright spark to pipe up and say that research has shown that tone-deafness exists and that people who have it are unable to enjoy or take part in music . . .

How can we find out more about the context of research findings? The summaries—known as abstracts—that researchers typically provide at the beginning of articles published in research journals, and also in conference proceedings, provide valuable insights into the context of research findings. They can help readers to understand what research findings mean, and help readers to decide whether to invest time in reading a full report. The following example, written by Gordon Cox, provides clear insights into almost all of the stages 1–7 of the research process listed above. It outlines some of the findings, explains the context in which they arose, and offers some cautious suggestions as to what they might mean.

Recollections and realities: conversations with student music teachers

Abstract

This study is based upon tape-recorded interviews with ten student music teachers who were studying at the University of Reading. It attempts to relate recollections and stories concerning their family background, musical education, decisions to enter university to read music, career choice, and early experiences of teaching. Through reflecting upon such insights lies the intention that we might develop a more effective training programme. The findings included some of the following observations: students are frequently defensive about their home backgrounds; recollections of their own music teachers fell into the three categories of positive, ambivalent and negative; their decisions to teach music were mixed, but could be divided broadly into those that were straightforward and committed and those that were provisional; initial experiences of teaching music were mixed, few accounts were unproblematic. Such group biographies should enable us to understand more fully the process of being a student music teacher, as well as the relationship of their personal experiences to such external forces as power, ideology and marginalisation which all affect the status of school subjects. (Cox 2002)

This is a summary of a paper of 2,000 or 3,000 words. Ironically, research projects that are written up as lengthy books rarely include this helpful sort of summary. It is easy to lose sight of the authors' research process as one works through several hundred pages of text, however diligently this process is signposted en route. And the understandable practice of reading only selected chapters of very long books can mean that the research process never becomes apparent to the reader.

The problems that this can cause are illustrated by the case of *Arts Education in Secondary Schools: Effects and Effectiveness*: an important, but very lengthy, book—referred to earlier (see p. 202)—that is based mainly on research in five secondary schools (Harland *et al.* 2000). The official summary published in the book has the flavour of some sorts of press releases, rather than that of an abstract. In particular, it emphasizes some (potentially newsworthy) seemingly negative findings about music, at the expense of the many positive findings about music that the book reports. For example, the official summary reports that music registered more 'no-impact' responses than other subjects, without explaining to readers that 'no-impact', within the context of this research, means something more specific, and much less worrying, than that students had said the subject had 'no impact' on them! Moreover, neither 'no-impact' nor 'impact' is listed in the index of the book, or included on the contents page, and so it is difficult for a time-pressed reader to find out about their special meanings within the context of this research.

The summary of this 602-page volume does not begin until p. 564 and so, in an ideal world, nobody would have read it until they had digested and reflected upon the preceding 563 pages. Thus readers would have been able to check the published summary against their own internal summary, and would have been aware of any spin in the published summary. In practice, of course, many readers turned straight to p. 564, read the summary and never got round to reading the rest of the book. And this mode of reading became the norm once it was a custom for the summary to be issued, without the accompanying book, as a handout at conferences. No wonder that music got a bad press from this book! And much time and effort has been wasted subsequently in planning how to resolve some particular problems with music that—to judge from the findings reported in the body of the book—may not exist.

How large does a sample need to be?

There is, of course, no simple answer to this question. It all depends on what a researcher is trying to do.

A researcher carrying out a case study of one 20-year-old woman who lives in Balham, London, and who wants to know about the frequency with which she listens to music of different types or for different reasons, over a period of a month for example, might simply ask her to fill in a listening diary that covers a month.

A second researcher who wants to find out why the students in a particular year group at the school where he teaches are, or are not, choosing to study a particular subject, or to go on a concert visit, or to apply for instrumental lessons, for example, might give out a questionnaire to all the students in the year group at the school.

Both of these researchers are trying to measure the full 'population' for their research. They have covered everyone who lies within the scope of this research. They have not done any sampling. End of story.

The need to sample arises when a researcher cannot measure everyone within their research population, and wants to generalize from the findings in a smaller number of people (a sample) to a population. Perhaps the first researcher wants to predict the listening patterns of all the 20-year-old women who live in Balham, or all the 20-year-old women who live in London, or all women everywhere, or all people everywhere. Clearly, a sample of one person would not be a reasonable basis for making any of these predictions. However, the sample of one becomes progressively less reasonable as one moves through this list of populations. The extent to which any one person could possibly be representative of the population becomes progressively less secure.

Perhaps the second researcher wants to know about the choices being made by students in the same year group in their local education authority, region of the country, or the whole UK. Similar issues arise, with the use of a sample of students from just one school becoming progressively less representative as one works through this list of populations.

But it is not just the size of a sample that matters, but also its structure. A sample of one hundred 20-year-old women who all live in the same group of streets in Balham, or who all attended the same school, or who all have the same or related ethnicity, might have listening preferences less representative of all the 20-year-old women in Balham than those of only fifty 20-year-old women who were chosen more carefully, i.e. formed a structured sample. Turning to the work of the second researcher, a sample of students of the right age drawn from five schools might be more representative of their LEA than a sample chosen from ten schools, provided that the five schools were chosen carefully.

A correspondence from the *Times Educational Supplement*[2] nicely illustrates this point:

High art: 'bald men with cellos'
Classical music concerts are 'baggy and sad', art galleries are 'quiet and boring', ballet is 'pointless' and historic buildings are 'not for young people'. The findings of a new study on teenage attitudes to high culture will make depressing, if predictable, reading for arts professional and educationists alike . . .

Twenty teenagers age 14 to 18, from widely differing backgrounds were asked by researchers from the National Foundation for Educational Research what they thought about art galleries, theatre, dance, classical concerts, historic buildings and museums. Only theatre generated any enthusiasm while the most commonly-used word to describe other forms of art was 'boring'. Many were seen as the preserve of the old and the rich. Only one of the 20 teenagers was positive about classical music.

Of classical concerts, [a] teenager said: 'You have to sit for ages in an uncomfortable seat, with the tiniest pair of binoculars, viewing some bald fellow with a cello.' (Warwick Mansell in the *Times Educational Supplement*, 17 December 1999)

Did the finding that few teenagers judge classical concerts appealing surprise you? Probably not. But did you nevertheless, like me, find your hackles rise as you learnt that the researchers had derived this finding through talking to only 20 young people? How dare they say something that, though probably true, is likely to dissuade even more teenagers from attending classical concerts in future, on the strength of such a seemingly impoverished piece of research? Surely, if the researchers were only asking the teenagers what they thought about art galleries, theatre, and so forth, they could have spoken to 200—or even 2000—of them?

In fact, the research (Harland & Kinder 1999) had rather more to it than the pre-Christmas write-up in the *Times Educational Supplement* may have led us to believe, and finding more than 20 young people to talk to might not have

[2] My thanks to Dr Janet Harvey for drawing my attention to this correspondence.

made the research any more representative, as the following tongue-in-cheek response shows:

We're not all old or bald
According to 'High art: bald men with cellos' (*TES*, December 17) the National Foundation for Educational Research draws conclusions regarding 'high art' and the attitudes of young people, based on questions to 20 teenagers.

While accepting that the opinions stated are those of the 20 young people, we would like to suggest that the sample is too small for the conclusions to be of value.

This letter is written jointly by nearly 200 young people of widely differing backgrounds who happen nonetheless to have an interest in classical music, popular music and many other art forms. Some of us are even cellists, some are male and none of us is bald!

We hope that, far from making 'depressing, if predictable, reading' for arts professionals and educationalists alike, the Gulbenkian Foundation and Arts Council will take no notice whatsoever of this report until they have a much larger and much more representative set of views.

(167 members of the Oxfordshire County Youth Orchestra and the Oxfordshire Schools Senior Orchestra in the *Times Educational Supplement*, 28 January 2000)

The first sample, of 20 young people, is too small for us to feel confident that their views about classical music are representative. The views of the second sample, of 167 young people, are no more convincingly representative. They are all members of an ensemble that performs classical music, and so form what statisticians and social scientists call a 'biased sample' in terms of views about classical music.

Symptoms or causes?

I have stated above that music education research should have the capacity to improve the learner's lot. In order to use it to improve the learner's lot, we have to be able to separate the causes of an effect from its symptoms.

In the film *Notting Hill*, Anna (Julia Roberts) observes to William (Hugh Grant) that men with big feet have big shoes. Big shoes are a symptom of having big feet, not a cause. If we give someone big shoes, this would not lead their feet to grow.

In research carried out with young people in the early 1990s, researchers based at the Universities of Exeter, Keele, and Sheffield found that high-attaining young instrumentalists have spent more time practising than instrumentalists who have not reached such a high standard (see, for example, Sloboda *et al.* 1996). It follows neither that everyone who practises for long hours will become a high-attaining performer, nor that insistence that a young instrumentalist practises for long hours will necessarily improve their chances of becoming a high-attaining instrumentalist. It does not even follow that practising for long hours is one of a package of behaviours that young instrumentalists must display (or usually display) if they are going to become very successful, as it is possible that there are more time-efficient approaches to developing instrumental skills that the high-attaining instrumentalists in the study did not know about, or chose not to adopt.

In my view, one of the main lessons from this research is the need to develop ways of practising that are as efficient as possible, so that nobody needs to spend more of their time on practice than they want, and also so that young people who do not have the opportunity to practise for long hours, perhaps because they have to spend much of their time outside school looking after younger siblings, or because there is nowhere for them to practise at home without disturbing their neighbours, still have the best possible chance of achieving their potential as instrumentalists. If more efficient ways of practising can be found and articulated—and I think it likely that many young instrumentalists use their practice time very inefficiently—then there will be nothing to stop young instrumentalists playing their instrument for long hours, where they wish to do this, and have the opportunity to do so. But this will be a matter of choice, not necessity.

Just as doctors look for medical symptoms when diagnosing a medical condition, teachers look for symptoms of the educational problems that hold back their students, so that they can 'treat' the problem, and help students to achieve more highly in future. Neither in education nor medicine are symptoms the same as causes, and it is the latter that have to be treated if the patient or student is to be cured, rather than just made more comfortable, or more accepting of their disadvantage.

In Chapter 8 I observed that some instrumental teachers select students for instrumental tuition according to the students' physical characteristics, because of a mistaken view that children with particular sorts of teeth, lips, hands, or arms, for example, will make superior players of certain instruments. In one of my first pieces of educational research I found a physical characteristic that predicted instrumental achievement better than any of the criteria which teachers were using: left-hand digital formula. To assess your left-hand digital formula, place your hand palm down on a flat surface, with your fingers together. Check whether your index finger or your ring finger reaches further up your middle finger. If your ring finger reaches further you have an I < R formula, along with about 70% of the general population. Otherwise, you have the less usual I > R formula (see Fig. 12). Among a sample of 84 successful young instrumentalists, hardly any of the violin or viola players had the I > R formula. Yet a majority of the other performers had the unusual I > R formula (Mills 1988b).

A little later, I wrote:

Digital formula is not customarily used in any type of musical selection. I came across it in an anatomy textbook (Jones 1941), not a music textbook. It is reasonable to suppose that the distribution of digital formula in children starting lessons on any instrument will be much the same as in the general population. It seems, though, that digital formula is predisposing some children towards success: the I < R formula benefits violinists and viola players, and the I > R formula promotes success on other orchestral instruments. Yet it would be preposterous to suggest that digital formula should become part of any selection procedure, for two main reasons:

◆ We do not know whether the apparent relationship between formula and success is inevitable, or the result of insensitive teaching. Think, for instance, of the left-hand positions which violinists of differing digital formula must adopt in order to rest all their left-hand fingertips on a string simultaneously. Much string technique is learnt by copying a teacher. If the teacher has an I < R formula, but has not noticed that a student has an I > R formula, is copying likely to result in the student developing a useful left-hand technique?

◆ Some people without the preferred formula are succeeding. So even if the general association between formula and success is nothing to do with teaching, screening according to digital formula would result in some potential professional musicians being denied lessons. (Mills 1991*e*: 160)

Digital formula is, I would argue, a symptom—not cause—of the ability to make fast progress in learning to play an instrument.

A rather different issue of cause and symptom arose in some research by Gary McPherson in Australia (see p. 81). He found that students aged 7–9 who were

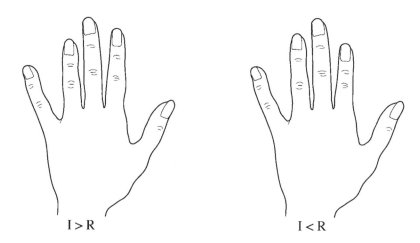

I > R   I < R

Fig. 12 Left-hand digital formula

interviewed shortly before they began instrumental lessons often predicted how long they would continue to take instrumental lessons, and how good they would become on their instrument (McPherson 2000). But was saying that one would continue learning for a long time and become a good player a cause or a symptom of this happening? Were it a cause, then teachers arguably have an ethical responsibility not to ask the question, as a child who answers it negatively is decreasing their prospects. Were it a symptom, and if we think that it is important that children sustain their instrumental lessons, then we need to look for the underlying cause of why some of them do not sustain them, and 'treat' that. One possibility is that the only children who know that instrumentalists typically have to play for quite a long time in order to do well are those with plenty of musical experience in their families, and who are being helped by this.

Teachers can learn from this research that any student who says that they are only going to continue lessons for a short time may need some special support and encouragement if they are to continue for longer. A student without anyone in their family, or among their friends, who has played for longer than a few months may not realize that one needs to do so if one is to become proficient. A student whose parents or older siblings have low expectations of them might need help in order to rise above what is anticipated. Teachers can also learn from this research that it might be unwise to ask children how long they are going to continue tuition, before they have even started. Why does the answer to this question matter to the teacher, or to the student, before the tuition—with all its attendant challenges and excitements—has even begun? And asking this question may lead children with low musical self-esteem to predict a lack of success that they are then likely to fulfil.

Researchers have responsibilities. The people who they research need to be left at least as able to learn as they were before the research began. Researchers take care not to damage students' image of themselves as learners, or to ostracize them in front of other students. I recently saw a UK television programme about the merits of independent boarding schools, when a group of young boys were asked to say which of them had cried most because they were homesick, and the boy who the rest of the group nominated looked seriously upset as his peers were allowed to mockingly parody—on national TV—behaviour that he had doubtless wanted to forget.

Researchers do not do this sort of thing to children deliberately. But it is easy to do it, on a small scale, inadvertently—by obliging children to think about something that they might not have thought about otherwise, and which results in them developing a new unconstructive judgement about themselves. Asking students how long they think that they will take instrumental tuition, before they have even had their first lesson, may be a case in point.

Doing research

Research is not an intrinsically difficult activity, the province only of those who are particularly 'clever', whatever this means. When music education research is disseminated to its main users—music teachers—in a form that is difficult to understand, this is typically because the researchers concerned are not effective communicators. Perhaps they are not very good at explaining logically and clearly what questions (relevant to learning) they sought to ask, how they went about answering them, what they found, and what conclusions they reached. Perhaps they patronize teachers by leaving out, or over-simplifying, parts of the 'story' that they think are 'difficult', with the result that it makes no sense. Perhaps they are doing both of these. If a story is complex, we need to be told this, and have the complexity explained to us, rather than be left feeling that we are stupid because we cannot see how the disjointed pieces of information that we have been given fit together. Some researchers have much to learn from many teachers about communication.

But while research is not intrinsically difficult, it does require organization, patience, ruthless logic, attention to detail, the confidence to decide which of many 'right' approaches to carrying out an investigation one will use, and the confidence to face a bevy of seemingly complex issues or seemingly conflicting facts, marshal them into some form that allows them to be interrogated thoroughly, and find the order (or at least one of many orders) within them. It also requires a willingness to carry on amending 'research instruments' such as questionnaires or interview schedules until they are as near to 'right' as possible, as many impromptu writers of questionnaires have found out to their cost. One cannot but feel sympathy with the music officers of the Qualifications and Curriculum Authority who, presumably accidentally, included the following admission in a newspaper account of what students had been found to do, think, and believe as a consequence of completing a QCA questionnaire:

Another finding was that even when a question looks straightforward, pupils can have a very different understanding of what is being asked. (*TES* Music Special, 16 November 2001, p. 4)

Experience of research may bring the ability to produce first drafts of questionnaires that are closer to the finished product, but does not remove the need to 'pilot test' them on a small group of people, whose answers are analysed with care, and who may be asked orally about what they understood particular questions to mean.

At times, of course, the attention to detail of even experienced researchers is not all that it could be. Perhaps particularly when presented with the opportunity to 'play to the gallery' at large conferences of practitioners, including teachers, who they may even over-confidently think are dazzled by the power of the researchers' brains—and especially when there are no other researchers around to listen—imprecise choices of forms of words can mislead an audience. Examples of this include the frequent suggestion that some secondary teachers are not very effective because of their 'classical conservatoire training'. We are intended to understand from this that secondary teachers whose training consisted entirely of the supposed 'master-apprentice' teaching of conservatoires know neither how to teach using a wider range of strategies, or anything of any music other than classical music. In considering this further, let us set aside the issue of whether or not it is helpful for any researchers whose last acquaintance with a secondary school was as sixth formers to be commenting on the effectiveness of contemporary secondary music teachers— or on conservatoires if they have never been to one at all. In fact, as almost any secondary teacher knows, very few of their number trained at a conservatoire. One might wish that it was otherwise, but currently only about one of the roughly 90 students who graduate each year from the Royal College of Music in London enter teacher training for either primary or secondary schools. And, as anyone who studies at a conservatoire knows, the days when one only learnt to play an instrument there, and the instrumental lessons were always 'master–apprentice' experiences, have long gone—if, indeed, they ever existed. In addition, no conservatoire could ever stop students from listening to, and playing, a wider range of music than classical music—although the courses that they provide may reflect the full range of students' interests less than perfectly. Contemporary conservatoire students listen to recorded music as they go about their daily business, just like other students, and their tastes and enthusiasms are often strikingly eclectic.

Interpreting research findings

A research investigation that has been organized thoroughly and implemented carefully will usually produce clear answers to the research questions that were posed. But what do these findings actually mean? And, given that educational research is carried out with a view to improving an aspect of learning, what should we—or somebody with another role—be doing in consequence?

Where we are presented with the mere disembodied findings of a research study, without being informed about its context, it can be impossible to work out what anyone could, or even should, be doing as a consequence. On the most basic level, if we do not know the age group of the people who were researched, or the country in which the research took place, we cannot tell whether the findings would be likely to relate also to the students who we teach. While research that has been carried out with another age group or in a different culture may still be relevant to our students, we need to know what the position is, so that we can appreciate how cautious our generalizations of the findings need to be. It is also helpful to know, for example, what sorts of questions students have been asked, so that one can understand the findings as fully as possible, and consider whether students of different age, or with a different cultural background, might have answered similarly. It is helpful for potential 'users' of research to know these sorts of things not so that they can evaluate the research (although some might also wish to do this) but so that they can use it as fully, but appropriately, as possible—in ways that are consistent with the 'story' that the research tells.

Presenting the disembodied findings of research brings risks for researchers too. With each successive telling of the findings, particularly at conferences of practitioners who are unlikely to be familiar with the original research, there is an increased danger of inadvertently strengthening the message to the point that it becomes inconsistent with the study. Thus a thoroughly researched (if unsurprising) finding that three-quarters of 750 UK secondary teachers have a degree that is 'based in classical music' (York 2001) became transmogrified, after several iterations by other researchers, into: 'Recent research suggests that many school music teachers have little respect for or understanding of the musical lives of those they teach' (Sloboda 2001). It is the reference to 'respect' that seems to me to be notably inconsistent with the original study. As well as being unfair, such flak does little for the image of secondary music teachers, and so is unlikely to encourage more music graduates—whatever the musical range of their degree—to consider music teaching as a career for themselves. This is an additional sense in which the research has not improved the learner's lot.

A few years ago it briefly became fashionable for researchers to state that their job ended with the production and explanation of their findings, and that it was up to teachers to decide what to do with them and to what extent they could be generalized. This is less of an issue now, and researchers often include helpful sections on 'what should happen next' at the end of their reports, and speak on this subject at conferences. And, as it has become something of a cliché to say only that what needs to happen next is more research(!), researchers now frequently suggest some possible action points for teachers. These are often very helpful. But beware the occasional researcher who spices up their list of suggestions with a few personal—but sometimes ill-founded—opinions about education that have little to do with the investigation in question, or who betrays limited knowledge about the education system in what they say. Ultimately it is up to the education system to decide what should happen next, as a consequence of the findings of research, in classrooms—bearing in mind the full range of evidence that is available.

Generalization of research findings is tricky for everyone: researchers as well as teachers and policy makers. Recently, researchers including Michael Bassey *et al.* (2001) have proposed 'fuzzy generalisation' as a way forward. Bassey offers the view that teachers and policy makers seek clear predictions such as 'do x in y circumstances and z will be the result', but that these are only very rarely deliverable because of the complexity of what is typically meant by 'y circumstances'. In other words schools, as social settings, have numerous influences on them—such as the quality of their accommodation, an outbreak of influenza, the size of their budget, or the economic advantage of their students—that may lie outside the scope of the research study, but nevertheless impact on whether or not 'z' happens.

Building on the principles of fuzzy logic, Michael Bassey suggests the use of 'fuzzy generalisations' or 'fuzzy predictions' of the form 'do x in y circumstances and z *may* result'. These may be coupled with *best estimates of trustworthiness* (BETs) that explain how likely 'z' is.

When applied to the Primary Assessment, Curriculum and Experience (PACE) project led by Andrew Pollard (2000), which monitored the impact of the changes occurring in English primary education in the years following the passing of the 1988 Education Reform Act, this led to fuzzy generalizations including:

1. If teachers and students are strongly constrained in their professional work, they are likely to become disenchanted and this probably affects recruitment and retention.

2. If students are strongly constrained in what they do in school, they are likely to become disenchanted and this probably affects their motivation and commitment to learning.

Andrew Pollard's BET was that these fuzzy generalizations were sufficiently substantial and fundamental to deserve the attention of governments or policy makers in any country where a national education system is being introduced. He argued that the generalizations were worth stating because policy makers in England had, in fact, not given them due consideration as possible, although unintended, outcomes of their policies.

One of the difficulties of fuzzy generalization is that the tentative nature of the predictions makes educational research even more open to the oft-made criticism that it simply restates the obvious. While (1) and (2) above are points that are worth making to policy makers, because they had not taken sufficient account of them previously, they will seem blindingly obvious to many teachers.

Of course, some people will ignore the results of research that conflicts with views that they hold strongly, or find convenient. An example of this is the erroneous view, which seems to have first become common in the late 1970s, that music is a 'right brain' activity with the capacity to save education from a 'left brain bias'. In fact, countless studies (e.g. Gruhn *et al.* 1997) have shown that music-making involves both hemispheres of the brain. There are many reasons for including music in the curriculum, some of which have been rehearsed earlier in this book, but the need to eliminate a 'left brain bias' is not one of them, as this does not exist. Nevertheless, music continues to be described as a 'right brain activity' in publications and at dinner parties. In an article on north America, Rudolf Radocy writes: 'The fact that music is a complex activity that uses many, if not all, brain areas, except in extremely simple situations involving processing of musical stimuli, [does] not deter the true believers' (Radocy 2001: 126). His comment could apply as easily to other countries, including the UK.

There is much that teachers can learn from research, just as there is much that researchers could learn from teachers. But researchers need to present their work so as to make it as straightforward as possible for teachers to use research well. And teachers need to look at research with an open mind, and enter into its process to as great an extent as possible, rather than just looking to research to reinforce their pre-existing views and beliefs, or present them with easy solutions.

Otherwise, some unfortunate things can happen . . .

In 2004, I wrote the following piece for *Link* magazine (Mills 2004*b*):

In defence of auditory learning

I enter the classroom. Pachelbel's *Canon* plays quietly in the corner. The children are working silently on number problems. I smile 'good morning' to the teacher, sit down by the files of lesson plans, individual education plans and assessment records that she has laid out for me, and begin to fill out my form:

> Year 6. Mathematics. 13 boys, 16 girls. Attainment target 2, levels 3–5. Pupils seated boy-girl in attainment groups with differentiated worksheets . . .

I can barely think. The Pachelbel is approaching the height of its beautiful, long, crescendo. I know this piece inside out. It draws me in . . . Get a grip on yourself, Mills. The teacher is playing this stuff because she believes it will help the children. They are coping. So can you.

But are they coping? It is the Minuet from *Berenice* now. A boy seated away from the CD player starts to caterwaul quietly with the melody. A girl nudges him to be quiet, with a worried look at me. I smile reassuringly. The boy looks to be in pain. He is struggling to complete his level 5 mathematics—at a fast pace, neatly and accurately—while this drug that is music courses through his mind. He is battling to concentrate, to do his work, to please his teacher, the girl, me . . .

A few minutes later, midway through a phrase of a Mozart horn concerto, the teacher turns off the music, and explains something mathematical to the whole class. She turns on the music again. It is the first movement of Vivaldi's *Winter*.

What is going on here? Why is this keen, experienced and very able teacher making it so difficult for at least some of her class to do their mathematics? Why is she polluting their learning environment with music? What is her evidence that this use of music is helping anyone with their mathematics? Let alone helping them to develop as musicians?

In another ethnically diverse school, in another city, some secondary teachers have just returned from a course on learning styles. A handout explains how to use music to promote learning in any subject. Teachers should play baroque music to students engaged in repetitive tasks in order to discourage their creativity, romantic music including the Brahms *Brandenburg Concertos* [*sic*] when seeking to encourage creativity, and music with 'explosions' before potentially dangerous experiments in science. 'Auditory learners' should be seated away from the music, or issued with ear plugs.

The world is going mad. Some rigorous and, as I understand it, distinct pieces of research into the effect of playing Mozart to some particular learners, and individual learning styles, have been hijacked by well-meaning people who did not understand them fully, and turned into dogma that teachers are, seemingly, expected to apply blindly. The advantages of sending children to school each day, rather than plugging them into computers at home, include that schools have teachers who think.

And why is it (nearly) always western classical music that gets turned into dogma? Is this because children who are played djembe drumming, hip hop or samba smile, or move their shoulders rhythmically with the music, so that we cannot but notice our educational problem?

I am writing this at the Royal College of Music. Student practice streams into my room from all directions. Mendelssohn, Puccini, Chopin, John Coltrane, and something excitingly spiky and avant-garde from the percussion suite . . . This doesn't distract me from writing. Why not? Perhaps because it is practice, rather than performance, so that I feel OK to drift in and out, even ignore it for minutes on end? But even as I suggest this, I can see holes. There are days when practice intrudes. This is partly a matter of mood, not what I am trying to do. And the sound of quiet practice at home, when I am trying to write, can drive me berserk.

Using music as a drug is educationally dangerous. We don't know what it does, but we do know that it does different things to different people, and different things to the same people at different times. And we can be fairly sure that different pieces of music do different things too. Education is not a career for witch doctors. As teachers, we need to understand what we are doing.

Music is not a panacea but an art. By teaching music in school, and teaching it in a way that is as positive, enabling, creative, and artistic as possible, we help children to make the most of music, for themselves, as they move through life.

Suggestions for further reading

Bray, D. (2000). *Teaching Music in the Secondary School*. Oxford: Heinemann.

Glover, J., & Young, S. (1999). *Primary Music: Later Years*. London: Falmer.

Mills, J. (1991). *Music in the Primary School*. Cambridge: Cambridge University Press.

National Association of Music Educators (2000). *Composing in the Classroom: The Creative Dream*. Bath: NAME.

Odam, G. (1995). *The Sounding Symbol: Music Education in Action*. Cheltenham: Stanley Thornes.

Paynter, J. (1992). *Sound and Structure*. Cambridge: Cambridge University Press.

—— & Aston, P. (1970). *Sound and Silence*. Cambridge: Cambridge University Press.

Philpott, C. (2001). *Learning to Teach Music in the Secondary School: A Companion to School Experience*. London: RoutledgeFalmer.

Young, S., & Glover, J. (1998). *Music in the Early Years*. London: Falmer.

References

Abeles, H. F., & Porter, S. Y. (1978). 'The Sex-Stereotyping of Musical Instruments', *Journal of Research in Music Education* 26: 65–75.

Acheson, D. (2002). *1089 and All That: A Journey into Mathematics*. Oxford: Oxford University Press.

Alden, A. (1998). 'What Does it all Mean? The National Curriculum for Music in a Multi-cultural Society'. Unpublished MA diss., London University Institute of Education.

Auh, M.-S., & Walker, R. (1999). 'Compositional Strategies and Musical Strategies when Composing with Staff Notations versus Graphic Notations among Korean Students', *Bulletin of the Council for Research in Music Education* 141: 2–9.

——— (2001). 'Korea'. In D. J. Hargreaves & A. C. North (eds), *Musical Development and Learning: The International Perspective*. London: Continuum.

Baldi, G. & Tafuri, J. (2000). 'Children's Musical Improvisations: Many Ways of Beginning and Ending', *Bulletin of the Council for Research in Music Education* 153–4: 15–21.

——— & Caterina, R. (2002). 'The Ability of Children Aged 7–10 Years to Structure Musical Improvisations'. In G. Welch & G. Folkestad (eds), *A World of Music Education Research* (pp. 25–34). Göteborg: School of Music and Music Education, Göteborg University, Sweden.

Bamberger, J. (1982). 'Revisiting Children's Drawings of Simple Rhythms: A Function for Reflection-in-Action'. In S. Strauss & S. Stavy (eds), *U-Shaped Behavioral Growth*. New York: Academic Press.

——— (1988). 'Les Structurations cognitives de l'appréhension et de la notation de rhythmes simples'. In H. Sinclair (ed.), *La Production de notations chez le jeune enfant*. Paris: Presses Universitaires de France.

Bandura, A. (1997). *Self-efficacy: The Exercise of Control*. New York: Freeman.

Barrett, M. (1994). 'Music Education and the Primary/Early Childhood Teacher: A Solution', *British Journal of Music Education* 11(3): 197–208.

——— (2002a). 'Invented Notations and Mediated Memory: A Case-Study of Two Children's Use of Invented Notations'. In G. Welch & G. Folkestad (eds), *A World of Music Education Research* (pp. 35–44). Göteborg: School of Music and Music Education, Göteborg University, Sweden.

——— (2002b). 'Taking Note: An Exploration of the Function of Invented Notations in Children's Musical Thinking Processes (Ages 4–5)', *Proceedings of the 7th International Conference for Music Perception and Cognition, Sydney*.

Barthes, R. (1977). *Image—Music—Text*. New York: Noonday.

Bassey, M., Hallam, S., Pollard, A., West, A., Noden, P., & Stake, B. (2001). *Fuzzy Generalisation: Transforming Research Findings into Fuzzy Predictions which can Inform Teachers', Policymakers' and Researchers' Discourse and Action*. Southwell: British Educational Research Association (BERA).

Bennett, N., & Carré, C. (1993). *Learning to Teach*. London: Routledge.

Bentley, A. (1966). *Musical Ability in Children and its Measurement*. London: Harrap.

Ben-Tovim, A., & Boyd, D. (1985). *The Right Instrument for your Child*. London: Gollancz.

Birmingham City Council (1996a). *Arts Guidance for the Birmingham Primary Guarantee*. Birmingham: Birmingham City Council.

—— (1996b). *The Birmingham Secondary Guarantee*. Birmingham: Birmingham City Council.

Blacking, J. (1976). *How Musical is Man?* London: Faber & Faber.

Board of Education (1931). *The Hadow Report*. London: HMSO.

Brand, E. (2000). 'Bridging the Gap between Research and Teaching', *Bulletin of the Council for Research in Music Education* 147: 30–5.

Brändström, S. (2000). 'For Whom is Music Education Intended?', *Bulletin of the Council for Research in Music Education* 147: 36–9.

Bridger, W. (1961). 'Sensory Habituation and Discrimination in the Human Neonate', *American Journal of Psychiatry* 117: 991–6.

Brittin, R. (2000). 'Preferences for Children's Music: Effects of Sequenced Accompaniments, School Culture and Media Association', *Bulletin of the Council for Research in Music Education* 147: 40–5.

Brophy, T. S. (2000). *Assessing the Developing Child Musician: A Guide for General Music Teachers*. Chicago: GIA.

Cage, J. (1962). *Silence: Letters and Writings*. London: Calder and Boyars.

Calouste Gulbenkian Foundation (1982). *The Arts in Schools: Principles, Practice and Provision*. London: Calouste Gulbenkian Foundation.

Cambridgeshire (1933). *Music and the Community: The Cambridgeshire Report on the Teaching of Music*.

Cattell, R. B., Eber, H. W., & Tatsouka, M. M. (1970). *Handbook for the Sixteen Personality Factor Questionnaire (16PF)*. Champaign, Illinois: Institute for Personality and Ability Testing.

Chaffin, R., & Imreh, G. (2001). 'A Comparison of Practice and Self-report as Sources of Information about the Goals of Expert Practice', *Psychology of Music* 29(1): 39–69.

Chang, H. W., & Trehub, S. E. (1977a). 'Infants' Perceptions of Temporal Grouping in Auditory Patterns', *Child Development* 48: 1666–70.

—— —— (1977b). 'Auditory Processing of Relational Information by Young Infants', *Journal of Experimental Child Psychology* 24: 324–31.

Colley, A., Comber, C., & Hargreaves, D. J. (1997). 'IT and Music Education: What Happens to Boys and Girls in Coeducational and Single Sex Schools?', *British Journal of Music Education* 14(2): 119–27.

Corredor, J. M. (1956). *Conversations with Casals*. London: Hutchinson.

Cox, G. (1997). ' "Changing the Face of School Music": Walford Davies, the Gramophone and the Radio', *British Journal of Music Education* 14(1): 45–56.

—— (2002). 'Recollections and Realities: Conversations with Student Music Teachers'. In G. Welch & G. Folkestad (eds), *A World of Music Education Research* (pp. 71–6). Göteborg: School of Music and Music Education, Göteborg University, Sweden.

da Costa, D. (1994). 'Background Listening', *British Journal of Music Education* 12(1): 21–8.

Daily Telegraph (2004). 'Take Five Year Plans with a Pinch of Salt', 21 July: 23.

Davies, C. (1986). 'Say it till a Song Comes (Reflections on Songs Invented by Children 3–13)', *British Journal of Music Education* 3(3): 279–93.

Davies, J. B. (1978). *The Psychology of Music*. London: Hutchinson.

Denton, C., & Postlethwaite, K. (1985). *Able Children*. Windsor: NFER-Nelson.

Denvir, B., & Brown, M. (1986). 'Understanding of Number Concepts in Low Attaining 7–9 Year Olds', *Educational Studies in Mathematics* 17: 15–36, 143–64.

DES (Department of Education and Science) (1978). *Primary Education in England: A Survey of HM Inspectors of Schools*. London: HMSO.

—— (1985). *Curriculum Matters 4: Music from 5 to 16*. London: HMSO.

DES (Department of Education and Science) and Welsh Office (1985). *GCSE: The National Criteria: Music*. London: HMSO.

DfE (Department for Education) (1995). *The National Curriculum: England*. London: HMSO.

DfEE (Department for Education and Employment) (1997). *Music Accommodation in Secondary Schools: A Design Guide: Building Bulletin 86*. London: The Stationery Office.

—— & QCA (Qualifications and Curriculum Authority) (1999). *Music: The National Curriculum for England*. London: HMSO.

Desforges, C. (2000). *Familiar Challenges and New Approaches: Necessary Advances in Theory and Methods in Research on Teaching and Learning: The Desmond Nuttall/ Carfax Memorial Lecture*. Southwell: BERA.

Dudley LEA (1996). *Moving on: A Key Stage 2/3 Curriculum Liaison Project*. Dudley: Dudley LEA Publications.

Ericsson, K. A., & Smith, J. (1991). *Towards a General Theory of Expertise: Prospects and Limits*. Cambridge: Cambridge University Press.

Everitt, A. (1997). *Joining in: An Investigation into Participatory Music*. London: Calouste Gulbenkian Foundation.

Farrell, G., Welch, G., & Bhowmick, J. (2000). 'South Asian Music and Music Education in Britain', *Bulletin for the Council for Research in Music Education* 147(51–60).

Ferreira de Figueiredo, S. L. (2002). 'Generalist Teacher Preparation: A Brazilian Investigation', *A World of Music Education Research: The 19th ISME Research Seminar, Göteborg, Sweden*. Göteborg: Göteborg University.

Finney, J., & Tymoczko, M. (2003). 'Secondary School Students as Leaders: Examining the Potential for Transforming Music Education', *Music Education International* 2: 36–50.

Fiske, H. (1977). 'Relationship of Selected Factors in Trumpet Performance Adjudication Reliability', *Journal of Research in Music Education* 25(4): 256–63.

FMS (Federation of Music Services), NAME (National Association of Music Educators), & Royal College of Music (2002a). *A Common Approach 2002*. Harlow: Faber.

—— —— —— (2002b). *A Common Approach 2002: Strings*. Harlow: Faber.

Freeman, J. (1998). *Educating the Very Able: Current International Research*. London: The Stationery Office.

Gane, P. (1996). 'Instrumental Teaching and the National Curriculum: A Possible Partnership?', *British Journal of Music Education* 13(1): 49–66.

Glover, J. (1998). 'Listening to and Assessing Children's Musical Composition'. In J. Glover & S. Ward (eds), *Teaching Music in the Primary School*. London: Cassell.

Glover, J. & Young, S. (1999). *Primary Music: Later Years*. London: Falmer.

Green, J. (1982). *The Book of Rock Quotes*. New York: Delilah/Putnam.

Green, L. (2001). *How Popular Musicians Learn*. Aldershot: Ashgate.

Griswold, P. A., & Chroback, D. A. (1981). 'Sex-Role Associations of Music Instruments and Occupations by Gender and Major', *Journal of Research in Music Education* 29(1): 57–62.

Gruhn, W., Altenmüller, E., & Babler, R. (1997). 'The Influence of Learning on Cortical Activation Patterns', *Bulletin for the Council for Research in Music Education* Summer 1997(133): 25–30.

Hallam, S. (1998). *Instrumental Teaching: A Practical Guide to Better Teaching and Learning*. Oxford: Heinemann.

Halsey, K., & Kinder, K. (1999). ' "I am New": Young People's Accounts of Accessing Cultural Venues'. In J. Harland & K. Kinder (eds), *Crossing the Line: Extending Young People's Access to Cultural Venues*. London: Calouste Gulbenkian Foundation.

Hamstead Hall School: Birmingham (2003). *Inspection Report*.

Harland, J., & Kinder, K. (1999). *Crossing the Line: Extending Young People's Access to Cultural Venues*. London: Calouste Gulbenkian Foundation.

—— —— Lord, P., Stott, A., Schagen, I., Haynes, J., Cusworth, L., White, R., & Paola, R. (2000). *Arts Education in Secondary Schools: Effects and Effectiveness*. Slough: NFER.

Harrison, A., & O'Neill, S. A. (2000). 'Children's Gender-Typed Preferences for Musical Instruments: An Intervention Study', *Psychology of Music* 28(1): 81–97.

Highfield, R. (2002). 'Tests Prove Tone Deafness', *Daily Telegraph*, 17 January.

Holt, J. (1984). *How Children Fail*. London: Penguin.

Imada, T. (2000). 'Out of logos: A Semiotic Approach of Music Education', *Bulletin for the Council for Research in Music Education* 147: 87–90.

Ings, R., Jones, R., & Randell, N. (1998). *Mapping Hidden Talent: Investigating Youth Music Projects*. Leicester: Youth Work Press.

Jones, F. W. (1941). *The Principles of Anatomy as Seen in the Hand*. London: Ballière and Cox.

Jørgensen, H. (2001). 'Instrumental Learning: Is an Early Start a Key to Success?', *British Journal of Music Education* 18(3): 227–39.

Juslin, P. N., & Sloboda, J. A. (2001). *Music and Emotion: Theory and Research*. Oxford: Oxford University Press.

Kelly, G. (1955). *The Psychology of Personal Constructs*. New York: Norton.

Kemp, A. E. (1996). *The Musical Temperament: Psychology and Personality of Musicians*. Oxford: Oxford University Press.

—— & Mills, J. (2002). 'Musical Potential'. In R. Parncutt & G. McPherson (eds), *The Science and Psychology of Music Performance: Creative Strategies for Teaching and Learning*. Oxford: Oxford University Press.

Kwami, R. (1998). 'Non-western Musics in Education: Problems and Possibilities', *British Journal of Music Education* 15(2): 161–70.

Lamp, C. J., & Keys, N. (1935). 'Can Aptitude for Specific Musical Instruments be Predicted?', *American Journal of Educational Psychology* 26: 587–96.

Lisboa, T. (2002). 'Children's Practice: A Multi-modal Approach to Teaching and Learning'. Paper presented at the 7th International Conference on Music Perception and Cognition, Sydney.

Macdonald, R., Miell, D., & Hargreaves, D. J. (eds). (2002). *Musical Identities*. Oxford: Oxford University Press.

McPherson, G. (2000). 'Commitment and Practice: Key Ingredients for Achievement during the Early Stages of Learning a Musical Instrument', *Bulletin of the Council for Research in Music Education* 147: 122–7.

—— (2003). 'Motivational and Self-regulatory Components of Musical Development', *SEMPRE Conference: University of Surrey Roehampton, April 2003.*

—— & Dunbar-Hall, P. (2001). 'Australia'. In D. J. Hargreaves & A. C. North (eds), *Musical Development and Learning: The International Perspective.* London: Continuum.

MacPherson, S. (1922). *The Musical Education of the Child.* London: Williams.

Mang, E. (2001). 'Intermediate Vocalizations: An Investigation of the Boundary between Speech and Songs in Young Children's Vocalizations'. *Bulletin of the Council for Research in Music Education* 147: 116–21.

Mansell, W. (1999). 'High Art: "Bald Men with Cellos"', *Times Educational Supplement*, 17 December: 5.

Maslow, A. H. (1954). *Motivation and Personality.* New York: Harper.

Mawbey, W. E. (1973). 'Wastage from Instrumental Classes in School', *Psychology of Music* 1(1): 33–43.

Mills, J. (1983). 'Identifying Potential Orchestral Musicians'. Unpublished D.Phil., Oxford University.

—— (1985). 'Gifted Instrumentalists: How Can we Recognise them?', *British Journal of Music Education* 2(1): 39–49.

—— (1988a). *Group Tests of Musical Abilities: Teacher's Guide and Recorded Test.* Windsor: NFER-Nelson.

—— (1988b). 'Tips for Teachers as Traps: An Example from Instrumental Tuition'. In W. Salaman & J. Mills (eds), *Challenging Assumptions: New Perspectives in the Education of Music Teachers.* Exeter: University of Exeter School of Education.

—— (1989). 'Generalist Primary Teachers of Music: A Problem of Confidence', *British Journal of Music Education* 6(2): 125–38.

—— (1991a). 'Clapping as an Approximation to Rhythm', *Canadian Music Educator* 33: 131–8.

—— (1991b). 'Out for the Count: Confused by Crotchets—Part 2', *Music Teacher* 70(6): 12–15.

—— (1991c). 'Confused by Crotchets', *Music Teacher* 70(5): 8–11.

—— (1991d). 'Assessing Musical Performance Musically', *Educational Studies* 17(2): 173–81.

—— (1991e). *Music in the Primary School.* Cambridge: Cambridge University Press.

—— (1994a). 'Music in the National Curriculum: The First Year', *British Journal of Music Education* 11: 191–6.

—— (1994b). *Musical Development—Conceptual.* Reading: International Centre for Research in Music Education.

—— (1995/6). 'Primary Student Teachers as Musicians', *Bulletin for the Council for Research in Music Education* 127: 122–6.

—— (1996a). 'Is Education in Decline? A View from the Joint Matriculation Board, 1954–1965', *Research in Education* 55: 29–38.

—— (1996b). 'Starting at Secondary School', *British Journal of Music Education* 13: 5–14.

—— (1998a). 'Music'. In J. Rose, P. Jones, G. Clay, J. Hertrich, & J. Mills (eds), *The Arts Inspected: Good Teaching in Art, Dance, Drama and Music.* Oxford: Heinemann.

Mills, J. (1998*b*). 'Response to Katie Overy's Paper, "Can music really 'improve' the mind?"', *Psychology of Music* 26(2): 204–5.

—— (2000*a*). 'The Quality of Provision of LEA Music Services 1999–2000': Address to Conference of the Federation of Music Services (FMS).

—— (2000*b*). 'Secondary Singing Inspected', *British Journal of Music Education* 17(1): 61–6.

—— (2002). 'Why Teach Music in School?', *Music Education International* 1: 152–3.

—— (2004*a*). 'Working in Music: The Conservatoire Professor', *British Journal of Music Education* 21(2): 179–98.

—— (2004*b*). 'Perspectives', *Link* (2): 50.

—— & Murray, A. (2000). 'Music Technology Inspected: Good Teaching in Key Stage 3', *British Journal of Music Education* 17(2): 129–56.

—— & O'Neill, S. A. (2002). 'Children as Inspectors? Evaluating School Music Provision for Children Aged 10–11 Years', *British Journal of Music Education* 19(3): 285–302.

—— & Smith, J. (2003). 'Teachers' Beliefs about Effective Instrumental Teaching in Schools and Higher Education', *British Journal of Music Education* 20(1): 5–28.

Mito, H. (2000). 'Tsumari Phenomenon and Tempo Acceleration Appeared in Keyboard Performance of Music Beginners', *Bulletin for the Council for Research in Music Education* 147: 132–7.

—— (2002). 'Performing at a Transposed Keyboard by Absolute Pitch Possessors'. In G. Welch & G. Folkestad (eds), *A World of Music Education Research* (pp. 181–8). Göteborg: School of Music and Music Education, Göteborg University, Sweden.

—— (2004). 'Role of Daily Musical Activity in Acquisition of Musical Skill'. In J. Tafuri (ed.), *Research for Music Education: The 20th Seminar of the ISME Research Commission.* Las Palmas: ISME.

Morley, T. (1952). *A Plaine and Easie Introduction to Practicalle Musicke.* London: Dent.

Murao, T. (1994). 'Concerning the Onchi in a Karaoke Society: Sociological Aspects of Poor Pitch Singing'. In G. Welch & T. Murao (eds), *Onchi and Singing Development: A Cross Cultural Perspective.* London: Roehampton Institute.

—— & Wilkins, B. (2001). 'Japan'. In D. J. Hargreaves & A. C. North (eds), *Musical Development and Learning: The International Perspective.* London: Continuum.

Musicians Union (2000). *Research into the Training Needs of Musicians.* London: Metier.

NACCCE (National Advisory Committee on Creative and Cultural Education) (1999). *All Our Futures: Creativity, Culture and Education.* London: DfEE Publications.

NCC (National Curriculum Council) (1992). *Music: National Curriculum Council Consultation Report.* York: NCC.

NIAS (Northamptonshire Inspection and Advisory Service) (1997). *Differentiation: A Guide for Music Teachers.* Northampton: Northamptonshire County Council.

Nielsen, S. G. (1999). 'Learning Strategies in Instrumental Music Practice', *British Journal of Music Education* 16(3): 275–91.

North, A. C., Hargreaves, D. J., & O'Neill, S. A. (2000). 'The Importance of Music to Adolescents', *British Journal of Educational Psychology* 70: 255–72.

Ofsted (1995). *Music: A Review of Inspection Findings 1993/94.* London: HMSO.

—— (1997). *Using Subject Specialists to Promote High Standards at Key Stage 2.* London: Ofsted.

—— (1998). *Standards in Primary Music: 1996–1997.* London: Ofsted Publications Centre.

—— (1999). *Primary Education 1994–98: A Review of Primary Schools in England.* London: Stationery Office.

—— (2003). *Inspecting Schools: Framework for Inspecting Schools.* London: Ofsted.

Okumo, C. C. (2000). 'Conceptualising African Popular Music: A Kenyan Experiment', *Bulletin for the Council for Research in Music Education* 147: 145–8.

Olsson, B. (2001). 'Scandinavia'. In D. J. Hargreaves & A. C. North (eds), *Musical Development and Learning: The International Perspective.* London: Continuum.

O'Neill, S. A. (2002). 'Young People and Music Participation Project': www.keele.ac.uk/depts/ps/ ESRC/esrcmenu.htm.

—— & McPherson, G. (2002). 'Motivation'. In R. Parncutt & G. McPherson (eds), *The Science and Psychology of Music Performance: Creative Strategies for Teaching and Learning.* Oxford: Oxford University Press.

Paynter, J. (1982). *Music in the Secondary School Curriculum.* Cambridge: Cambridge University Press.

—— (1992). *Sound and Structure.* Cambridge: Cambridge University Press.

—— (1997). 'The Form of Finality: A Context for Musical Education', *British Journal of Music Education* 14(1): 5–22.

—— (1999). 'Embodied Meaning: Commentary on Correia', *Psychology of Music* 27(1): 102–4.

—— (2000). 'Making Progress with Composing', *British Journal of Music Education* 17(1): 5–32.

—— & Aston, P. (1970). *Sound and Silence.* Cambridge: Cambridge University Press.

Persson, R. (2001). 'The Subjective World of the Performer'. In P. N. Juslin & J. A. Sloboda (eds), *Music and Emotion: Theory and Research.* Oxford: Oxford University Press.

Petch, J. A. (1966). 'Whither Education? (Wilde Memorial Lecture)', *Memoirs & Proceedings of the Manchester Literary and Philosophical Society* 108(4): 1–13.

Plummeridge, C. (1997). 'The Rights and Wrongs of School Music: A Brief Comment on Malcolm Ross's Paper', *British Journal of Music Education* 14(1): 23–8.

Pollard, A., Triggs, P., Broadfoot, P., McNess, E., & Osborn, M. (2000). *What Pupils Say: Changing Policy and Practice in Primary Education.* London: Continuum.

Priestley, E., & Fowler, F. (1962). *The School Recorder: Books 1 and 2.* Leeds: E. J. Arnold.

Primos, K. (2001). 'Africa'. In D. J. Hargreaves & A. C. North (eds), *Musical Development and Learning: The International Perspective.* London: Continuum.

QCA (Qualifications and Curriculum Authority) (2000). *Schemes of Work for Music at Key Stages 1, 2 and 3.* www.standards.dfee.gov.uk/schemes. Retrieved, from the World Wide Web: www.standards.dfee.gov.uk/schemes.

Radocy, R. (2001). 'America'. In D. J. Hargreaves & A. C. North (eds), *Musical Development and Learning: The International Perspective.* London: Continuum.

Rauscher, F. H., Shaw, G. L., & Ky, K. N. (1993). 'Music and Spatial Task Performance', *Nature* 365: 611.

—— —— Levine, L. J., Wright, E. L., Dennis, W. R., & Newcomb, R. L. (1997). 'Music Training Causes Long-Term Enhancement of Preschool Children's Spatial-Temporal Reasoning', *Neurological Research* 19: 2–8.

Ritterman, J. (2000). 'Learning What it is to Perform: A Key to Peer Learning for Musicians' In D. Hunter & M. Russ (eds), *Peer Learning in Music.* Belfast: University of Ulster.

Roadknight, P. (2000). 'The 'time machine' and the Voice—Looking Back on a KS3 Music Project', *NAME magazine* 4: 4–7.

Robinson, G. (2000). 'The Creative Imperative: Investing in the Arts in the 21st Century'. Paper presented at the New Statesman Arts Lecture 2000.

Rose, J., Jones, P., Hertrich, J., Clay, G., & Mills, J. (1998). *The Arts Inspected: Good Teaching in Art, Dance, Drama and Music.* Oxford: Heinemann.

Salaman, W. (1988). 'Personalities in World Music Education No. 7—John Paynter', *International Journal of Music Education* 12: 28–32.

SCAA (School Curriculum and Assessment Authority) (1996). *Musical Ideas (Unit 2 of Key Stage 3 Optional Tests and Tasks for Music).* London: SCAA.

Schenck, R. (2000). *Spelrum: en metodikbok för sång- och instrumentalpedagoger.* Göteborg: Bo Ejeby Förlag.

Schools Council (1968). *Enquiry 1, Young School Leavers.* London: HMSO.

Seashore, C. E. (1938). *The Psychology of Music.* London: McGraw-Hill.

Seddon, F., & O'Neill, S. A. (2001). 'An Evaluation Study of Computer-Based Compositions by Children with and without Prior Experience of Formal Instrumental Music Tuition', *Psychology of Music* 29(1): 4–19.

Shaw, H. W. (1952). *Music in the Primary School.* London: Dennis Dobson.

Shepard, R. N. (1982). 'Structural Representations of Musical Pitch'. In D. Deutsch (ed.), *The Psychology of Music.* New York: Academic Press.

Shuter-Dyson, R., & Gabriel, C. (1981). *The Psychology of Musical Ability* (2nd edn). London: Methuen.

Sloboda, J. A. (1989). 'Music as a Language'. In F. Wilson & F. Roehmann (eds), *Music and Child Development.* St Louis: MMB Music.

—— (2001). 'Conference Keynote. Emotion, Functionality and the Everyday Experience of Music: Where does Music Education Fit?', *Music Education Research* 3(2): 243–53.

—— (2002). 'Musical Peak Experiences—What is the Educational Relevance?' Paper presented at the Annual conference of the Federation of Music Services.

—— Davidson, J. W., Howe, M. J. A., & Moore, D. G. (1996). 'The Role of Practice in the Development of Performing Musicians', *British Journal of Psychology* 87: 287–309.

Spychiger, M. (1993). 'Music Makes the School', *Die Blaue Eule.* University of Freiburg.

Sunday Times (2001). 'Sweet George', 2 December.

—— (2002). 'Musical Girls Hit a Male Note', 21 April: 13.

Sundin, B. (1998). 'Musical Creativity in the First Six Years: A Research Project in Retrospect'. In B. Sundin, G. McPherson, & G. Folkestad (eds), *Children Composing.* Malmö: Malmö Academy of Music.

Swanwick, K. (1968). *Popular Music and the Teacher.* Oxford: Pergamon Press.

—— (1999). *Teaching Music Musically.* London: Routledge.

—— & Tillman, J. (1986). 'The Sequence of Musical Development: A Study of Children's Composition', *British Journal of Music Education* 3(3): 305–39.

Taylor, S. (1973). 'Musical Development of Children Aged Seven to Eleven', *Psychology of Music* 1(1): 44–9.

TES (Times Educational Supplement) (2000). 'We're not all Old or Bald', 28 January: 18.

—— (2003). 'Year 8 is Boring' (p. 9) 'Enriched Teens' (p. 28), 4 April.

van Niekerk, C. (2002). 'Music Education Unit Standards for Southern Africa (MEUSSA): A Novel Team Research Project, 2000–2001', *Proceedings of the 19th Research Seminar of ISME, Göteborg, Sweden.*

Welch, G. (2001). *The Misunderstanding of Music: Inaugural Lecture*: Institute of Education University of London.

—— Ockelford, A., & Zimmermann, S.-A. (2001). *Provision of Music in Special Education (Promise): A Report on a Research Project Funded by the Esmee Fairbairn Trust with Support from the Royal National Institute for the Blind (RNIB)*. London: University of London Institute of Education and RNIB.

Wiggins, T. (1996). 'The World of Music in Education', *British Journal of Music Education* 13(1): 21–9.

Willans, G., & Searle, R. (1953). *Down with Skool!* London: Max Parrish.

Williamon, A., & Valentine, E. (2000). 'Quantity and Quality of Musical Practice as Predictors of Performance Quality', *British Journal of Psychology* 91: 353–76.

—— (2002). 'The Role of Retrieval Structures in Memorising Music', *Cognitive Psychology* 44: 1–32.

Wragg, E. C. (2003). 'The Four Awful Truths'. *Times Educational Supplement,* 12 September: 40

York, N. (2001). *Valuing School Music: A Report on School Music.* London: University of Westminster and Rockschool Ltd.

Young, S. (1995). 'Listening to the Music of Early Childhood', *British Journal of Music Education* 12(1): 51–8.

Youth Music. (2003). *Youth Music Action Zones: Sound Strategies for the Future.* London: Youth Music.

Index of Authors

General Index